TEACHING THE WORD, REACHING THE WORLD

BY

ROBERT G. FLOOD

AND

JERRY B. JENKINS

MOODY PRESS

CHICAGO

© 1985 by
THE MOODY BIBLE INSTITUTE
OF CHICAGO

All rights reserved. No part of this book may be reproduced in
any form without permission in writing from the publisher,
except in the case of brief quotations embodied in critical articles
or reviews.

While attempts were made to update alumni information where
possible, those mentioned may have moved to other assignments
or ministries since press time.

Library of Congress Cataloging in Publication Data

Flood, Robert G.
    Teaching the word, reaching the world.

    Includes bibliographical references.
    1. Moody Bible Institute.   I. Jenkins, Jerry B.
II. Title.
BV4070.M76F575   1985   207'.77311   84-27340
ISBN 0-8024-8567-7

    1 2 3 4 5 6 7 Printing WO Year 89 88 87 88 86 85

Printed in the United States of America

07. 77311
771
6

L.I.F.E. College Library
1100 Glendale Blvd.
Los Angeles, Calif. 90026

034675

CONTENTS

CHAPTER

	Foreword	8
1	The Word to the World	10
2	Moody: The Man and the Ministry	18
3	Moody's Chicago School	34
4	The R.A. Torrey Years	46
5	The James M. Gray Years	56
6	The Will Houghton Years	66
7	The William Culbertson Years	78
8	The George Sweeting Years	88
9	Oasis in the City	98
10	People: The Lifeblood of the Institute	106
11	Shaping the Church in America	116
12	Discipling Young America	128
13	Salt in Society	136
14	Over Land and Sea	142
15	To Every Nation	150
16	On the Air	176
17	Missionaries of the Skies	188
18	Science and the God of Creation	198
19	Books for Today's World	210
20	The Making of a Magazine	218
21	The Nation's Classroom	224
22	Moody After Hours	232
23	From Sankey to Satellite	238
24	A Century in Christ's Service	250
	Board of Trustees	254
	MBI Management	256
	Appendix A: Doctrinal Statement	255
	Appendix B: Buildings and Grounds	257
	Appendix C: WMBI Milestones	259
	Appendix D: MIS Historical Highlights	261
	Bibliography	263

FOREWORD

One hundred years ago a man of humble origins, who had become by God's grace the best known evangelist and preacher of his day, dedicated a portion of the property God had given his ministry to start a school to equip laborers to reap the plentiful harvest.

The man was Dwight Lyman Moody, and the school that he founded that day was the Chicago Evangelization Society, later to be known as the Moody Bible Institute.

D. L. Moody was a man of special vision. He saw that the preaching of God's Word could not end with his generation, that there had to be new Spurgeons and Whitefields and Taylors to grasp the torch and run the race, continuing the work of God. While the messengers always changed, the message remained the same: Every soul is eternally lost, but Christ has come to redeem those souls.

No one knew better than Mr. Moody that God is sovereign over the affairs of man. But he also knew that God appoints men and women to tell the world of the Savior, to be agents of the convicting work of the Holy Spirit. Moody would agree with the thoughts of J. I. Packer in his book *Evangelism and the Sovereignty of God:*

> Whatever we may believe about election, the fact remains that men without Christ are lost and going to hell. . . . "Except ye repent," said our Lord to the crowd, "ye shall all . . . perish." And we who are Christ's are sent to tell them of the One (*and only One*) who can save them from perishing. Is not their need *urgent* . . . does that not make evangelism a matter of urgency for us?

The eternal consequences of sin were always prominent in the heart and mind of D. L. Moody. The *urgency* that weighed upon him convinced this man of action that if the work was to continue the men and women that God raised up had to be trained to perform their labors. Moody resolved to build a school that would forge the zeal of the eager witness with the knowledge of the learned professor. The need was *urgent*, and Moody responded.

Billy Graham once said that if he was given only three years to minister, he would devote the first two years to preparation. The Institute believes in the idea of being thoroughly prepared. Our students ready themselves through three years of vigorous classroom training with committed educators.

At the same time, through their Practical Christian Ministries, students are constantly reminded that being a Christian is essentially being a witness to the death, burial, and resurrection of Jesus Christ. Teams of our young people minister in nursing homes, missions, Sunday schools, youth clubs, open-air groups. Through these experiences they are greeted with the stark reality that the need is still *urgent*, that people are dying without knowing Christ.

Right now more than 23,000 former students are serving Jesus Christ full time throughout the world. But the task is incomplete; it is our unfinished duty! Of 4.7 billion people living on this earth, only one billion claim to be Christians. Very few organizations have the opportunity and responsibility that we have to make the difference and to blaze new trails in missions, the pastorate, academics, education, and communications. Moody Bible Institute must continue to lead the way, because God has entrusted to us the mission of teaching the Word and reaching the world.

Claiming Hebrews 11:6, "without faith it is impossible to please God," we will endeavor to conclude our first century and charge into our second with a strong, victorious faith and a clear renewed conviction of urgency. We will strive to be honorable stewards of God's blessing by trusting him to mold and inspire the laboring servants of the future, sending them to the far corners of the globe.

I can imagine Mr. Moody, sitting in his leather chair, opening his old, well-worn Bible, putting on his spectacles, and being stirred the way I am when I read Habakkuk 2:2, *"Write the vision*, make it plain upon the tablets that he may RUN that readeth it."* We want the Lord to create new runners through our witnesses, and we have to do it now!

The celebration of our one hundredth anniversary provides a paramount opportunity to reaffirm to the world the urgent, all-consuming vision of D. L. Moody: World evangelization in this generation.

GEORGE SWEETING
President
Moody Bible Institute

Chapter 1

THE WORD TO THE WORLD

One hundred years ago, evangelist D. L. Moody planted a small Bible school on the north side of Chicago. God took what the young man started and made it global. Even in Moody's day it did not take long for the school to adopt a world vision. Years before, Moody himself had become an international figure, drawing audiences in the British Isles alone that totaled more than five million.

Wherever Moody went, he made the Bible a living Book, and brought the common man in touch with the Living God.

Some thought Dwight L. Moody simplistic, a charge that is frequently leveled against those who insist on the basics. Yet, as in the world of athletics, the victorious are those who major on the fundamentals.

It would be impossible to measure the full impact of the Moody Bible Institute upon America. For one hundred years it has fed the churches of America with pastors and Christian workers dedicated to the Word and to Jesus Christ.

For nearly a century Moody has poured Christian books into the marketplace and built one of the nation's foremost evangelical magazines, now reaching a quarter-million homes a month.

A half century ago, the Institute pioneered Christian radio in America. Now in this decade, space age technology has opened Moody radio to the nation. No city, town, or hamlet is out of potential reach, thanks to communications satellites that can beam Moody programming to the skies and back to down-link receivers in only a fraction of a second.

After one hundred years, Moody Bible Institute continues to bring the Word to the world.

And it has stepped far outside American borders to bring the Word to the world.

How a person perceives the nature of Moody Bible Institute often depends on what prong of its outreach may have touched his life.

If his pastor is a Moody graduate, he may imagine the Institute as a seminary. If he has seen a Moody Institute of Science film, he may imagine a great laboratory. If he has been converted to Christ under a Moody-trained missionary, the Institute may seem like a great church filled with other fine missionaries.

The skeptic approached by Moody students on the streets of Chicago might perceive them as nice religious kids or even fanatics. The graduates of Moody Bible Institute are laboring around the globe. One has dedicated years to child evangelism in Nazareth, where Jesus Himself "grew in favor with God and with man." Another opened a Christian bookstore in Turin, Italy, location of the shroud that is reputed to have been the linen in which Jesus' body was wrapped.

Still others work in places like Micronesia in the South Pacific and Seychelles in the Indian Ocean—islands so tiny and obscure that very few maps identify them.

The careers of some Moody graduates have included ministries in several countries. These few simple lines from a 1981 edition of *Moody Alumni* say it well: "Paul J. Andreason, Class of 1916, died in Continental Divide, New Mexico. He was a former missionary to India, Vietnam, Korea, Cypress, and Java."

These servants have pursued not the wealth of this world, but "the wealth of His riches in glory." Mr. and Mrs. Earl Dix are another example of this. *Moody Alumni* states that the Dix's "have been church planting in Zaire for Africa Inland Mission since 1929. They left New York on the day the stock market crashed, and until 1984 they were still active among the Zande tribe, a field they pioneered in 1931."

Probably no single institution has had as much impact on the world missionary movement in the past century than has the Moody Bible Institute. It can be documented that about one of every fifteen Protestant missionaries from North America on the field today have been trained, at least in part, at Moody.

The greatest number have gone to Africa, where Christianity is growing rapidly. When MBI's late president, Dr. William Culbertson, toured the mission fields of Africa in 1960, he wrote back, "There were some missionaries there whose fathers and mothers went to Africa from MBI. These people really affect the world they live in. It is almost impossible to realize the changes that can be wrought by the gospel until you see the difference yourself."[1]

Some gave their lives to open Africa to the gospel (see chapter 15). Among the earlier pioneers were graduates like Reg and Zan Reynolds. For more than forty years they labored with the Africa Inland Mission. The missionary history of these two modern disciples of Christ in the land of Livingstone reads like the journeys of the apostle Paul.

Second only to Africa have been the number of graduates who have gone to Latin America. Tribal linguists have ventured into thick jungles to live among the peoples, unlock unknown tongues, tend medical needs, translate the New Testament, and share the love of Jesus. Many of the earlier pioneers had to ride mule or horseback over steep mountain trails, paddle dugout canoes, or trek long distances over dusty or muddy trails to extend the spiritual frontier. This early breed of missionary planted churches wherever he could and pushed forward. Nothing prodded his pioneer spirit more, nor burdened him more, than to spot another village in the back country without the gospel.

While Moody graduates labored side by side with thousands of missionaries trained elsewhere, including those from other continents, they helped lay the foundations for the phenomenal surge of evangelical Christianity seen in parts of Latin America today.

In Quito, Ecuador, high in the Andes mountains, the powerful transmitters of radio HCJB beam the gospel not only throughout Latin America, but around the world. Moody graduate Clarence Jones established HCJB more than a half

1. *Quarterly Fellowship Newsletter* (June 1961).

century ago, and has been called the pioneer of missionary radio itself. He founded the World Radio Fellowship, and today scores of MBI-trained missionaries serve under its auspices.

HCJB and other superpower stations, such as those of Trans World Radio and the Far Eastern Broadcasting Company, penetrate deeply into communist lands. Millions behind the Iron and Bamboo Curtains are listening, and a groundswell of spiritual revival is in process.

In earlier days, most missionaries who headed for Asia went to China. Of Moody's twenty martyrs for the cause of the gospel, eight died there.

When the Communists took over in 1948 and drove the missionaries from the mainland, it appeared to some that years of toil and sacrifice would go down the drain. The Communists murdered Christians, closed their churches, and declared religion an "opiate of the people."

For years, Red China shut out the rest of the world. Christians in the West speculated whether anything remained of the church for which so many had given their lives. Finally, a few reports began to trickle out. Yes, there was still a remnant of the church in China—at least underground. But how big? And how vigorous? Dying or healthy?

As doors once again began to open, the real story emerged. Estimates of the number of Christians in China ran as high as fifty million—ten times the number of believers missionaries had left when they were expelled years earlier! The majority seemed to be meeting secretly in house churches, and an accurate count is still impossible, but clearly God had worked mightily.

The political turmoil that forced missionaries from China has never ceased. The uprise in the Congo (now Zaire) that killed missionary Paul Carlson in 1964 sent hundreds of other missionaries fleeing. The wars in Lebanon have closed most work there. Missionaries to Afghanistan have had to take other assignments. Tribal linguists have been forced from some Latin American countries. But in the interim of missionary absence, God does His work.

John Beekman was told by doctors in 1944 that his bad heart could take his life within a year. But embued at Moody with the missionary spirit, he would not let that stop him. After a year of linguistics study at the University of Oklahoma, Beekman and his wife, Elaine, plunged into an area deep in Mexico near the Guatemalan border, home of the Chol Indians.

They translated the Scriptures into Chol, won converts, and taught them to evangelize others. John and Elaine Beekman left the Chols in 1962 for other translation assignments and for reasons of health. When they returned to the tribe fifteen years later, they found some 20,000 Christians!

Hundreds of other Moody graduates have seemed to vanish from civilization into all-but-forgotten pockets of the world to invest their lives among peoples most do not even know exist. They have gone convinced that even the smallest tribe has a right to hear the gospel and that God will eventually fulfill His promise to redeem men "out of every kindred, and tongue, and people, and nation" (Revelation 5:9).

As dedicated scientists in linguistics, these missionaries have undertaken one of the most painstaking tasks imaginable. It can take years to reduce a primitive language to written form. The linguist must first discover some pattern in the welter of sounds that strikes his ear—sounds that often have no parallel in English. When he has finally reduced the language onto paper, he faces the awesomely meticulous task of translating the Scriptures into that language—verse by verse.

Kenneth Pike—longtime chairman of the Department of Linguistics at Michigan State, Wycliffe Bible Translators associate, and 1982 candidate for the Nobel Peace Prize—points out that a tiny alteration in tone can completely change the meaning of a word. One example is the Mexican Mixtec word *chaa*, which can become either "man" or "come" or "smoke a cigarette." (Imagine if one should err in translating a passage such as Matthew 8:7—"And Jesus said unto him, I will *come* and heal him"!)

In the past few years, more Moody Bible Institute graduates have joined Wycliffe Bible Translators than any other mission. Wycliffe, with more than five thousand missionaries, is the

Irwin Moon and his wife, Margaret, rejoice as Life *magazine (May 9, 1938) discovers "Sermons from Science." In later years Eastman Kodak will give him its Gold Medal Award and commentator Lowell Thomas will call him "a particularly gifted man."*

largest mission in the world. The late William Cameron Townsend, the tribal linguistics pioneer who founded the mission, attended Moody Bible Institute's Evening School, as did his wife, Elaine.

It is no secret that exported Hollywood films help shape the minds of men abroad. Around the world, also, from the islands of Indonesia to the villages of Poland, from the executive boardrooms of American industry to the universities of Europe, an average of a half million people a day view films produced by the Moody Institute of Science.

It all began with the dream of one man, Irwin Moon, who saw the potential of wedding biblical truth to scientific truth. His breakthrough came at the San Francisco World's Fair in 1939, when tens of thousands watched his live demonstrations. After World War II, Moon began to put his science and faith material on film to reach a wider audience.

When Moon retired in 1972, the internationally-known news commentator, Lowell Thomas, said, "To me, Irwin Moon is something of a phenomenon, a particularly gifted man. I wish he could go on and on for at least another five or six decades."[2]

In the decade since then, Moody Institute of Science has continued to expand its film line and to put existing films into scores of languages. Its most exciting years may yet be ahead (see chapter 18).

Paul Robinson, a former Louisiana State football player, also had a dream. He wanted to become a missionary pilot. Mission boards turned him down because he was too old. So Robinson decided to start a missionary aviation school. With the approval of the Moody Bible Institute board, the dream became reality, and today Moody Aviation trains more than 60 percent of the world's missionary pilots.

From a story by Wes Pippert of United Press International:

> In the foothills of the Great Smoky Mountains in the eastern tip of Tennessee, Moody Aviation is teaching young men to fly everything from tractors to vegetables to medicine to live cattle in small planes to the world's remotest nooks and crannies. The motivation that makes these student pilots clock hundreds of hours in some of the most difficult conditions it's possible to simulate is the Great Commission of Jesus Christ—to go into all the world and preach the gospel.[3]

George Verwer fanned the flames of

2. *Moody Memo* (17 November 1972), p. 2.
3. Wesley Pippert, "The Making of a Jungle Pilot," *Moody Monthly* (March 1972).

Chicago's skyscrapers, including the John Hancock Center, the nation's fourth tallest building, reflect in the glass that encloses Moody Bible Institute's arch entryway. Dwight Moody planted his school in the midst of the city, and it still stands there after a century.

Paul Robinson sees the potential of the airplane on the mission field and persuades Moody Bible Institute to train pilots.

George Verwer's Operation Mobilization buys the Doulos *(above) and sends thousands of young people into major port cities.*

evangelism in the hearts of many fellow students when he studied at Moody Bible Institute in the early sixties. His classmates remember well the all-night prayer meetings he directed, and his single-minded spiritual enthusiasm. Verwer went on to found Operation Mobilization, taking teams of young literature evangelists into country after country.

OM raised $700,000 for an ocean liner, somewhat antiquated, that would sail from port to port, loaded with several hundred young missionaries and tons of gospel literature.

Critics said the idea was foolish—a waste of God's money. But they were wrong. Much of the world's population, Verwer pointed out, can be found in the major seaports. By the time his ship, the Doulos, doubled as a floating hotel, Bible school campus, bookstore, and conference center, it turned out to be one of the most efficient missionary investments of modern times. OM later bought an even larger ship, the *Logos*, which has spent most of its time in the Pacific, while the original ship evangelizes countries of the Atlantic.

Meanwhile, Moody graduate Jerry Moritz has become deputy chaplain of the United States Marine Corps, with a force of 270 chaplains under

him. The assignment followed two years as chaplain of the 3rd Marine Division in Okinawa, and several years as the second ranking Navy chaplain in Pacific, where he helped meet the spiritual needs of 50,000 men in port and at sea (see chapter 14).

Michael Guido is a bandleader turned evangelist. John Haggai founded Evangelism International. Both happen to base their far-flung ministries in Georgia and are graduates of Moody Bible Institute. But from their US headquarters, the gospel goes into the nations of the world.

The books of Moody Press can be found around the world, thanks in part to a growing international book market and the long-established outreach of the Moody Literature Ministries. One children's book, Ken Taylor's *Bible in Pictures for Little Eyes*, is now in sixty languages, with total sales of more than a million copies.

D. L. Moody first conceived of the inexpensive religious paperback decades before the paperback became standard in the book industry. Since then, God has used millions of Moody Press paperbacks to change men and women around the world.

One day in 1982, thirteen hundred

John Haggai of Evangelism International shakes hands with Anwar Sadat. From Haggai's base in Atlanta, he trains internationals to reach their own countries with the gospel.

students of the Moody Bible Institute joined hands and entirely circled their campus—about eight city blocks. Then the students silently prayed for the world outreach of their school.

Since the campus is on one of Chicago's busiest intersections, about a mile north of Chicago's Loop, the school promptly received a call from a city journalist.

"What's going on over there," he asked, "a protest or something?"

When the reporter was told what it was all about, he was no longer interested. Good news is non-news. He remained, like so many, unaware that the thousands for whom these students were praying were literally changing nations.

Not every newsman misses the story. Bob Faw, a reporter for Chicago's CBS affiliate WBBM-TV, came to the Moody campus to "find out how, in a world of secularism, a place like MBI could exist, much less flourish."

After ten hours of filming, he described MBI students as "latter days soldiers for Christ" and concluded, "Here there is hope."[4]

A visitor from Japan wanted to see the school about which he had heard so much. He also wanted to tell his own story to its students and employees.

He had been converted after World War II through reading a tract handed to him by an American missionary in a Tokyo railroad station. Its salvation message had overwhelmed him, and Christ transformed his life. The Japanese guest had become a global evangelist, telling people of other nations, and even world leaders, of Jesus Christ.

Who was the Japanese visitor?

Mitsuo Fuchida, who had led the attack on Pearl Harbor that plunged America into World War II in 1941.

He was living proof of the difference the gospel of grace and forgiveness can make. He is one of the reasons why Moody Bible Institute continues to take the Word to the world.

4. Bob Faw, WBBM Radio, as quoted in *Moody Memo* (18 September 1974).

Chapter 2

MOODY: THE MAN
AND THE MINISTRY

The sound of the woodchopper echoed through the trees in extreme northwest Massachusetts, within sight of New Hampshire and Vermont. The young boy wielding the ax seemed to abound with energy.

He knew how to work. It took that kind of person to survive on those rocky New England farms, where someone once quipped that "there are sufficient stones to build four fences to the acre."

Dwight L. Moody's birthplace in Northfield, Massachusetts, overlooking the distant hills of Vermont. Here Moody enjoys his family but grows restless and leaves home for Boston.

While Dwight Lyman Moody was a mere boy, his father died, leaving nine sons and daughters. The oldest of the boys ran away, and the broken-hearted widow, doubly bereft, began an heroic struggle against poverty.

Her little son Dwight grew up with scanty education but an unusually imaginative mind. Reminisced the *Chicago Tribune* on the centennial of his birth, "Moody received many maternal blisterings, for he was rather wild and wound up with tricks."[1]

The youngster delighted to play Indian and frighten fidgety Squire Alexander's cattle at night. In school he delivered Marc Antony's funeral oration over Caesar and for effect used a miniature coffin containing a much frightened tomcat as the corpse of Caesar.[2]

At seventeen, Moody went across the state from Northfield to Boston, where he went to work in his uncle's shoestore.

Moody turned out to be a first-class salesman. No shoddy pair of shoes walked past him without a challenge. Nor was he content to let prospects come to him. He stood out on the sidewalks and went after the crowds. You have to go where the people are, he believed.

In Boston, at the persuasion of his uncle, Moody attended the Mount Vernon Congregational Church. There he sat under a Bible teacher named Edward Kimball. And Kimball followed up on his pupils. Concerned about Moody's soul, Kimball hastened to the shoestore one day and brought Moody right to the point. Jesus had died for him, Kimball pressed, and it was time for Moody to make a decision. The timing was right. Moody responded.

But a short time later, when the Mt. Vernon Congregational Church interviewed him for membership, Moody was unable to answer simple questions. When asked what Christ had done for the world he shocked his sponsors: "A great deal, but I don't know of anything he has done in particular."

A later interview showed more promise.

1. Frank Cipriani, "The Sinner Saver," *Chicago Sunday Tribune* (24 January 1937), p. 9.
2. Ibid.

Church entry 1131 on March 12, 1856, read: "Mr. Moody thinks he has made some progress since he was here before, at least in knowledge. He maintains his habits of prayer and reading the Bible. . . . Is fully determined to adhere to the cause of Christ always."[3]

Moody's spiritual life began to blossom.

Then just as suddenly as he had left the hamlet of Northfield for Boston, Moody left Boston on impulse for Chicago, not telling his family. Upon his arrival in the fall of 1856, he dashed them off a quick note with the startling information that "God is the same here as in Boston."

A bootstore promptly hired Moody and made him their traveling representative. The ambitious Moody immediately set his goal: a fortune of $100,000.

But shoes were no longer his only product. He also wanted to tell people about God. He rented a pew in Plymouth Church and went out onto the streets to fill it. He not only filled one pew, but four. Nor did he pick and choose his prospects. Everyone from beggars to business executives were eligible for a Moody approach:

"Are you a Christian?"

Unless the prospect could retort promptly with a convincing answer, he would find Moody in quick pursuit.

"Why not?"

Moody's reputation spread. One man handled Moody's stock question with, "That's none of your business."

3. Ibid.

Moody's North Market Hall Sunday school class (Moody at rear center, James Farwell in top hat). His class eventually grows so large that it attracts a visit from Abraham Lincoln—on his way to Washington, D. C., to be inaugurated as president of the United States.

"Oh yes, it is," Moody snapped back.

The man eyed him warily.

"Then you must be Moody."

Moody's approach took courage. The streets were tough. Vice flourished. Temptation abounded. But Moody let nothing swerve him from his mission.

When he asked to teach a Bible class, he was told there was nothing open. He went out on the streets and recruited his own class—urchins of all sorts. He picked them as he found them.

Some of his early converts included Madden the Butcher, Red Eye, Rag-Breeches, Cadet, Black Stove Pipe, Old Man, Darby the Cobbler, Jackey Candles, Smikes, Butcher Lilray, Greenhorn, Indian, and Gilberic. That's exactly as Moody knew them. And he had a way with them all.

But Moody could relate also to the top ranks of Chicago's social class. As God is no respector of persons, Moody took men as they were.

As Moody's fame grew, journalists called him "Brother Moody." "Some of the heretics in the street had a different name—'Crazy Moody.' "[4] Bad press, though, could not daunt him. Moody used the press to advertise and help fill his pews.

When Moody rode the streets on an Indian pony, handing out candy apples and rounding up kids for his Sunday school, critics wrote it off as a publicity stunt. But Moody wanted to draw attention to himself only because he wanted to bring everybody he could to the Savior.

Moody was a man of impulse. A family might hear a perfunctory knock at the door, then have Moody burst in.

"I'm D. L. Moody. Are you Christians? Do you pray? Have you any coal in the house? Come, kneel down with me. Pray!"

The family would kneel and pray. The next day they might find their coal bin replenished.[5]

As the work grew, Moody searched for bigger quarters. He rented a grimy hall on North Market Street, and promptly filled it with more than five hundred a Sunday. It was hardly the place in which you would want to host a

dignitary. But word of Moody's success in the inner city reached Abraham Lincoln. The president-elect dropped in to see it for himself on his way from Springfield to Washington for his inauguration.

Before Lincoln left, he told the crowded Sunday school class, "I was once as poor as any boy in the school, but I am now President of the United States, and if you attend to what is taught you here, some one of you may yet be President of the United States."[6]

Moody proved to be the primary catalyst for a movement that would soon become known as the Young Men's Christian Association—YMCA—of which he was president for a time.

By 1860, Moody was making a major impact on Chicago. During the war, Moody was an abolitionist and for the Union, but he could not bear to "shoot down a fellow human being." So in Chicago he conducted missionary services among the Union soldiers at Camp Douglas, and later among some nine thousand Confederate prisoners, after the camp had been converted into a war prison.

But it had always been Moody's bent to go where the people were, and most soldiers were not in Chicago, but on the front lines. Moody offered himself as a volunteer chaplain and headed South—to Shiloh, Murfreesboro, Chattanooga. He was one of the first to enter Richmond. But he used the boom of his voice, not that of a cannon, to mount his spiritual assault. And the Bible was his ammunition.

In the presence of death, Moody aided the wounded and pressed men about their eternal destiny. General O. O. Howard of the 4th Corps praised Moody for his service and said Moody had proved "how a soldier could give his heart to God."[7]

During the war, Moody fell in love and in 1862 married Emma Revell, sister of publisher Fleming H. Revell, a name still prominent in Christian publishing. Though Emma was only nineteen, Moody had found a partner entirely in

4. Ibid.
5. Ibid.
6. Ibid.
7. Ibid.

tune with the call of God upon his life, one he saw as the "divinely appointed balance wheel" of his existence.

Though his ministry at times took him far from home, Moody's tender letters home reflected his character as a family man. Emma, too, smoothed his rough edges and brought to the marriage a decidedly superior education.

Emma Revell Moody and Dwight shortly after their marriage, he at age twenty-five and she at nineteen.

Back in Chicago after the Civil War, two movements took much of Moody's attention: the YMCA and the spread of the Sunday school throughout the Midwest. With the former, he worked closely with Chicago merchant John V. Farwell and raised money to build the first "Y" hall in America. Cyrus McCormick, inventor of the reaper, gave Moody the first $10,000 for the project. It burned four months later, but before the embers had cooled, he had agents out raising funds to replace it. Yet the greatest fire was still to come.

Moody knew how to tap the well-to-do for funds, but it was not for his own welfare. It was for the welfare of others and the advance of the gospel. By then, Moody had shifted his priorities and scuttled his ambition for personal wealth. He could have become a millionaire, said his close friends, but the Wall Street panic of 1857 convinced him he should not regard faith as primarily "an aid to fortune." Of his merchant associates in Chicago, Moody once said, "I felt I could equal any of them, except one—and that one was Marshall Field."[8]

In turning to full-time Christian service,

Moody forsook any guarantee of regular income and formed no board or society to assure his living expenses. He determined to trust God alone, confident that since the Lord had called him to the work, He would also support him in it. If not, he could go back to selling shoes, for had not the apostle Paul made tents to pay expenses?

In 1860, at the age of twenty-three, Moody was earning $5,000 a year—big money in those days. Soon after Moody gave up his business for the Lord's work, John Farwell discovered him sleeping on a settee in a room at the YMCA and eating in cheap restaurants to stretch his savings. One year later, his income shriveled to $150.

As the number of Moody's converts grew, he realized he would have to build an edifice where spiritual growth could be nourished. So in 1864, with twelve charter members, Moody opened the Illinois Street Independent Church, with an auditorium seating fifteen hundred, and with also several classrooms. The church called the Reverend J. H. Harwood as its pastor, while Moody served as one of the deacons.

Another event that set the stage for

8. Ibid.

Cyrus S. McCormick, evangelical Christian, inventor of the reaper and founder of what would become International Harvester, presents the gospel to the laboring class and financially backs Moody's venture. His son Cyrus McCormick, Jr., becomes one of the school's seven original trustees.

Ira Sankey, an internal revenue collector whom Moody recruits in Indianapolis to become his soloist and songleader. The team of Moody and Sankey soon moves the hearts of millions in Great Britain.

several successful decades of ministry happened in Indianapolis at a convention of the Christian Association. There Moody met Ira Sankey, an internal revenue collector who would become his famous soloist for the next quarter century.

The first time Moody heard Sankey's booming voice lead a morning prayer meeting in "There is a fountain filled with blood," he sought out Sankey after the meeting.

"I want you."

"What for?"

"To help me in my work in Chicago."

"But I can't leave my business."

"You must. I have been looking for you for eight years."[9]

The combination of the short, bearded evangelist and the tall, side-whiskered Sankey proved a spectacular success. One report called it "something like the words-and-music combination of Gilbert and Sullivan." It turned out to be an unbeatable combination, both at home and abroad.

Sankey's voice was resonant, well-controlled. His enunciation was excellent. The songs he chose, and sang, touched the hearts of all—songs like the militant "Hold the Fort," the narrative "Ninety and Nine," and the simple tune and message of "I Am So Glad that Jesus Loves Me."

"Whosoever Will" echoed the joyous welcome of salvation to any who would respond to the work of Calvary. "Rescue the Perishing" gave thousands of Christian workers their marching orders and campaign song.

The crowds at Farwell Hall grew, and the Lord's work prospered.

Then, on a Sunday evening in October 1871, as Moody was preaching in the evening service, ominous flames erupted on Chicago's South Side. The story of Mrs. O'Leary's cow stands as only legend, but by midnight the populace was fleeing in panic. The inferno swept

9. J. C. Pollock, *Moody—The Biography*, p. 88.

On the evening of October 8, 1871, smoke billows up from Chicago's Near South Side. Fire engines clang. People flee. The fire races northeast through tinder business establishments and wooden frame houses. By the next morning Chicago lies in ashes. Dwight Moody loses both his church and his home.

northward block by block, reducing the city to ashes.

Even as fire bells sounded and smoke began to fill the air, Moody was preaching on the text, "What will you do with Jesus who is called the Christ?" Soloist Ira Sankey then sang "Today the Saviour Calls."

Moody urged his audience to consider choosing Christ and to return the following Sunday to make a decision.

When the courthouse bell rang out the alarm and the first horse-drawn fire engines rushed toward the scene, Moody was just concluding his service. Hearing the commotion outside, he and his soloist, Ira Sankey, promptly dismissed the capacity crowd. Hundreds in the gathering rushed to aid others or their own families.

As Moody made his way toward his own home, hurricane-like southwest winds from the fire blew sparks down around him, touching off first one house, then another. "The city's doomed," he told his wife, Emma, as he arrived home.

The Moodys thought their own home was perhaps far enough from the blaze to escape, but in the early morning hours police urged a fast getaway. Dwight and Emma dispatched their two children to the suburbs with a neighbor and began gathering a few belongings.

Among them happened to be a cherished portrait of D. L. Moody by G. P. A. Healy, the most famous portrait artist of that day. Healy had given it to Moody upon his return from a family vacation in Great Britain, where Moody later held dramatically successful campaigns.

Emma urged Moody to save the painting.

"Take my own picture," he laughed. "That would be a joke. Suppose I meet some friends in the same trouble as ourselves and they say, 'Hullo Moody, glad you have escaped. What's that you've saved and cling to so affectionately?' "[10]

Looters already on the scene obligingly cut it out of its frame and handed it to his wife.

Throughout his life Moody abhorred any veneration of himself, either in painting or photo. That is one reason why few photographs of him were ever taken.

This painting of Moody by famous portrait artist G. P. A. Healy barely escapes the Chicago fire. When wife Emma discovers looters about to make off with it, they politely take it from its frame and hand it to her.

The great Chicago fire destroyed Moody's lovely home that had been provided and furnished by friends less than a year earlier. The harrowing experience turned Mrs. Moody, then just twenty-eight, gray almost overnight.

The fire destroyed also the YMCA and Moody's church. While greatly disappointed, in Moody's eyes it was not the worst catastrophe that could happen to man. Far worse that anyone should not hear clearly the gospel. The Chicago fire impressed upon him a new urgency. Farwell Hall, along with most of Chicago, had burned to the ground, and three hundred died.

From that time forward, Moody vowed he would press the decision for salvation not sometime later, but now.

Two weeks after the fire, Moody and his family visited the scene of devastation. He poked through the ruins of his home and found in perfect condition a toy iron stove belonging to his little daughter. It is among the mementos still displayed at the Moody Birthplace and Museum in East Northfield, Massachusetts.[11]

10. Bernard R. DeRemer, "D. L. Moody and the Chicago Fire of 1871," *Moody Alumni* (Winter 1981-1982).
11. Pollock, p. 90.

With his typical endless energy, Moody again sprang into action. He rebuilt his church within a few weeks, named his new building the North Side Tabernacle, and turned it into a relief center to help feed and clothe the thousands who had lost their homes in the fire.

When Moody returned for a Christmas Eve dedication of his new tabernacle, only a few rough shanties had yet arisen in the area—usually on the sheltered side of a blackened, crumbling wall. Streets were blocked with rubbish. Holes gaped where homes and business had been.

Moody himself took up residence in the tabernacle for a time, and spent his mornings scouting for neighborhood refugees. He would say to some half-starved, shivering man who came for help, "Here, take these clothes; help yourself to these provisions—all you can carry; and promise me to thank God for them, on your knees, before you eat the flour and potatoes or put on the coat and trousers." And as Moody met physical needs, hundreds also responded to the gospel.

While in New York City to raise money to rebuild, Moody's heart was set aflame. As he walked along a street in New York City, he received the answer to his prayer for the infilling of the Holy Spirit.

Of it he said, "I was crying all the time that God would fill me with His Spirit. Well, one day in the city of New York—O what a day! I cannot describe it. I seldom refer to it. It is almost too sacred an experience to name. I can only say God revealed Him to me and I had such an experience of His love that I had to ask Him to stay His hand! I went to preaching again. The sermons were not different, yet hundreds were converted."[12]

Moody was soon to take the gospel to Great Britain. That Moody-Sankey campaign got its first spark from a spur of the moment invitation. Moody was invited to speak in a London church. At the close he asked those who wanted "to have your lives changed by the power of God through faith in Jesus Christ as a personal Saviour" and who "wanted to become Christians" to rise. People rose everywhere.

Moody thought they had misunderstood and tried to clarify his invitation. Scores still came forward as Moody and the host minister

looked on, astonished. The phenomenon repeated itself the next night.

Moody returned to the States, now envisioning a British Isles campaign. He and Sankey laid plans, but somehow Moody faulted in his usual administration efficiency and failed to communicate his intentions to his contacts in Great Britain.

When Moody and Sankey arrived at Liverpool in June 1873, they found no one to meet them. Worse yet, Moody soon learned that all three of his prime contacts had died. So he asked a flustered friend in York to set up some evangelistic meetings in that city.

One morning as they waited for something to happen, Moody quipped to his associate, "I say, Sankey, here we are, a couple of white elephants!"

The ministers of York were suspicious. Americans? "Why do they want to come to York?" "What's the YMCA up to?" "Whoever heard of a mission in midsummer?"[13]

Meetings did begin, however, in York's Corn Exchange. Little seemed to happen at first— at least on the surface. Britons were not used to Moody's informal style of preaching or to Sankey's portable organ. They winced at the American evangelist's accent and his sometimes poor English, but the Spirit of God began to work.

D. L. Moody sharply denounced sin, but also made clear to his audiences—many of Calvinistic bent—that God loves even the worst of sinners. Listeners heard him blend the warmth and affection of Jesus as Friend with the awe and reverence of the Lord as God.

" 'To as many as received Him,' " he would quote, " 'to them gave He power to become the sons of God'—Him, mark you. Not a dogma, not a creed, not a myth, but a *Person*."[14]

Sankey's music caught hold. Crowds grew. The campaign extended into weeks, then months. Stores by the thousands displayed revival posters. Government leaders, including British Prime Minister William Gladstone, complimented and endorsed Moody. Communists denounced his

12. Horace Thorogood, "Moody—Salesman of Salvation," *Evening Standard*.
13. Pollock, p. 105.
14. Ibid., p. 106.

work as a "bourgeois plot to import intellectual opium."[15]

Gladstone appeared at one of the great meetings during the campaign, and Moody later summarized their conversation: "He said he wished he had my shoulders, and I said I wished I had his head on them."[16]

Moody and Sankey moved on to Scotland, where anti-ritualistic Scots at first raised their eyebrows at Sankey's organ and criticized Moody's grammar. But revival soon took hold. Moody drew tremendous gatherings in Glasgow. When an auditorium overflowed, he addressed an estimated 50,000 outside from a buggy. He later moved on to Ireland, touching Belfast, Londonderry, and other cities and winning friendly words from the leading Irish Catholic newspapers.

Then he took on London.

It turned out to be his greatest triumph. The figures: Camberwell Hall, sixty meetings, 480,000 in attendance; Victoria Hall, forty-five meetings, 400,000; Royal Haymarket Opera House, sixty meetings, 330,000; Bow Road Hall, sixty meetings, 600,000; and Agricultural Hall, sixty meetings, 720,000. Total: in excess of 2.5 million.[17]

The impact of the campaign would be felt throughout England for decades. It had started with England's middle class, spread to the poor, and eventually permeated even the aristocracy, including the Princess of Wales. When the campaign closed after two years, all Great Britain was talking about Moody and Sankey.

One Birmingham minister, who had prayed for revival but did not expect it to come through two Americans, dryly told Moody, "The work is most plainly of God, for I can see no relation between yourself and what you have done."

Moody laughed. "I should be very sorry if it were otherwise."[18]

Moody and Sankey returned to America as

15. Alfred Balk, "The Man Who Spoke to 100,000," *Sunday Digest* (24 July 1960).
16. Thorogood.
17. Cipriani.
18. Pollock, p. 145.

In 1874 nearly three-quarter million people turn out to hear Moody in a series of sixty meetings at London's Agricultural Hall. Moody's campaigns not only bring countless thousands to salvation but also help unite Great Britain and the United States in common spirit.

1876: Royalties from the Moody-Sankey hymnbook help build the old Moody Church on the corner of Chicago and LaSalle, future site of Moody Bible Institute. Years later the congregation will move a mile to the north, and the Institute's bookstore and women's dormitory (Houghton Hall) will rise on this site.

world famous figures. While many newspapers affirmed the campaign's impact on Great Britain, other journalists scorched the evangelist, assumed unworthy financial motives, and inevitably criticized Moody's English. Jealous clergy spread rumors Moody had to head off, but he had predicted such.

"There will be many bitter things said, and many lies started," he assured, "and as someone has said, a lie will get half round the world before the truth gets its boots on!"[19]

Moody-Sankey hymnbooks sold like hotcakes—both in Great Britain and later in America. Royalties began to pile up, leading to rumors that Moody and Sankey were growing rich on them and that Barnum, the circus magnate, was backing them.

Moody sent the first British royalties, totaling $35,000, home to Chicago to complete his newest church at Chicago Avenue and LaSalle. By the turn of the century the Moody-Sankey

hymnal had generated well over one million dollars in royalties, but it was all channeled into evangelistic and philanthropic causes. Moody and Sankey made not one penny of personal profit.

Neither Moody nor Sankey let the success of the British Isles campaign spoil them. They clearly understood the source of the spiritual power that had swept Great Britain. And if it could happen there, it could also happen in America. Moody began to outline an American revival. The nation needed it. The Civil War, like all wars, had disrupted social morality. People chased after easy wealth. Corruption penetrated high political office.

Target cities were New York, Brooklyn, and Philadelphia—with Brooklyn the opener in October 1875. Rich and poor alike poured in, though the press gave mixed reviews. While some again ridiculed Moody's grammar, the *New York*

19. Ibid., p. 151

Tribune said, "Christianity is not a matter of grammar."[20] And thousands came to Christ.

It was a similar story in Philadelphia, where merchant John Wanamaker let Moody preach in the old freight depot of the Pennsylvania railroad, which Wanamaker had purchased and would later make into a store. One evening, President Grant and several of his Cabinet members sat on the platform.

Then followed great campaigns in New York, Chicago, Boston, Baltimore, Cleveland, Cincinatti, Richmond, Denver, Colorado Springs, St. Louis, and San Francisco. Canada and Mexico also wanted him, but his schedule just didn't permit it.

If those who turned out for Moody expected to hear polished eloquence, they were disappointed. Yet Moody communicated superbly. He was in tune with the common man and also in tune with God. "He knew only two books," Henry Drummond once said, "the Bible and Human Nature. Out of these he spoke; and because both are books of life, his words were afire with life; and the people to whom he spoke, being real people, listened and understood."[21]

Moody treated the Bible as a living Book. He knew it not so much as a scholar, but by intuition. Its historic characters were his personal friends or enemies. They were not misty outlines of legendary lore. Wrote one observer of Moody's day, "He touches them and they live, move and meet you face to face."[22]

"As a public speaker," wrote John H. Elliott, "Mr. Moody impressed me tremendously by his downright earnestness, not expressed by shouting, but by a sort of restrained force that made his words come out red-hot and without affectation. You didn't smell sulphur and brimstone in his sermon. He just talked to his flock on the common sins and urged them to turn away from them."[23]

Moody preached with a clear, resonant voice and with a conversational tone. "He did not affect the orator," Elliott observed. "Rather he seemed to try to use simple words and plain, pronounced in a way that the common people could understand without explanation. He did not intone or shout, nor did he gesture much; but

every movement counted for something worth while."[24]

Once asked "How do you overcome nervousness in the pulpit?" Moody replied, "Be yourself. I detest the kind of people who take a religious tone when they begin to talk to you on the subject of religion, and have a peculiar whine. Be natural. Talk on the subject as you would any other."

C. I. Scofield, known for his Scofield Reference Bible, said of Moody's methods: "[He] never began to preach until he had gathered his

20. Cipriani.
21. P. W. Philpott, "Moody Mighty Reconciler, Like Lindbergh," *The Chicago Tribune* (5 February 1928).
22. S. Parkes Cadman, "Famous Revivalists of the United States," p. 441.
23. *The Chautauquan* (20 January 1895).
24. John H. Elliott, "An American Great-Heart," *Christian Endeavor World* (14 December 1911).

Dwight Moody and associates on the platform at Northfield, Massachusetts, site of large Bible conferences in the second half of the Nineteenth Century. Ira Sankey leads the singing. Moody shuns oratory, speaks mostly in conversational tone.

audience into almost perfect rapport with himself."[25]

And a columnist for the *Chicago Daily News* who had heard Moody a number of times wrote: "He was the most rapid speaker I ever heard, yet every word was distinctly uttered, and in spite of the volume of his utterance there were no useless repetitions. . . . He was the same brusque, cheerful, offhand talker in private that he was on the platform."[26]

Moody excelled at recruiting others. Even in the early days of his work, he was always trying to get new speakers for his mission, and he would hail almost anyone. "Come over to my Sunday school tomorrow and talk Jesus to the children!" He wanted the school kept ablaze with interest.

In a tribute to Moody at his death in 1899, the *Chicago Times Herald* wrote:

Moody found that the sacrificial atonement of the Nazarene had power to touch the hearts of men, and he preached it as Paul preached it in Syria and Macedonia, without embellishment or studied rhetoric. He drew not upon archaeology or cryptograms, but upon the human heart, the daily life, for his proofs of the doctrines of redemption and immortality.

He left the battle of the creeds to be waged by the cloistered scholars. His profession was not theology. He was about his Master's business. While theologians emptied pews with dogmatic controversy, Moody filled great auditoriums with the masses of the people who were hungry for the simple consolations of religion."[27]

Moody's campaigns were the most elaborately planned, advertised, prayed about, and promoted of any to that date. He introduced advance planning by prominent laymen. Moody also used committees, but he always relied on his own choice of individuals for each job. "If there had been a committee," he contended, "Noah's ark would never have got built!" In large cities, his crusades typically involved as many as five hundred ushers and a thousand choir members. Yet in the final analysis it was always the gray-haired, 280-pound Moody who dominated. After hymns by Sankey had established the atmosphere, Moody, Bible tucked under one arm, would step forward to deliver an anecdote-filled half-hour sermon from a short, scribbled outline.

The great evangelist frowned upon hysterical outbursts or claims of miraculous healing, encouraged by many revivalists. Normal interruptions he skillfully integrated into his sermons—especially lost or crying youngsters. "My friends," he would shout, "we are *all* lost children, like that one there!" Altar-call exhortations, while impassioned, were as simple as, "All you must do is come and take, T-A-K-E, take!"

Moody initiated methods that have since become a part of the fabric of today's evangelistic

25. Paul Hutchens, "D. L. Moody's Platform Methods," unpublished paper.
26. Emma K. Parrish, "Early Days on the Great West Side," *Chicago Daily News* (7 February 1929).
27. "Dwight L. Moody" obituary, *Chicago Times Herald* (23 December 1899).

Moody preaches in the cities and towns of America. Today Moody Bible Institute's librarian can open a file of letters and newspaper clippings, filed chronologically, and tell an inquisitor where Moody was on almost every day between 1837 and 1899.

crusades. He may well have been the first evangelist to intelligently use the inquiry room. He could use the Bible effectively with inquirers, and he trained others to do the same. Moody also knew the importance of longer-term follow-up. He encouraged new converts to join a good church, and then to start doing something tangible for the Lord.

And what of his organizational ability? John Elliott comments:

It was of the first order. During the World's Fair campaign in Chicago I had abundant opportunity to see Mr. Moody at his best as an organizer and handler of men. There were times when he had so many in hand that with most men confusion would have surely resulted; but he was perfectly at home, and planned everything so wisely that every man

had his work, and did it, or Mr. Moody speedily knew the reason why.[28]

Yet there were times when Moody, too busy for the detail, frustrated those whom he simply expected to "go do it."

Moody seemed able to handle problems almost intuitively—like the man who once droned on in public prayer from his platform. Moody had a good sense of pace in his public meetings, and he simply could not let the situation get out of hand. Finally, he announced: "While our dear brother finishes his prayer, let us go on with the service."[29]

Moody could handle almost any crank with great skill. A man who wanted to use Moody to forward some personal scheme called on him at his office.

Moody listened for a time. "Do you mind my lying down on my back on this settee?"

"Not at all," replied the man.

"Now go on with your story," said Moody.

The man, thinking he now had great opportunity, proceeded with great assurance.

In less than five minutes Moody was sound asleep. The visitor, feeling at least some sympathy for so tired a man, slipped out.[30]

Moody's British and American campaigns, demanding as they were, still seemed to leave him ample time for other Christian pursuits. Among them were schools he established at Northfield, his birthplace. In 1879, nearly a decade before Moody Bible Institute would become a reality, he opened the Northfield Seminary for Young Women. Two years later in the same town he started the Mount Hermon School for Young Men. These high schools offered a practical curriculum, with the Bible at the center. Later Northfield would become the scene of great summer conferences—the largest of their kind in the world.

Moody went abroad again for another British revival in 1881. It was every bit as great as the first one, and again the city of London gave him the greatest reception. During the campaign

28. Elliott.
29. Pollock.
30. Elliott.

1893: A World's Fair, the Columbian Exposition, comes to Chicago. Dwight Moody mobilizes the city's evangelical forces, turns his school into "campaign headquarters," and preaches to more than two million before the fair closes.

he spoke to two million persons. A third campaign followed.

P. W. Philpott, late pastor of Moody Memorial Church, wrote in the *Chicago Tribune*, "Moody's three triumphant tours of Great Britain had a tremendous influence in drawing England and America closer together."[31]

Moody also, noted Philpott, "worked prodigiously for reconciliation and unity among the Protestant churches." He had no patience with squabbles over nonessentials and preached only the kingdom of heaven as Christ had preached it. "His greatest work of reconcilation, though," said Philpott, "was between individual souls and their God."[32]

A second American campaign built momentum for an era of crusades across the nation that would span almost another two decades—before Moody's death in Northfield in 1899.

Moody preached not only in the big cities, but also in many smaller towns across the nation. If you should want to know, out of curiosity, if and when Dwight L. Moody ever came to your town, the Moody Bible Institute librarian can tell you to the day. And he may even be able to come up with a newspaper clipping of what he said that day! The Institute's Moodyana collection includes over 1,200 Moody

letters in nine bound volumes, indexed and arranged chronologically. From these letters and other sources, the library has compiled a chronological summary of Moody's life, detailing where he was and what he did on almost every day between 1837 and 1899!

Moody's success might have gone to his head, but it didn't. "I am the most overestimated man in the country," he said. But no one believed him. Those who came within the range of his personality felt the touch of God. He brought God to men, and men to God.

Two famous men started from Illinois about the same time. One was Robert G. Ingersoll, the other Dwight L. Moody. Ingersoll went forward with oratory, brilliance, genius, intellect. Moody stepped out with poor education, imperfect grammar, little promise of success. The contrast, in every respect, was like night and day.

The two criss-crossed America, and even roamed the world. The one tore down. The other built up. One called the Bible idiotic, a delusion. The other held the Bible high as God's Word of truth and salvation. Meanwhile, the world looked on. People read their writings, heard them speak. The two men died the same year. Ingersoll was

31. Philpott.
32. Ibid.

1895: Moody takes members of his family on a buggy ride at his home in Northfield, Massachusetts.

buried in New York, and Moody in an obscure New England town that he himself made famous.

Ingersoll left nothing—no hospital, no school, no following to rise up after he was gone and call him blessed.[33]

When Moody's life ended, America, Europe, the world, mourned. God had used him to change millions of lives and to leave a spiritual legacy that continues to impact the world. The stocky man with broad shoulders left his indelible imprint upon a major Midwest city. Chicago at one time claimed this mighty preacher, but by the time he died the whole world claimed him.

The press had called him "Brother Moody" in derision. But he persevered, on behalf of the gospel, until his friends and companions were many of the greatest people in letters, science, and government in every part of the civilized world.

"Never has a man made more of his talents than did D. L. Moody," wrote Philpott. "Lacking eloquence and with an unimposing platform presence, he became the greatest preacher of the age. Meagerly educated himself, he rose to be one of America's foremost educators. Knowing little of business, he developed into a great executive successfully administering a gigantic project. Born in poverty and dying a poor man, his philanthrophy mounted into the millions."[34]

On a chilly day in December 1899, D. L. Moody was buried at the top of a round knoll only a hundred yards from his Northfield birthplace. But in those intervening sixty-two years, Moody had traveled a million miles for the sake of his Savior, and preached to one hundred million people.

The world has never been quite the same.

33. *Quarterly Fellowship Newsletter* (March 1960).
34. Philpott.

Chapter 3

MOODY'S CHICAGO SCHOOL

Dwight L. Moody's dream of a school in Chicago simmered on a back burner for nearly two decades before 1886. It might never have come about had it not been for the influence of three women in his life.

One was the principal of a college.

One was the wife of a famous industrialist and inventor.

The other was his wife.

One winter Sunday morning in 1873, Moody trudged across the Clark Street bridge over the Chicago River, heading for his tabernacle. On the bridge he joined Miss Emma Dryer, an Illinois educator, also on her way to the tabernacle.

The two had met in 1870, through mutual friends. From the outset Moody had been impressed both with Emma Dryer's education and with her knowledge of the Bible. As principal of Illinois State Normal University, she administered a college whose sole purpose was to train teachers for the schools of Illinois.

When the great Chicago fire broke out in October 1871, Emma Dryer was in Chicago visiting friends. She promptly left her educational position to throw her energies into Moody's relief work, as superintendent of the Chicago YWCA.

As the two now walked together, Moody tried his best to persuade Emma Dryer to remain in Chicago, to join his church, to get into the work and to stay with it the rest of her life.

He reminded her of a Christian girls' school in Great Britain, called Mildmay, which had impressed him, and which he had earlier described to her. Moody envisioned a similar kind of school in Chicago. He was going to Great

For nearly two decades Illinois educator Emma Dryer (above) tries to persuade Dwight Moody to start a Bible school in Chicago.

Britain again for eight or ten months, he said, but upon his return he would make the school top priority.

Emma Dryer told Moody, however, that she thought such a school should include men. It should be co-educational, she insisted. But Moody wanted a school for women only, lest he seem to compete against seminaries.

It was years before the idea advanced further. Moody found himself in a British campaign that extended two years, then came home to undertake his American campaigns and develop his schools at Northfield.

Emma Dryer did remain in Chicago and developed what she called the "Bible Work." It expanded, the staff grew, and wealthy financial supporters backed her. During this time Mrs. Cyrus McCormick became a very close friend.

Moody tried again in 1876 to follow through with his promise to Emma Dryer, but the pressures of his schedule sidetracked him once more.

1886: Formation of the Chicago Evangelization Society becomes the official birthdate of the Moody Bible Institute, but the meeting for incorporation takes place in 1887 at the Grand Pacific Hotel (shown above after the Chicago Fire).

By 1882, Miss Dryer decided to make some moves of her own. She had been impressed with the teaching of Dr. W. G. Moorehead, professor at Xenia Seminary (later its president). Why not invite him to Chicago to conduct a short-term Bible institute, she thought, and test the waters for something more permanent?

Emma approached Charles A. Blanchard, pastor of Moody's Chicago Avenue Church. Blanchard assured her he would have no trouble raising $500 for the project. Dr. Moorehead accepted, and the institute opened in May 1882 with fifty students. It was an unqualified success, and what became known as the "May Institutes" were repeated each year until 1889, when the new "Training School of the Chicago Evangelization Society" initiated year-round classes.

1883: Emma Dryer helps bring Dr. W. G. Moorehead of Xenia Theological Seminary to Chicago for several weeks of Bible lectures. This "May Institute" becomes an annual event and leads to Moody's permanent Bible school.

The Chicago Evangelization Society grew out of two special meetings held at Farwell Hall in Chicago to discuss city evangelization. Moody spoke at the first one in 1885. To that group of interested Chicago citizens, he laid it on the line. If they wanted to start a Chicago training school, they first had to raise the money for it.

And while Moody was enthusiastic about the project, he made clear that his schedule would not permit him to stay around Chicago and raise the funds himself. Chicago would have to do it. But was Chicago ready? Moody confided to Emma Dryer that perhaps it should be started in New York.

Upon leaving Chicago, Moody left her

with the challenge: "Keep it before them," he said, "that I won't come until they raise that $250,000" (the sum they had determined necessary).[1]

It did not take long to come up with more than half of the money. Nettie (Mrs. Cyrus) McCormick and her son promised $50,000. John V. Farwell offered $100,000 in stock. On January 22, 1886, Moody returned to Farwell Hall for a second meeting. A Chicago newspaper carried a stenographic report of Moody's address. In part it read:

> I tell you what I want, and what I have on my heart. I would like to see $250,000 raised at once; $250,000 for Chicago is not anything. Some will be startled, but see how the money is pouring in upon you. See how the real estate has gone up, and how wealth is accumulating, and how you are gaining in population . . . .
>
> Take $50,000 and put up a building that will house seventy five or one hundred people, where they can eat or sleep. Take the $200,000 and invest it at 5 percent, and that gives you $10,000 a year just to run this work. Then take men that

have the gifts and train them for this work of reaching the people.

> But you will say: "Where are you going to find them?" I will tell you. God never had a work but what he had men to do it. I believe we have got to have gap-men—men to stand between the laity and the ministers; men who are trained to do city mission work.

Moody told how every city mission work he had seen in Europe had all but failed—because the people were not trained.

> We need the men that have the most character to go into the shops and meet these hardhearted infidels and skeptics. They have got to know the people and what we want is men who know that, and go right into the shop and talk to men. Never mind the Greek and Hebrew, give them plain English and good Scripture. It is the sword of the Lord that cuts deep. . . .[2]

Moody said he did not want to be misunderstood, nor did he want to criticize good

1. Gene Getz, *The Story of Moody Bible Institute,* pp. 35-36.
2. *Chicago Tribune* (23 January 1886), p. 3.

Though unable to be on campus much of the time because of his evangelistic campaigns, Moody visits the school frequently. Here he reads correspondence in his office.

education, but he said that often the typical student "comes out of a theological seminary knowing nothing about human nature; he doesn't know how to rub up to these men and adapt himself to them, and then gets up a sermon on metaphysical subjects miles above these people. We don't get down to them at all; they move in another world."[3]

Clearly Moody no longer objected to men in the Bible institute program. Though the move might offend some seminaries and clergy, to him the great need outweighed the risk.

A little over a year later, Moody met with a group in his room at the Grand Pacific Hotel in Chicago. A constitution for the "Chicago Evangelization Society" had been drafted, and at the meeting a committee was appointed to secure a charter. That became the official first document, or birth certificate, of the Moody Bible Institute.

Six highly qualified men had been appointed as trustees:

Nathaniel S. Bouton, one of the West's most prominent producers of architectural iron and railway castings. As Chicago's former Superintendent of Public Works, his administration had given Chicago its first paved streets.

John V. Farwell, one of Chicago's most prominent dry goods merchants (his firm would be bought out by Carson Pirie Scott & Co. in 1925). Farwell was also vice-president of the Chicago Board of Trade, presidential elector on the Lincoln ticket in 1860, and later Indian Commissioner under President Ulysses Grant. Moody and Farwell were such close friends that someone once called Farwell "the inventor of Dwight L. Moody." "I didn't create him," Farwell countered, "God did."

T. W. Harvey, one of Chicago's pioneer lumbermen and at one time the greatest retail lumber dealer in the world. In Michigan, Harvey built the first logging railroad ever constructed. He also founded the town of Harvey, twenty miles south of Chicago's Loop.

Elbridge G. Keith, one of the organizers and president of Chicago's Metropolitan National Bank, and later president of the Chicago Title and Trust Co. Keith served as Moody Bible Institute's treasurer for eighteen years.

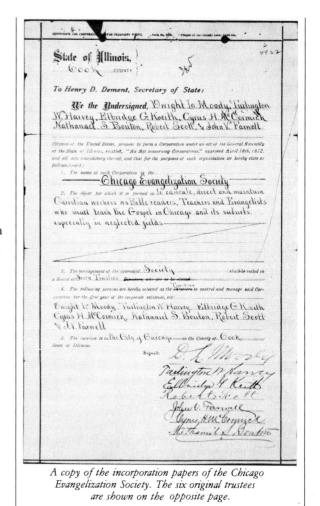

A copy of the incorporation papers of the Chicago Evangelization Society. The six original trustees are shown on the opposite page.

Cyrus H. McCormick, Jr., son of the inventor, who was also a friend and Moody supporter, president, chairman of the board, and executive of the International Harvester Co. for thirty-three years. One of the wealthiest men in the country, he built the present Chicago YWCA building on North Dearborn in memory of his wife, served on a dipolomatic mission to Russia, was a trustee of Princeton University, and served as director of McCormick Theological Seminary.

Robert S. Scott, senior partner in what is now Carson Pirie Scott & Co., still one of Chicago's foremost department stores.

The Chicago Evangelization Society absorbed Emma Dryer's "Bible Work" and began to reach out to the city in tent meetings, thousands of home calls, Bible classes, and the like. But there were growing pains. It was a

3. Ibid.

T. W. Harvey, founder of the town of Harvey, south of Chicago and at one time the greatest retail lumber dealer in the world.

John V. Farwell, prominent Chicago dry goods merchant and vice-president of the Chicago Board of Trade.

Cyrus H. McCormick, Jr., son of the reapers's inventor and International Harvester chief executive for thirty-three years.

Elbridge G. Keith, president of Chicago's Metropolitan National Bank and later president of the Chicago Title and Trust Co.

Nathaniel S. Bouton, who as Chicago's superintendent of Public Works gives the city its first paved streets.

Robert S. Scott, senior partner in what is now Carson, Pirie, Scott, and Co., still one of Chicago's most prominent department stores.

pioneer work, with no previous pattern. Tensions developed, particularly between Moody and Emma Dryer. Moody's long absences and lack of communication, Miss Dryer's penchant for meticulous detail and her health problems all seemingly contributed to her eventual resignation.

Though a great organizer of people, Moody assumed others would handle the details. Wrote Charles Blanchard:

Mr. Moody was an inspirer, not an organizer of work. He was so great a man that he could not debate with fellow workers. He directed them, and persons who did not care to do what he wanted them to were not associated for any length of time with him or his work. This is not a criticism, it is a statement of fact, the truth of which all who knew Mr. Moody personally will recognize.[4]

4. Getz, p. 38.

The work proceeded, but it almost collapsed again in July 1887 when, in a moment of haste, Moody himself resigned.

A letter from Mrs. Cyrus McCormick had precipitated the action. She had written Moody to express discontent regarding the constitution of the Chicago Evangelization Society and to offer ideas for improvement. Moody momentarily misread her intentions.

When in 1887 Dwight Moody resigns in a moment of haste, Mrs. Cyrus McCormick persuades him to reconsider and carry on.

Emma Moody wrote Mrs. McCormick a lengthy note and explained that Moody had made his decision to resign because he believed it would be to the best interest of the group. Mrs. McCormick wrote Moody back, aghast, offering to resign in his place. He realized his mistake and reconsidered.

In an article on the origin of Moody Bible Institute, James Findlay throws further light on Mrs. Moody's role:

> Emma Moody was shy and retiring in the extreme, and few people knew the influence she exerted on her husband. Little record is left of the esteem Moody held for his wife's opinions and the deep affection that existed between them. In her own special way Emma Moody acted constantly as a counterbalance to her ebullient spouse. No better

illustration is available to demonstrate how quietly yet effectively she aided her husband.[5]

Though Emma Dryer withdrew from the work, she continued to admire D. L. Moody and show keen interest in the Moody Bible Institute until her death in 1925. Had she not "kept the vision of the school before him" for sixteen years, and then applied her educational and organizational expertise to its earliest existence, there might not be a Moody Bible Institute today.

Mrs. Dwight (Emma) Moody, though shy and retiring, provides just the right counterbalance to her ebullient spouse.

The short-term "institutes" associated with the Chicago Evangelization Society still had not developed into a full-time school. Nor did that work have its own building or resident campus.

One evening John Morrison, an usher in the Chicago Avenue Church, stepped outside the church's northwest door for a breath of air.

"Is that you, Morrison?" asked Moody, who was to preach that night. "Do you see that lot? Let us pray the Lord to give it to us for a school."

5. James Findlay, "Moody, 'Gapmen,' and the Gospel: The Early Days of Moody Bible Institute," *Church History,* 31 (September 1962), p. 331.

The two men knelt and prayed right there.

In their wildest imaginations, those two could not have envisioned how God would answer that prayer, nor the vast complex that would stand on that very lot and the surrounding properties a century later.

Soon the plans for the largest May institute to date unfolded, and Moody left for the West Coast, leaving orders to "push it."

At a press interview in San Francisco, he was asked:

Do you intend to fit workers for the foreign field?

"Any field on earth that God calls to. I think the training will be good for foreign work. Persons who cannot lead souls to Christ in America, can't do it in Africa or China."

Why not start such an enterprise right here in San Francisco?

"I think Chicago is more central and less expensive to reach. San Francisco is too far to one side."

Will you take persons of any nationality?

"Yes, any one who can understand the English language."[6]

Back in Chicago for the May conference, Moody found an even greater crowd than he had anticipated. Enthusiasm for the school ran high, so Moody promised to return for another conference in September.

Meanwhile, the board moved quickly to buy the three houses next to the Chicago Avenue Church, and the lot for which Moody and Morrison had prayed. The existing structures were remodeled, and construction began on a three-story men's dormitory and main office building at 80 West Pearson Street. A few years later, when Chicago introduced its new street-numbering system, the structure became 153 Institute Place—the building that named a street. The building would become known around the world, and in actuality it would mark the beginning of the strongest force behind the entire Bible institute movement.

Moody himself was the school's president, but he could not administer its day-by-day operation. Moody selected as superintendent the brilliant, young Dr. Reuben A. Torrey, graduate of Yale College and Seminary, who had also studied abroad. Torrey had gotten his first taste of soul-winning in Moody's great New Haven campaign on the threshold of Yale University.

At the dedication of the 153 Building on January 16, 1890, Moody outlined the purpose of the school—to train men and women for city visitation and foreign missions, and to train both evangelists and musicians. A lengthy newspaper interview outlined his philosophy of education. Asked what studies would be pursued in the new training school, he replied:

> Mainly three. First I shall aim to have given a sufficient knowledge of the English Bible; so far as may be, a practical mastery of it. Second, I would have workers trained in everything that will give them access practically to the souls of the people, especially the neglected classes. Third, I would give a great prominence to the study of music, both vocal and instrumental. I believe that music is one of the most powerful agents for good or for evil.[7]

Although Moody's schedule allowed him on campus only occasionally, there was always excitement when he arrived. He often took charge of classes.

Early student and later matron Annie Rosie remembered those times well. "He would not lecture us but talked in a fatherly way about practical things. He told the students to make 'rest day' different from every other day, to put away books—no studying to be done. . . . He told the men students not to try to preach like someone else but to maintain their own individuality. He also told them not to lie on the pulpit when preaching but to stand erect and keep their hands out of their pockets."[8]

William Evans, who would become world famous as an author and Bible teacher, became Moody Bible Institute's first graduate in 1892. Evans had first heard Moody preach at New York City's Fifth Avenue Presbyterian Church. After a forceful sermon from Luke 5, Moody urged young

6. Getz, pp. 42-44.
7. Bernard R. DeRemer, *Moody Bible Institute: A Pictorial History,* p. 30.
8. Ibid., p. 31.

The original Moody Bible Institute, after two stories are added to accommodate the influx of Christians mobilized for the 1893 Chicago World's Fair. Inset: The graduation class of the Summer of 1890.

men and women to give their lives to the Lord's service. Then with his usual uncanny insight, he looked down at the audience and singled out Evans.

"Young man, I mean you."

Again after the meeting Moody said to Evans, "Young man, somehow or other God told me He meant you. Have you never been called to give your life to the service of Jesus Christ?"

Evans, a young convert and a typesetter for the *New York World,* would have to give up a comfortable position. The sacrifice seemed too great. Evans pleaded not enough money.

"Did I say anything about money?" Moody retorted. "Young man, you pack up your trunk and go to my school in Chicago. Never mind about money."

Within a few days Evans was on his way to Chicago, where he found an allowance of twenty-five dollars a month waiting for him.[9]

From the very outset, Moody students have been able to tell story after story of how God has met financial needs. One hundred years later such stories continue to abound. For many this area has always been a test of faith.

The 1893 Chicago World's Fair (Columbian Exposition) gave Moody and his Bible institute the perfect arena for putting evangelism into action. Despite doctor's warnings to slow down, Moody planned the largest single campaign of his career.

Two floors were added to the 153 Building to accommodate visitors and the increasing enrollment that Moody anticipated the fair would bring. The city's evangelical forces mobilized behind him, with the Moody "campus"—such as it was—his campaign headquarters. Clinics on evangelism were set up in

9. Ibid., pp. 32-34.

Tent meetings of the Chicago Evangelization Society bring hundreds to a faith in Jesus Christ as Dwight Moody's school on Chicago's North Side puts down its roots.

Moody persuades William Evans (above) to resign from his typesetter's job with the New York World *and attend his Chicago school. He becomes its first graduate and later a world-renowned Bible teacher.*

eighty churches, tents, theaters, missions, and halls throughout Chicago. Foreign language interpreters were recruited.

By the time the fair was over, Moody's meetings at the exposition had drawn nearly two million people.

The school grew and prospered spiritually. Benefactors like the McCormicks saw that it had the needed funds. Moody constantly scoured the horizon for good Bible teachers, and his contacts were many. By the turn of the century, an almost constant cross stream of figures from the world's evangelical *Who's Who* had preached and taught on campus. These included men like F. B. Meyer and G. Campbell Morgan of London, Andrew Murray of South Africa, C. I. Scofield of Dallas, China missionary J. Hudson Taylor, and many others.

Even then many called the school "Moody's," as some today do. Yet it was not officially named Moody Bible Institute until after the evangelist's death. Moody would not have allowed it.

The school prospered, but on December 22, 1899, newspaper headlines across the nation and even abroad shouted the news that Moody had died while in the midst of a campaign in Kansas City.

His followers reeled in shock.

Fifty years after Moody's death in 1899, Pulitzer Prize winning cartoonist Vaughn Shoemaker draws this cartoon for the Chicago Tribune. Moody Bible Institute had become not only a Chicago "institution," but a world-renowned one.

Chapter 4

THE R. A. TORREY YEARS

The twentieth century was the perfect time for a new run at the future. But only a week before the new year began, the one who so admirably inspired "shoe-leather evangelism" had suddenly passed from the scene. Quaker Oats executive Henry Parsons Crowell said that when Moody died, "it seemed as if the life had gone out of the Institute."[1] R. A. Torrey, however, assured that the work would go on.

Could the school Moody founded take on the new century without him? Would those who had so earnestly supported it still do so without Moody on the scene? And what directions would it take?

"The monument I want when I am dead and gone," Moody had once said, "is a monument on two legs going about the world."[2]

Many also wondered if the Institute could stand true to its biblical doctrines as the winds of theological controversy blew across the land.

R. A. Torrey soon proved himself the right man for the times.

Though raised in a godly home, Torrey had by college days acquired only a veneer of Christianity. At Yale he buckled under social pressure and became a heavy drinker. In his senior year, however, he found personal salvation. When Moody came to town, Torrey involved himself in the crusade.

Torrey's conversion, however, had not settled all his intellectual doubts—even as he pursued theological studies at Yale Seminary. "The professors. . .were all orthodox," Torrey said, "but I was not."[3]

Could he really believe in the resurrection, as told in the Scriptures? Torrey dug into the evidence in depth, and found it overwhelming. "That conclusion," he said, "carried everything with it that was essential."[4]

But Torrey had also followed the transcendental thinkers and read heavily in Unitarianism. Questions remained. From Yale, Torrey pursued studies in Leipzig and Erlangen, Germany, and faced head-on the arguments of the "higher critics." Abroad he settled the question once and for all. Yes, he could trust the Bible, its infallibility, its full authority. And he knew why. Torrey never wavered again.

Yale-educated R. A. Torrey is converted in one of Moody's crusades, studies further in Europe, superintends a Minneapolis rescue mission, then assumes the presidency of Moody Bible Institute.

On return from Germany, Torrey became superintendent of the city mission in Minneapolis.

1. Dorothy Martin, *God's Power in Action*, p. 40.
2. Ibid.
3. Ibid., p. 41.
4. Ibid.

He gave up his salary and deliberately put himself out on a financial limb. City work gave him further seasoning and exposed him to the gospel's power in the lives of men. Such background produced a man who could handle himself and the Scriptures well, whether on skid row or among the theological scholars. Said one biographer, "He could kneel beside a drunk, in a mission or explain the gospel at an elegant dinner table."[5]

It was this combination that gave Dwight L. Moody's successor the credentials to formulate a solid school curriculum and answer the arguments of the higher critics, while at the same time enthusiastically directing the school's city outreach.

Torrey perceived well what he needed to do with the Institute. Moody had relied heavily on guest teachers. Torrey saw the danger that students might look more to prominent men than to the Scriptures themselves. The school needed a resident faculty and a curriculum with more continuity. Guest teachers often differed in certain details of doctrinal viewpoint.

In its aggressive outreach to the city, the Institute originated, under Torrey, what became known as the "gospel wagon." These horse-pulled wagons each held a small organ, a desk for a pulpit, and a few seats for a choir. It was designed to "go where the people were." Here and there it would stop for fifteen or twenty minutes for an outdoor meeting. If the people would not step inside a church, then Moody Bible Institute would take at least a semblance of the church to the people. Within a few years the gospel wagon was seen across Europe.

Others besides Reuben Torrey helped shape the Institute in those early years.

Shortly after Moody's death, his only son-in-law, A. P. Fitt, was elected to the board (for a short while he even held the title of president). Fitt handled executive duties in the transition period. He proved to be an excellent liaison with Moody's friends around the world and also between Chicago and the Northfield schools, which had been entrusted to Moody's oldest son, Will.

5. Ibid., p. 44.

Like Dwight L. Moody, Torrey can relate both to the educated elite and the man on the street. He pushes the concept of the "gospel wagon," taking the gospel to people where they are. Horse-drawn wagons like the ones above later give way to the automobile (see page 69).

The faculty in 1911. Front row: J. H. Ralston, Miss A. M. Taylor, Miss C. A. Cary, Miss D. M. Sellers, William Norton. Middle row: J. H. Hunter, H. W. Pope, J. M. Gray, D. B. Towner, William Evans, A. F. Gaylord. Back row: J. B. Trowbridge, E. A. Marshall, E. O. Sellers, George S. Schuler, W. C. Coffin, W. L. Gilpin.

More prominent names were added to the board. Publisher Fleming H. Revell, Moody's brother-in-law, became a trustee in 1900. Among other great men who later joined were world-famous gynecologist Dr. Howard A. Kelly of Baltimore and William Whiting Borden, wealthy New England heir, later immortalized in missionary annals as "Borden of Yale." Borden gave almost his whole million-dollar fortune to the cause of missions—$100,000 of that going to Moody. When he died at age twenty-five, Princeton Seminary said, "Probably in the history of the Christian church, no man of his years has ever provided so largely for the evangelization of the world."

Then there was Thomas S. Smith, "apple king of the Midwest." He walked forward in the Chicago Avenue Church one night when D. L. Moody was preaching. Moody took his hand, looked in his face, and said, "Young man, God has a place for you!"

Again, Moody was prophetic. Thomas Smith served on the Moody Bible Institute board for forty-three years, twenty as vice-chairman. Quiet and unassuming, he arose every morning at 4 A.M. for his quiet time—before going to the old South Water Street market. Smith's son, Wilbur M. Smith, became a Moody professor, noted Christian author, and long-time *Moody Monthly* magazine columnist.

James H. Todd was named the first superintendent of men. A. F. Gaylord, a student in 1891, became business manager that same year and held the job for forty-four years.

Henry Parsons Crowell, founder of Quaker Oats, also stepped into the Institute scene in those early transitional years and helped chart its future.

How did a cereal magnate find his way into the mainstream of Moody Bible Institute? Crowell had never met Moody, but he had heard him preach once. The Chicago business executive lived on Rush Street, only a few blocks from the Institute, and was active at nearby Fourth Presbyterian Church on Michigan Avenue. A godly man, it was no surprise that he should

1901: Henry Parsons Crowell, founder and chief executive officer of Quaker Oats, serves as chairman of the Board of Trustees for more than forty years.

become interested in the work of the Moody Bible Institute.

Crowell and his wife invited Moody Bible teacher William R. Newell (lyricist of the famous gospel song, "At Calvary") into their home to conduct a weekly Bible class. The experience revolutionized their lives.

Crowell was elected to the board of trustees in 1901 and became president three years later—a position he would hold for forty years. As a hard-working trustee with keen business acumen, Crowell poured himself into the challenge heart and soul.

As Crowell got close to the inner-workings of the organization, he realized the school lacked a broad financial support base. D. L. Moody had relied heavily on the gifts of well-to-do businessmen. Crowell himself gave very generously, but he also saw the danger in doing so.

Even as he joined the board, financial woes were piling up. Bills on daily operational costs exceeded income. Property repairs went unattended. Some donors loyal to Dwight L. Moody, but not to the school itself, had stopped giving.

Crowell gave of his own wealth to help keep the Institute going, but he knew that was only stop-gap. Crowell envisioned thousands of donors across the country who would give to the school on a regular basis, even if the gifts were in small amounts. And with a broad financial base, the Institute would also have a broad prayer base. He theorized that people would pray more for the success of a project if their money was in it.

With godly wisdom and concern, Crowell saw another aspect. A broad base of support would help hold the school to its purpose, its biblical doctrine, its evangelical zeal. If these ever swerved or faded, support would also fade. As Crowell put it, "if the fire no longer burned, the Institute deserved to die."[6]

An expanded board of trustees also helped solidify the organization in transition. The large board became, at times, a bit unwieldy, so for the urgent high-level decisions necessary between

6. Ibid., p. 51.

board meetings, Crowell suggested the establishing of an executive committee from within the board. The idea has been followed ever since.

Lean financial years following Moody's death precipitated a cautious fiscal policy. With rare exception, the Institute refused to build new buildings unless the money was first in hand.

That secure approach to building endures at MBI today. At times, especially during high inflation, some have questioned the wisdom of that policy. "Construction costs have spiraled while the Institute waited for all the funds." "Does this not show lack of faith in the fact that God will provide the balance, once the step has been taken and the building is underway?" Yet it has saved millions of dollars of mortgage interest over the decades. The exercise of faith still operates when building needs arise. And one look at the Moody campus today hardly suggests that God has withheld His blessing.

This insight, and the business ethics established from the very beginning of this century, can be traced to the godly wisdom of Henry Parsons Crowell.

When the Institute set its course at the outset of the century, it put gospel music high in the curriculum. Though Moody himself could not carry a tune, he recognized music as a powerful medium for the gospel—a medium men could put either into the hands of God or into the hands of Satan. Obviously, he used it well in his own crusades. Soloist Ira Sankey's health did not hold long enough for him to remain with Moody in latter years. But Hugh McGranahan, nephew of then famous composer James McGranahan, was tapped to head Moody Bible Institute's first music department. A rich heritage of gospel music blossomed as the years passed (see chapter 23).

No event at Moody Bible Institute draws greater crowds than the annual Founder's Week. The week-long Bible conference in early February brings thousands to the campus. By 1984, even the 4,000-seat Moody Church could no longer accommodate the response on the closing Sunday afternoon of the conference, and Moody moved this event to Chicago's new 18,000-seat indoor Horizon Stadium in suburban Rosemont.

1909: The school breaks ground for a men's dormitory (152 Institute Place, later named Norton Hall). The apartments in the background are now the site of Torrey-Gray Auditorium.

A men's dormitory room at the turn of the century.

Founder's Week started in 1901 as a one-day observance of Moody's birthday—February 5. Legend has it that Moody himself dashed into a classroom—or dining room—one February 5 and declared, "It's my birthday. Let's go for a sleigh ride." In 1901, after Moody's death, the Institute initiated a Founder's Day observance—classes were canceled, and students shared a day of recollections about D. L. Moody, in prayer and social activities. Some years, at least, that included a sleigh ride. Special Founder's Week conferences in 1911 and 1917 led to an established week-long event by 1926.

The Institute schedule at the turn of the century kept a fast pace. Mornings were filled with classes, afternoons in most cases with

An early Founder's Week celebration in Old Moody Church. More than three-quarters of a century later the closing 1984 Founder's Week service will draw more than 15,000.

practical work "appointments" (five each week) for every student—a rescue mission, children's meeting, open-air meetings, or a visit to a hospital, jail, or home. This was designed to "test students, as well as train them. Many do not know the gift that is in them until they are put on trial."

Classes ran Tuesday through Saturday. Monday was rest day. That was the time for a picnic lunch in the park, a boat ride on Lake Michigan, ice skating or sledding in Lincoln Park, or perhaps a game of tennis on the Clark Street courts near Newberry Library.

Students had to fulfill one hour's domestic duty daily ("dum work," as it was called). That might be washing glasses and silver, dusting

1898: A student tennis game, with Chicago's Newberry Library in the background. Moody Bible Institute is two blocks away.

A turn-of-the-century scene in the library (first floor of the original building). A close study shows students properly spaced, all holding their poses for the photographer.

November 1905: The first graduating class of Moody Bible Institute.

offices, or one of many other chores. It not only helped establish household discipline, but it also saved the Institute money. The practice continued until World War II.

Men and women ate in different dining rooms. The evening tea bell always rang at six o'clock, recalled Margaret Blake Robinson, former newspaperwoman and author of *A Reporter at Moody's* (1900). "We have chicken and ice cream for dinner. Every former student knows it is Wednesday," she wrote, "for that is the day the brown hen comes down from her perch in the family coop to gladden the student's heart."[7]

An evening "Bible talk" might follow, then "dum work" and socializing in the parlor. Faculty and students prayed together the first Tuesday of each month. Friday morning Missionary Study and Prayer Union often brought together students with missionaries on furlough. In such sessions many committed their lives to the mission fields.

Reuben A. Torrey kept a close eye on student life until, after nearly a decade as president, he resigned in 1909 for full-time evangelism. The crusades of R. A. Torrey brought further millions under the sound of the gospel during his career—with the impact upon Australia as great as upon any continent. In 1912, Torrey became dean of the Bible Institute of Los Angeles (now Biola University), where he served until 1924. When he died in 1928, he had written more than forty books. Some of them, like *What the Bible Teaches* and *The Divine Origin of the Bible*, are still in print.

When Torrey left in 1909, the mantel fell on James M. Gray, who would guide Moody Bible Institute until it was almost a half century old.

7. Margaret Blake Robinson, *A Reporter at Moody's.*

Reuben A. Torrey and his staff keep the Moody Bible Institute afloat after Moody's death, but Torrey is away much of the time on evangelistic campaigns as distant as Austrailia. In 1909 he resigns. Three years later he becomes dean of the Bible Institute of Los Angeles, now Biola University.

Chapter 5

THE JAMES M. GRAY YEARS

The authority of the Bible was the main issue in a fundamentalist-modernist division that split the 1920s.* Denominations with creeds based on the Word of God crumbled before the new spirit that intellectually pitted man against God and seemingly found God wanting.

Evangelicals were naturally alarmed at the denial of basic Christian doctrines by ministers and seminaries. Some reacted with shrill denunciations, but many able evangelical preachers and teachers held their ground during those tempestuous years. They did not bury their heads in the sand nor take an anti-intellectual, irrationally angry stand. *The Fundamentals*, a series of twelve booklets, gave a clear explanation and a defense of essential Christian doctrines. Dr. Torrey and Dr. Gray were among the leaders who presented the conservative view of Scripture in a scholarly, reasonable way.

During those years faith missions were established. Other Bible schools and Bible colleges joined Moody to vigorously challenge the liberal teaching in schools originally established by Christians.

But it cannot be denied that liberals had the loudest religious voices in the 1920s and 1930s. Other groups and cults busily pushed their ideas as well. Christian Science added thousands of converts, and Russellism spread rapidly. Emile Coue's host of followers faithfully repeated his slogan, "Day by day, in every way, I am getting better and better."

The excesses of the Roaring Twenties reached a crescendo in Chicago. Even school children knew about the houses of prostitution and the gambling dens. Henry Crowell's original Committee of Five became a Committee of Fifteen as other businessmen joined the effort to control the appalling vice. Chicago became the center of a vicious era of control by gangsters.

Suddenly the foundation of society abruptly crumbled with the stock market in 1929, and the economy crashed in on the city. The financial crisis was so bad in 1930 that the police were not even paid. But Chicago hoped the money that the throngs of visitors spent at the Century of Progress Fair, opened in 1933, would cure its depression. It didn't.

Naught have I gotten but what I received;
Grace hath bestowed it since I have believed;
Boasting excluded, pride I abase;
I'm only a sinner saved by grace.

These words of the gospel song, *Only A Sinner,* came from the pen of James M. Gray. They reflect the spirit of the man who would lead Moody Bible Institute through perilous times, early financial crisis, upheaval of world war, theological confusion, then the collapse of Wall Street.

For more than a quarter century Gray commanded the ship skillfully through rough waters. Yet it could hardly be said that he fit the image of a man who had ambitiously pushed himself up into the executive ranks.

And that may have been one reason for his success: he was completely uninterested in pushing himself.

* The following information on religious, political, and social events is excerpted from *God's Power in Action,* by Dorothy Martin (Moody Press).

"Whom am I serving?" he often asked. [1]

Gray was born in New York City in 1851 and converted as a young man. In 1879, at twenty-eight, he was called to the First Reformed Episcopal Church in Boston. There he pastored for a quarter century and also taught Bible courses at what is now Gordon College.

Though a specialist in Bible exposition, Gray also set a fast pace in community affairs. At that time the major issue was anti-liquor legislation. Because Gray felt preaching against sin also meant taking action in the marketplace, he became an ardent prohibitionist.

As a student in New York, Gray sang in Moody's meetings at the Hippodrome and heard him preach many times. When Moody asked him to speak at his Northfield summer conference, Gray made the Book of Job come alive to laymen. Moody was so impressed that he invited him to teach at the Institute during summer months. In fact, he put Gray in charge of the total operation while Torrey was away for four months on an evangelistic campaign.

By 1904, the Institute was still groping for a plan that would solve the dilemma of its day-by-day leadership, especially during Torrey's frequent absences. In one plan, writes William M. Runyan in *Dr. Gray at Moody Bible Institute,* "Each dean was to give four months a year, or one term, to teaching in the Institute and eight months to Bible teaching or evangelism on the field." [2] Gray, who had served as a regular summer lecturer, was to be one dean, Torrey another, and it was hoped that C. I. Scofield would be the third.

It was not good organizational strategy, and fortunately the plan never materialized. Also, Torrey and Gray had theological differences, although they were not insurmountable.

The far-sighted administrative counsel of Henry Parsons Crowell saved the day. Crowell urged that Gray accept the position of full-time dean. Gray was reluctant—he did not want to handle the top position alone. But Crowell's gentle persuasion prevailed.

Gene Getz, in *The Story of Moody Bible Institute,* describes this move, in retrospect, as a

1. Martin, p. 66.
2. William M. Runyan, *Dr. Gray at Moody Bible Institute,* p. 139.

In its early tradition of outreach to the city, Moody Bible Institute gathers children from the neighborhood for its Vacation Bible school.

pivotal decision. "It is highly possible," he says, "that without Gray's leadership, the institute may have moved in one or two directions—either toward fanaticism with an emphasis on 'healing' and 'emotional demonstrations' or toward theological liberalism, as happened in the Northfield Schools."[3]

Technically, Gray did not become "president" of Moody Bible Institute until 1923, for until that time the chairman of the executive committee, Henry Crowell, carried that title. But in reality, Gray served a presidential role.

The man who did not really want the top job not only demonstrated his administrative expertise, but he also proved a strong spokesman for biblical orthodoxy.

While the era of Dwight L. Moody had had its own doubts and skepticism, the drift from orthodoxy intensified after the turn of the century. Gray's abilities as a superb Bible teacher and expositor stood him well in the role of Christian

apologist and defender of the faith.

Gray also employed the tools of a Christian journalist. During his years in Boston, he had seen firsthand the hold of Christian Science on sincere, earnest people. So he wrote *The Antidote to Christian Science*. He attacked not the people, but the belief.

With Harry Emerson Fosdick, though, it was a different story. Fosdick had denied the faith he was ordained to uphold, and his book, *The Peril of Worshipping Jesus*, had documented his apostasy. Gray published a scalding reply in his book, *The Audacity of Unbelief*. Among Gray's other books in defense of the faith were *Why I Believe the Bible Will Stand*, *Why a Christian Cannot Be an Evolutionist*, and *Modernism, a Foe to Good Government*.

A push for an "inter-church world movement" emerged after World War I. Gray

3. Getz, p. 77.

The executive committee of Henry Parsons Crowell, James M. Gray, and Thomas S. Smith, (the latter called by some the "apple king of the Midwest") guides the affairs of Moody Bible Institute through almost a quarter century. Thomas Smith's son, Wilbur, later becomes a renowned Moody Bible Institute professor and popular Moody Monthly columnist.

spoke out for denominations and the role of the local church. The Moody Bible Institute had always been interdenominational, and it would back those local churches who still stood for the fundamentals of the faith.

The term "fundamentalism" itself, of course, did not originate until shortly after 1909, when Gray and Torrey and the orthodox scholars contributed to *The Fundamentals* as a defense of historic biblical doctrines. Over the years the Institute has held, without compromise, to the fundamental doctrines of evangelicalism.

Although James M. Gray defended the faith without compromise, he did so as a gentleman. It would have contradicted his quiet, dignified nature to do otherwise. Yet his words struck with power.

In 1914, with the world on the brink of World War I, the Institute sponsored a historic Prophetic Bible Conference at Moody Church to reaffirm the doctrines of historic Christianity, both for the church at large and for the Institute itself. Ministers gathered from across the country and went home feeling its great impact. Although newspapers that week criticized the conference for what it saw as a pessimistic tone, the ominous events of the world at that time, observed Dr. Wilbur M. Smith, "compelled journalists to resort to the very apocalyptic vocabulary that they decried."[4]

Gray was a Bible scholar, but he also knew how to make what he taught, and what he wrote, very clear. It was Gray who introduced the "synthetic" method of Bible study, which helped students see the Bible as a whole, and each Bible book as a whole. His *How to Master the English Bible* became a classic. Other Bible institutes, colleges, and seminaries throughout the world used his method.

R. A. Torrey had already pioneered a study-by-mail program, and Gray's synthetic Bible study approach gave the fledgling Moody Correspondence School a boost. Moody quickly added correspondence courses in Introductory Bible, Christian Evidences, and Evangelism. Close on the heels of those came Dr. C. I. Scofield's three-volume course, which covered the entire Bible.

Meanwhile, the Evening School also grew. At one point its curriculum duplicated the Day School, but it soon became impossible to crowd all of those same courses into evening hours. Evening School was forced back into its original format and purpose—to train laymen in local churches, not necessarily full-time Christian workers.

"The English Bible," said Moody's 1922-23 catalog, "is the great and fundamental textbook. It is felt that simply from an intellectual point of view a clear and comprehensive acquaintance with its contents is in itself a liberal education. But from the spiritual side, to know it thoroughly and to be able to

4. DeRemer, p. 56.

1914: At this historic Prophetic Bible Conference at Moody Church, MBI declares the "fundamentals of the Christian faith," both for its own posterity and for clear delineation to the nation and the world.

handle it rightly in preaching, teaching, and in personal work is absolutely indispensable to Christian workers of every class."

The Institute chose for its scriptural motto 2 Timothy 2:15: "Study to show thyself approved unto God, a workman that needeth not to be ashamed, rightly dividing the word of truth."

Not only did Moody Bible Institute weather the fundamentalist-liberal storm and save its own destiny, it molded opinion as well. Wrote one Jasper Mossee in The World Book in 1923, "In my judgment, the constituency that has gone out from the Moody Bible Institute during the last ten years has saved the evangelical churches of the country."[5]

The usual blend of quiet dignity and firm authority that Gray possessed was described well by student Betty Scott (later Mrs. John Stam, who with her husband would be martyred in China). In a letter to her missionary father in China during her first term at Moody she wrote:

> Dr. Gray did not wait for me to make myself known, but fairly early in the fall sent me a nice note asking if I could come to his office at a certain hour. How charming and lovable a man he is! I just love him. And he inspires me with awe. More than any other person I ever heard, he gives the sure impressions of "speaking with authority," like the old prophets. Yet nobody could ever accuse him of being conceited. . ."[6]

Behind Gray's dignity also lay a penchant for an amazing amount of humor. Often he took the occasion of an offering to tell one of his funny stories. "God pity the man," he once said to his secretary, "who takes his work too seriously."

Gray of course did have his serious side. Students who walked in late to chapel were sure to feel the cold stare of James M. Gray. At times some thought Gray's watchful eye saw too much. But beneath it all he was looking after the welfare both of students and employees.

Gray built and maintained a faculty that was equally committed to the Scriptures. One of those he recruited was P. B. Fitzwater, who at one time was the most widely read newspaper writer in the world with a syndicated column appearing in 2,600 papers across the nation. Fitzwater, an able Bible scholar, served as dean and then director of general course and the pastors' course for more than thirty years—until his retirement in 1954. The main classroom building on campus bears his name.

Gray insisted that his faculty live near the campus to be present at Institute functions. He wanted both a close family atmosphere and a close management team.

In 1905, Gray combined the men's and women's departments, which had been separate. But men and women still continued to sit on separate sides in classes—and in the dining room.

5. Rollin Lynde Hart, "The War in the Churches," *The World Book* (September 1923), p. 472.
6. DeRemer, p. 49.

1913: P. B. Fitzwater, one of the nation's most popular newspaper columnists, joins the faculty and stays for nearly forty years. In 1960, the school dedicates Fitzwater Hall to his memory.

He also added English to the curriculum, which until that point had been a feature of only the Evening School—to accommodate immigrants and help them understand the Bible.

From the school's outset, entrance requirements had been minimal. In Moody's day many people, though intelligent and self-educated, had not pursued formal study beyond the fifth or sixth grade. Now times were changing. Secular educators set higher standards. Gray insisted that minimal entrance requirements did not mean inferior education. But to move with the times, he proposed requiring a high school education for entrance.

The move triggered a storm of protest. Even Torrey feared that it would keep out many for whom the school was originally intended. But the move was made anyway, and the storm eventually subsided.

The earliest days of Gray's regime saw little monies to expand the campus. But after a time the Institute acquired adjacent properties, and in 1909 it built an additional men's dormitory (152 Institute Place), renamed Norton Hall in 1951. Nearly two decades later, the building—which stood approximately where the underground student dining hall is today—was

The faculty in 1927. Now two years after the Scopes Monkey Trial in Tennessee, theories of evolution gain popularity in the marketplace. Moody Bible Institute holds firm. Years later even reputable scientists will challenge the premises of evolution.

torn down to develop the new campus. In the early seventies the Norton name was transferred to a newly-acquired building near Evanston.

In 1912, the Women's Building (830 N. LaSalle) arose. Now Smith Hall, it houses offices on the first three floors, and married students and single women students on the upper floors. The building has been so modernized that it is now difficult to tell that it was one of the school's earliest buildings.

The old Moody Church on the corner of LaSalle and Chicago was the Institute's next major purchase. It became the school's auditorium. (The Moody Church congregation in 1915 built a 5,000-seat tabernacle, with sawdust floor, on North Avenue a mile to the north, and then dedicated its present 4,200-seat edifice on that same site in 1925.)

Students eagerly descend upon the post office looking for mail from home. The scene will repeat itself daily for the decades to follow. Only the clothing styles will change.

James M. Gray gave Moody Bible Institute its school song in 1909, with music professor D. B. Towner supplying the tune. In years to come it would become loved by thousands all over the world. Gray wrote many other hymns and gospel songs, some of which remain standards in American hymnals.

By 1912, Moody had more than two-hundred students from about forty denominations. By 1916 it had an alumni association. And by then the buildings of the Institute totaled six and one-half acres of floor space. One visitor to the campus said, "I have seen many things grown on

a space of six acres, but none that gave the results of your institution."[7]

These stairs of the 153 Building lead past a beautiful stained-glassed window of "The Sower" (see page 6). Years later it will backdrop the information desk of Crowell Hall. Below: Conversation at the old information desk in 153.

In the mid-twenties the nation had begun to pioneer a new medium called radio. Henry Coleman Crowell, son of the Quaker Oats founder, had just joined the Moody staff. With the foresight characteristic of his father, he realized the potential.

Gray at first did not think Christians had any business tampering with the airwaves. Scripture defines Satan as "prince of the power of

7. Ibid., pp. 57-58.

the air," and Gray, along with some other Christians of his day, saw it as a potentially dangerous realm, though he had other reservations as well. The story may leave us amused, but even Gray shortly changed his mind. When in 1926 a North Dakota resident wrote to Moody Bible Institute and asked, "Is radio of God or the devil?" President Gray answered, "We think it is of God."[8]

The years of Dr. Gray spanned dramatic changes in women's fashions, from pre-World War I ankle-length dresses to the flapper era of short skirts, rolled silk stockings, and heavy makeup. School officials had to decide where to draw the line. On such sensitive issues students and administration sometimes clashed. Dorothy Martin writes:

> We look back and smile at the "sleeves to the elbow" rule. The girls then did not all smile, of course, and some found ways of getting around it. One could always put elastic in the sleeve and pull it up or down as the situation required. And the men grumbled at wearing coats and ties in the

dining room in Chicago's blistering heat. Life was regimented, but after all, was not this the "West Point of Christian Service"?[9]

When James M. Gray retired from the presidency in 1934, depression still lay heavy across the land. A year earlier, in an attempt to bolster spirits, Chicago had staged its 1933 Century of Progress Exposition. But it was a bit like whistling in the dark. Gloom prevailed. Moody Bible Institute felt the economic impact of the time, but its own mission, its spirit, its vigor, stood above temporal events.

Already Moody Bible Institute was almost a half century old, and some of its graduates had already spent a good portion of their lives in Christian service at home or abroad. The rich heritage that Moody, Torrey, Gray, their associates, and the school's alumni had already passed on would lay the foundations of the next half century.

8. James M. Gray, "Radio," *Moody Bible Institute Monthly* (March 1926), p. 309.
9. Martin, p. 77.

Founder's Week, from the time of its origin, has brought the greatest expositors of the time to Moody's campus. Pictured above are the 1930 celebration's speakers. Front row: H. A. Ironside, Charles Abel, William Lamb. Middle row: Abraham Machlin, Francis Russell, H. W. Beiber, A. Hudson, Elias Newman. Back row: M. H. Reynolds, Harry Strachan, H. W. Hudson.

1935: James M. Gray at Lake Michigan, one year after he retires. His administration spans three decades, from the era of Theodore Roosevelt to Franklin Roosevelt. Moody Bible Institute is now almost a half century old.

Chapter 6

THE WILL HOUGHTON YEARS

Young Will Houghton had a natural talent for the stage. In his teens, and against his mother's objections, he signed with a touring company. He developed into a seasoned vaudeville actor, circuiting the country with his own comedy act.

His theatrical career came to an abrupt end at age twenty-three when a sermon in his mother's church brought him under conviction. Though he had already received Christ during an evangelistic crusade at fourteen, Houghton now surrendered all. He abandoned the stage.

After further education, Houghton launched into the ministry, gaining practical on-the-job experience with itinerant evangelists in the New York area. He became a songleader, gospel singer, and budding preacher. He eventually came to the attention of Dr. Reuben A. Torrey, who saw great potential in the young man and took him under his tutelage. When Houghton took his first church, nine people were converted at his trial sermon, the first of thousands during his career. Large crowds turned out to hear his most popular sermon, "From Stage to Pulpit."[1]

Adelaide, Houghton's wife of two years, took suddenly ill in the summer of 1916 and died that autumn, leaving him with two infants. Two years later Houghton married Miss Elizabeth Andrews, whom he had met while serving as a chaplain to World War I troops leaving for the front lines.

God's hand seemed to be upon all that Houghton undertook. He pastored a church near Philadelphia with stunning results. After preaching to great crowds in Ireland, he accepted a call to the Baptist Tabernacle in Atlanta, one of the South's most influential congregations. Three years later he left that church at its peak attendance of 4,000 to pastor the Calvary Baptist Church of New York City, across the street from Carnegie Hall.

Main entrance of the Calvary Baptist Church of New York City, where James M. Gray finds the man to succeed him as president. Will Houghton leaves Calvary's pulpit to assume his new call to Chicago.

There Will Houghton—evangelist, church builder, and Bible teacher—had to follow John Roach Stratton. Church attendance had plummeted upon Pastor Stratton's death. Calvary's new skyscraper church-hotel complex stood half completed when the stock market crashed.

Houghton rebuilt the congregation and saw completion of the new auditorium, embedded

1. William R. DePlata, *Tell It from Calvary,* p. 59.

inside the church's 320-room Hotel Salisbury. Houghton soon found himself in the role of pastor and hotel president. He filled both the church and the hotel.

Crowds packed Calvary's downtown Manhattan church on Friday nights for youth rallies that foreshadowed the Youth for Christ movement still nearly two decades away. Calvary's radio outreach sent both Houghton's sermons and his melodious baritone voice out across New York City. The city was Houghton's great burden, and so he wrote a book of poetry called *Rhymes from a City Tower*. In its preface he wrote:

"The people! The people! How our Lord loved the people of the crowded city. He yearned for them and wept over them. . . . Who in Christ's name will love the people of our city today?"[2]

The economic storm rumbled ominously just over the horizon and broke in 1929. The national picture in James M. Gray's closing years as president of MBI was grim.

March 1933 had turned out to be the low point in the nation's morale as unemployment figures soared. Bread lines shuffled men along cold sidewalks in city after city. No one was prepared for the shock of the depression that boiled out of the world's failure to settle its

economic problems after World War I.

During the thirties, certain forces shaped the country's attitudes and actions. These were philosophical and religious rather than material and political. They did not hit as sharply as the depression, but they had a lasting influence on American culture and religion.

The decline in moral values of the Jazz Age was coupled with the alarming flood of gangsterism and lawlessness. The repeal of prohibition in 1933 proved a bitter blow to Protestant groups which had thought it would control the abuse of liquor.

The social gospel proponents seemed to some to be right after all in preaching that this life needed more attention than the afterlife. Many churches joined to condemn the social order and advocate even more extreme measures than the New Deal had taken. New groups formed such as Frank Buchman's Oxford Movement, reaching "up-and-outers" with a do-good philosophy.

The neo-orthodox theology movement rose out of the circumstances shaping those years. It stressed a return to the Bible, but not to the doctrine of scriptural inerrancy. Evangelicals stood for the reliability of Scripture and the need for

2. Ibid., p. 64.

The faculty in 1943. Neo-orthodoxy, the Oxford movement, and other liberal trends continue to erode America's churches, but Moody continues to send solid young men and women into the Christian ministry both at home and abroad.

1935: Gospel wagons disappear. Enter the V-8 gospel car. A crowd assembles for the dedication of these vehicles to the cause of the gospel. New president Will Houghton leads the ceremonies.

personal salvation through Jesus Christ alone.

The chaotic economic, social, and religious conditions affected American churches in different ways. Some closed during the unsettling times; others merged to conserve buildings and programs and finances. Still others found attendance increased as people searched for meaning to their hard lives.

Into his eighties, James M. Gray decided to retire as MBI president and handpick his successor. Neither the board nor Gray could seem to find just the right man. Then in early 1934 Gray chaired a Moody-sponsored Bible conference in Calvary Baptist Church. At the Sunday morning service he heard Dr. Will Houghton preach. Immediately Gray decided, "There is the man to follow me at the Institute."[3]

For Houghton it was another call to the city, this time the "city with broad shoulders." It was also a call to the pulpit, a call to the Word of God he loved so well, a call to young people, to radio, to writing—all of which Houghton had handled well. And his experience in the building program in New York City brought further expertise into his new role.

Moody Bible Institute now had over 900 students, a radio station, a correspondence school, a magazine, and a book publishing operation. Houghton characterized himself as a "creator of ideas." But he knew the future dare not be built on his mere human ingenuity. When he had taken the pastorate of New York City's Calvary Baptist, he told the congregation, "I want to build around the Lord, not around myself." When he arrived at Moody, his first move was to call the Institute to prayer, including its alumni around the world. "God alone," he said, "is equal to the needs."[4]

Only a month after Houghton's inauguration, the martyrdom of MBI graduates John and Betty Stam in China shocked the Christian world. On December 7, 1934, Communists looted their mission station at Taingtech, Anhwei Province, took them hostage and demanded $20,000 ransom. The next day, before negotiations could be completed, their decapitated bodies were found along the road.

At the news of the tragedy, many offered their lives to spread the gospel abroad.

In memory of the Stams, Will Houghton wrote a poem, "By Life or By Death," later set to music by George S. Schuler.

> The world moves on, so rapidly the living
> The forms of those who disappear replace
> And each one dreams that he will be enduring—
> How soon that one becomes the missing face!

3. Ibid., p. 65.
4. Martin, p. 100.

Henry Coleman Crowell (at center, wearing glasses) leads one of WMBI's popular outdoor broadcasts. These airings were held in front of Crowell Hall and draw hundreds of observers.

Help me to know the value of these hours,
Help me the folly of all waste to see;
Help me to trust the Christ who bore my sorrows,
And thus to yield for life or death to Thee.[5]

Houghton was a master promoter, and the Institute needed all it could get to keep its head above water in the rough seas of economic depression. Two events gave Houghton the ideal occasion: the fiftieth anniversary of the Institute and the centennial of Moody's birth. He called for a massive two-year celebration, with a strong evangelistic emphasis.

The Institute pushed plans to observe the two events both in the United States and in Great Britain, the scene of Moody's greatest evangelistic campaigns. Churches in every state and thirty foreign countries observed "Moody Day," Sunday, February 7, 1937. Twelve thousand crowded the Chicago Coliseum February 5, Moody's birth date. Secular magazines and newspapers as well as Christian publications rehearsed his life and work. Newspapers like the *Chicago Tribune* and the *New York Times* gave the story a page or more. Even the liberal *Christian Century* paid Moody a two-page editorial tribute.

Those two years saw Moody-sponsored rallies and conferences from New York's Carnegie Hall to Royal Albert Hall in London. There were many conversions, and in some instances revival. The extent of all that prompted Wilbur M. Smith

to ask, "Has anyone, except a few national leaders like Abraham Lincoln, ever been so honored on the 100th anniversary of his birth?"[6]

Even as the nation still struggled to extricate itself from economic woes, the Institute broke ground for a twelve-story administration building, greatly needed to accommodate its expanding business and educational offices—then scattered in half a dozen buildings over an entire city block. It also needed additional classrooms, a larger library, and studios for radio station WMBI.

Half the money for the building came from Henry Crowell, who years earlier had vowed to give 60 percent of his income to the Lord's work. Houghton urged Crowell to permit the words "Crowell Hall" to be cut in stone over the arch entryway on LaSalle.

There was silence for perhaps two minutes. Then Crowell lifted his head, and said

5. DeRemer, p. 96.
6. Ibid., p. 80.

Moody's new Administrative Building rests on bedrock beneath Chicago's sometimes shifty lakefront subsoil, but the "foundation of God" stands even more sure. In cornerstone ceremonies on May 27, 1938, are Dr. Houghton; F. J. Thielbar, architect; and Henry P. Crowell.

1938: The first class to march through the arch of Moody's newly-completed twelve-story Administrative Building, renamed Crowell Hall in 1945.

quietly, "No (pause); no (pause); years ago I told the Lord that if He would allow me to make money for His service, I would keep my name out of it, so He could have the glory."[7] It was not named Crowell Hall until after his death.

The LaSalle Street frontage of the Moody campus changed dramatically in the late thirties. When the city had widened LaSalle Street in 1930 to accommodate increased automobile traffic, that put some of the Institute's buildings almost in the street. One of those was the historic auditorium, formerly Moody Church, on the corner of LaSalle and Chicago. It was finally razed in 1939—as soon as construction workers had completed the basement of Torrey-Gray Auditorium. The solution for what is today Smith Hall was not so simple. In 1939, fourteen feet had to be cut off from the front of the building, top to bottom for all eight floors!

In the mid-thirties, Moody issued its first student newspaper (1935), introduced caps and

7. Ibid., pp. 80-82.

gowns at graduation (1936), and published its first yearbook (1938).

By the end of the thirties, the circulation of *Moody Monthly* had begun to climb, with Houghton as both its editor and prime promoter. As a former actor and "creator of ideas," Houghton knew how to handle words in print.

When Will Houghton stepped into the Moody presidency, WMBI had been on the air eight years, but was sharing time with another station. Those had been exciting, but chaotic, years as radio expanded across the country. Hundreds of applicants competed for air space. The government assigned frequencies one moment and canceled them the next. As stations proliferated, once-clear channels found other voices crowding in.

Henry Crowell and other Institute officials made countless trips to Washington, D. C., to keep WMBI on the air. In 1934, the government established the Federal Communications Commission (FCC) to bring order out of the chaos. Fortunately, in its very first year the FCC gave WMBI a good rating, in part because the station refused to offend the listening public with crass financial appeals and attacks on other religious viewpoints.

As war exploded in Europe, Houghton put radio to work in the growing world crisis. The Moody Bible Institue, he felt, should be a

Looking down Institute Place from Wells Street. In the 1960s all of these buildings except Crowell Hall will be razed, Fitzwater Hall will rise at the near right, and the rest of the land seen will become the school's landscaped Alumni Plaza.

leader. So he initiated a chain broadcast called, "Let's Go Back to the Bible," that was aired across the nation.

In 1941, WMBI began broadcasting a full-day's schedule, and for the first time Moody enjoyed its own exclusive channel. It expanded into cultural and educational programming and applied for an FM license. When war restrictions on the radio industry were lifted in 1943, WMBI signed off the air at sunset, but Moody's new WDLM-FM picked up from there and broadcast until 9 P.M. (see chapter 16).

In the meantime, Houghton had discovered a man on the West Coast who would introduce an entirely new medium to evangelism.

In California, a young and creative minister, Irwin A. Moon, set out to show his congregation that the wonders of creation were not the result of evolution, but the work of God. To illustrate his sermons, he staged simple scientific demonstrations. The enthusiastic response prompted Moon to resign his church to give full time to this new calling. People jammed college and civic auditoriums to see and hear his "sermons from science" demonstrations.

In 1938, at the Church of the Open Door in Los Angeles, Houghton saw Moon in action and pressed him to join the extension staff of the Moody Bible Institue. At first Moon was not interested—he thought a Moody affiliation would

In 1938, Will Houghton discovers Irwin Moon in Los Angeles and persuades him to link his "Sermons from Science" to Moody Bible Institute. At the 1939 World's Fair in San Francisco Moon becomes a sensation. By the 1950s Moody Institute of Science films are reaching a worldwide audience.

The 1946 post-graduate faculty features some of the most prominent names in evangelical academia.
In the front two stand B. D. Estill, Kenneth Wuest, Wendell Loveless, Carl Amerding, Will Houghton,
William Culbertson, and Wilbur Smith.

limit his access to the secular public. But Houghton eventually convinced him that the opposite was true.

On loan from Moody to the Christian Businessmen's Committee International, Moon proved to be one of the sensations at the San Francisco World's Fair. With the bombing of Pearl Harbor, Moon headed off toward the warfront, not with ammunition, but with the paraphernalia of a scientist. He gave live demonstrations to servicemen all over the world—and many found salvation.

But Moon knew he could reach only so many people face to face. The military, he noted, was putting all the training it could onto film, in order to speed the educational task. Why not put some of his own material onto film?

Moon teamed up with F. Alton Everest, former professor of electrical engineering at Oregon State University, to reach evangelical Christians woefully ignorant of the scientific laws that supported the very gospel message they believed and wanted to share with others.

The first film, *The God of Creation*, received rave notices in both Christian and secular reviews. Moon's time-lapse photography portrayed many facets of creation in accurate detail. These films later won awards in both the scientific and photographic world. Suddenly the Moody Institute of Science stood on the brink of a far-reaching ministry that would resound around the world (see chapter 18).

The war years left their mark on Moody Bible Institute. Suddenly there were fewer men students than women. Graduates went off to war, a few as chaplains, and fifteen alumni gave their lives for the cause of freedom and for the gospel (see chapter 14). The school and its related ministries forged ahead. Not even a second world war could seriously interrupt its long-standing mission. It only underscored its urgency.

As the war came to a close, Dr. Houghton brought British Lt. General Sir William G. S. Dobbie and Lady Dobbie to the United States under the auspices of Moody Bible Institute. Dobbie had distinguished himself as the

1939: With the widening of LaSalle Street in 1930 (see next page), fourteen feet finally has to be removed from all seven stories of the women's dormitory (now Smith Hall). Though built in 1912, the building will still stand in 1985, thoroughly modernized within.

heroic defender of the island of Malta, so strategically important to Allied power in the Mediterranean. He was widely known not only as a great military man, but also as a devoted Christian.

During their four-month tour, the Dobbies addressed at least 150,000 people in forty cities from coast to coast. The ministry was aimed at middle and upper classes—those from political, business, professional, and social arenas largely unreached by the gospel message. At exclusive clubs, university gatherings, and high society teas, as well as mass meetings, the Dobbies bore a unique testimony for the Lord Jesus Christ.[8]

That was the kind of creative planning in which Houghton excelled.

In Washington, D. C., the Dobbies addressed House and Senate breakfast groups and were luncheon guests of Mrs. Franklin D. Roosevelt in the White House, the president being out of the city. Mrs. Roosevelt was so impressed that she referred to them three separate

8. Ibid., p. 93.

times in her nationally syndicated newspaper column.

With the war over, a climate of economic boom lay ahead. So did new frontiers for Moody Bible Institute—especially in the field of missionary aviation. But Houghton now faced a health crisis.

For thirty years he had suffered from migraine headaches, which at times had tremendously drained him. In June 1946, he suffered a heart attack. Though he temporarily recovered, he was unable to carry the heavy duties

of his office. For a time he kept in close touch with the work through the dean of education, but eventually even that became impossible. Dr. Houghton died in June 1947.

> In all my ways be glorified, Lord Jesus,
> In all my ways guide me with Thine eye;
> Just when and as Thou wilt, use me, Lord Jesus,
> And then for me 'tis Christ, to live or die.[9]

9. Ibid., p. 96.

The advent of heavy automobile traffic forces the widening of LaSalle Street. Buildings of the Moody Bible Institute, now sporting a radio antenna system, rise in the background. By the 1980s the intersection of Chicago and LaSalle, just beyond the distant automobiles, will become one of Chicago's busiest, and LaSalle Street will become LaSalle Drive.

Chapter 7

THE WILLIAM CULBERTSON YEARS

ill Houghton had himself brought to the Moody campus the man who would succeed him. He came first as a Founder's Week speaker in 1939, then as Dean of Education in 1942. *Newsweek* magazine carried the announcement of William Culbertson's arrival, and called him a "large, plain, and cheerful man."[1]

Like Houghton's predecessor, James M. Gray, he was a member of the Reformed Episcopal Church—in fact, he was its bishop over the New York and Philadelphia synods. Like Gray, he was scholarly, well educated. His convictions about the absolute dependability of Scripture were unshakable. While he refused to criticize fellow believers for small differences in viewpoint, he had no patience with those who did not accept the "supremacy of God's Living Word and God's Written Word."

Therefore, in no way could he support the National Council of Churches and the World Council of Churches, which he felt represented a

1. *Newsweek*, (7 September 1942).

Torrey-Gray Auditorium has only a basement level when Dr. Culbertson assumes the presidency in 1942. A large sign on the roof shows passersby how it will appear when finished. But war intervenes, and it will be 1954 before construction resumes.

"unity of disbelief." The further drift of those organizations even since his time has substantied the wisdom of that position.

When the board of trustees selected Culbertson from a field of twenty-six men, he was surprised. "Very frankly," he said, "I didn't have in mind the presidency. I was content in the education field."[2]

Dr. Houghton had brought William Culbertson to Moody because he saw in him his strong gifts as a Bible teacher. In his initial years at Moody, Culbertson exercised those gifts in the classroom and established a good rapport with his students, many of whom are still scattered around the globe as missionaries, pastors, and Christian leaders. Especially interested in Jewish evangelism, he made several trips to one of his favorite areas, the Holy Land. Even with his multi-faceted duties as president, he continued to teach one course on campus: Geography of Bible Lands.

From this solid base and after a year as acting president when Houghton's health failed, Culbertson stepped into the top job in 1948. Students and employees stood to greet the announcement with applause and the singing of the Doxology.

Culbertson took over at a crucial time in world history. The extent of the World War II atrocities against Jews horrified the world as emaciated figures stumbled through the opened gates of German concentration camps.* As a result, the sympathy of much of the world supported the birth of the State of Israel in 1948.

Economic experts warned that the early 1950s would be critical years in the world's history. In spite of affluence, people were jittery.

In 1954, the words "under God" were added to the Pledge of Allegiance, and that same year the Supreme Court outlawed segregation in public schools.

In 1955 the Prudential Building went up in Chicago, the first new office building since 1934, and the tallest in the city. Among other items in its cornerstone was a map showing the number of former Moody students and their location on mission fields. That same year Richard J. Daley was elected to his first term as mayor of the city.

By the 1960s people glibly used terms like "new morality," "population explosion," "death of God," and "post-Christian era." Among the most prominent distinctions of the 1960s was the surging interest in mysticism, astrology, the occult, and eastern religions. LSD and other drugs were hailed as substitutes for a religious experience.

A variety of religious moods swept people back and forth. The power of positive thinking gained vast followers through books by Norman Vincent Peale, Fulton J. Sheen, and Anne Morrow Lindbergh. Extentialism intrigued many with its revolt against absolutes, particularly—as in all ages—against the absolutes of Scripture.

Dr. Culbertson chats with Billy Graham in the early years of the evangelist's rise as a national and international figure.

But not all the news was doubt and protest. The late forties and fifties had brought a revival among many young people. Youth For Christ and InterVarsity Christian Fellowship

---

* The following information on religious, political, and social events is excerpted from *God's Power in Action*, by Dorothy Martin (Moody Press).

2. Kay Oliver, "In the Steps of D. L. Moody," *Moody Monthly* (September 1971).

actively promoted Bible study on high school and college campuses. Billy Graham's influence grew phenomenally from 1949 into the 1960s. Campus Crusade for Christ reached collegians with its emphasis on sharing Christ, as did the Navigators with their strong Scripture memory program.

The Dead Sea Scrolls discoveries in caves in Jordan, especially the famous Isaiah scroll, evidenced the validity of Scripture to those who needed such confirmation.

Meanwhile, out of the late sixties grew the Jesus movement, with its varying depths of experience, some genuine, some superficial.

In some ways Dr. Culbertson stood in contrast to his predecessor. Houghton had been a promoter. He would not hesitate, for instance, to hawk *Moody Monthly* magazine from the pulpit—wherever he went. Dr. Culbertson did not feel at ease in that kind of role.

Yet the choice turned out to be right for the time. Major decisions on the school's curriculum and educational philosophy lay ahead, and that was Dr. Culbertson's forte. Neo-orthodoxy and other views of Scripture, short of inerrancy, surfaced in some once conservative denominations. Culbertson held the Institute's position firm.

"As president of the Moody Bible Institute," he said in his 1966 Founder's Week message, "I want to sound again the word of warning. If we as orthodox, as evangelicals, as fundamentalists move from this doctrine—the inspiration of the Word of God—we are doomed to disaster."[3]

Although the postwar years brought a booming economy, the new president of Moody Bible Institute faced hard problems.

The GI Bill of Rights had triggered a surge of applicants, but the Institute did not have the classroom or dormitory space to accommodate them.

Salaries of faculty and employees had not kept pace with spiraling living costs. There was no adequate retirement and pension plan.

The neighborhood around the campus had deteriorated. It was no longer safe to walk LaSalle Street alone. Pressures mounted for the school to move out of the city and build in the suburbs.

Some pressed that Moody Bible Institute should become a Bible college or full-fledged Christian liberal arts school. Yet the majority of the school's constituents would have loudly protested such a move.

Theological drift in segments of the church at large, though not new, worried some onlookers. Would Moody Bible Institute hold the line?

The board of trustees debated and discussed at length whether Moody Bible Institute should remain in the city. Thoughts of a serene campus somewhere outside the city made the option attractive. The downtown campus, strategically located, would undoubtedly bring a fine price.

1960: Dr. Culbertson completes a world tour of mission fields and is greeted by Moody Bible Institute executive Henry Coleman Crowell, son of the Quaker Oats founder.

But after long discussion and much prayer, the board voted to remain on LaSalle Street. The proximity of inner Chicago as a training ground and mission field could not be ignored. The city of Chicago promptly seemed to confirm the decision by vacating Institute Place, the street that jutted into the campus, and selling the whole block to Moody.

And so for the next third of a century,

3. William Culbertson, 1966 Founder's Week message.

the Moody campus would undergo its own gigantic urban renewal program that continues today.

By 1950, a beautiful ten-story women's dormitory was rising on the corner of Chicago and LaSalle, where the old Moody Church once stood. It was dedicated in 1951 and fittingly named Houghton Hall. That year women moved from the old 830 Building (now Smith Hall) and several small buildings into the new edifice. Men moved into the vacated 830 Building, with overflow assigned to an entire floor of the Lawson YMCA, two blocks away.

The Moody Bookstore moved from Wells Street, on the back side of the campus, to the first floor of Houghton Hall. This street-level location on the corner of one of Chicago's busiest intersections, with spacious display windows, gave the store new visibility and a well-lighted, modern atmosphere.

In 1951, Mrs. Will Houghton helps lay the cornerstone for the ten-story women's dormitory named for her late husband. The architect, MBI board chairman Frank F. Taylor, and Dr. Culbertson stand at her side.

The basement level of Torrey-Gray Auditorium had already been completed as far back as 1939. Atop the auditorium's shallow, flat-roofed entrance on LaSalle stood a billboard showing how the structure would eventually appear.

Gifts to the building fund, always kept separate from daily operational funds, had long

been accumulating toward the completion of Torrey-Gray Auditorium. But a gift from the family of the famous gospel composer, William Howard Doane (see chapter 23), together with a sizable bequest, suddenly expanded the plans. It would now be possible to attach a four-story

music building to the rear of the auditorium, with offices, classrooms, and more than thirty-five practice rooms. The Doane gift would also provide the organ for the auditorium. Work on the complex began immediately, and it was completed in time to dedicate at Founder's Week 1955.

Compressed by the effects of a telephoto lens, Moody Bible Institute seems under assault by industrial pollution and urban decay. By the 1960s the school will have to decide whether to stay in the city or flee to the suburbs. It will stay, and the neighborhood will begin to rebound.

Just a year after Houghton's death in 1947, the Institute had purchased the rest of the block along Chicago Avenue, Wells Street, and Institute Place (which included sixteen stores and sixty-four apartments). The buildings were razed in 1953 to create more on-campus parking.

A campus once outdated now changed dramatically. The LaSalle Street frontage, which was what most passing motorists saw, seemed impressive. But behind that lay a mix of the old and the new. Blighted old brick buildings and apartments still huddled up against the campus on the north and west sides. The old original 153 Building sat in the middle of the crowded campus; nostalgic to many, but very much in the way. It finally had to come down.

Meanwhile, the trustees approved property purchases for bookstores in other parts of Chicago and for radio stations in other cities.

Dr. Culbertson and his staff tackled the issue of Institute salaries and benefits. It could be argued that Moody Bible Institute had always been a ministry, and for the privilege of serving there, one could expect to be paid somewhat less than he might earn in a secular job. But was that view fair? Even James M. Gray had hammered away at the trustees to upscale salary levels for his employees, though he never worried about himself. Now in postwar, many had to commute from the suburbs, adding to personal expenses.

Moody salary levels began to rise, slowly at first, but surely. Step by step, the Institute introduced improved benefits and also began to put greater stress on mid-management skills.

As the school emerged from World War II, though, more than its campus had become outdated. So also was the school's schedule. A two-year program, with only one month of break each year, did not interface well with other schools. In 1951, the Institute moved to the semester program, gave the students a full summer break, and extended the course of study to three years. This freed students to take summer jobs and to put their Moody training to work in summer camps, home mission fields, or home churches.

It meant they could also transfer more easily into or out of other schools. A three-year program (ninety-six semester hours) allowed the Institute to receive college accreditation. Meanwhile, a six-week summer school drew others not regularly enrolled and kept facilities from lying idle. With the new three-year schedule came also an overhaul of curriculum.

The end of War World II brought new technology into Moody's long-standing missionary program. The sons of an evangelical pastor, Wilbur and Orville Wright, had ushered in the era of flight. Now, in God's timetable, aviation would be used for the cause of the gospel.

God had used a visionary country preacher to initiate the Moody aviation program in 1946 (see chapter 17). It soon outgrew its Quonset hut facilities at Elmhurst Airport, in Chicago's western suburbs, and had to find a new home at Wood Dale Airport, just two miles from O'Hare Field.

The Missionary Technical Course put students through a major in aviation flight and mechanics, but in 1954 added a second major— radio and communications. Isolated mission fields needed specialists trained in point-to-point radio communications.

Dr. Culbertson eventually had a chance to ride with some of the school's Moody-trained pilots into some of the most remote pockets of the world. On a 30,000-mile tour in 1960, he sat with cannibal chiefs in New Guinea and also visited Australia. In 1957, he reviewed firsthand the work of Moody graduates in the heart of Africa. At Tangiers, Morocco, he met the oldest active Moody-trained missionary. H. P. Elson operated the Raymond Lull orphanage in Tangiers, but at age ninety-five (he had known Moody personally), Elson was ready to turn the work over to younger MBI grads.[4]

4. "Inside Moody Bible Institute," *Moody Monthly* (December 1960).

After World War II, Paul Robinson (center) sees his dream of a missionary flight school become reality. Eventually it will train more than half the world's missionary pilots. It will also move from the busy skies near O'Hare Field to the edge of Tennessee's Smoky Mountains.

In the jungles of New Guinea, during his 1960 tour, Dr. Culbertson sits with a native and cradles a human skull—the victim of a headhunter. He sees firsthand on several continents how the gospel can totally change lives.

Upon Culbertson's return from that world trip, the Institute stood on the brink of the sixties. And in that decade Dr. Culbertson would face his greatest challenges.

More voices were insisting that Moody become a Bible college and grant degrees. After all, were not degrees essential in the mid-twentieth century? And no matter the actual quality of specialized education at Moody, how could a graduate without a degree convince those on the outside? To many, it seemed to make sense.

Yet was not Moody's finely-tuned emphasis on the Bible, without liberal arts accoutrements, the very thing that had set it apart from other Christian schools and helped make it great? Would not the change to a Bible college diffuse that emphasis, subtly change the campus atmosphere, spread resources too thin, and sacrifice the distinctives of its rich heritage?

In grappling with these issues, Dr. Culbertson formulated his personal philosophy of education:

> Bible institutes from the time of their origin, have stressed those things needed for vital Christian witness: the study of the English Bible, the winning of souls, spiritual living, missionary outreach, gospel hymnody. While certain elements have been added to the course of study, these basics remain intact. As I see it, the Bible institute is a specialized school, distinct from the liberal arts college, from the theological seminary, and from the scientific institute. Some speak of it as a religious, undergraduate, professional school.[5]

5. Martin, p. 134.

As debate swelled, Moody decided to poll its alumni. It sent out a detailed questionnaire, asked graduates to evaluate their education, and posed the question of degrees. The replies came back: alumni regarded their education at Moody highly, but, they said, the Institute must give a degree.

Administration and faculty pondered their options. A four-year degree program, they decided, was not the answer.

The uniqueness of Moody Bible Institute, decided the board, must be preserved. It must not succumb to pressures that it change its course, that it become like thousands of other schools, which surrounded it in the nation.

The Institute announced its solution. It would continue to give diplomas to those who graduated from the three-year course. But a student with three years of credit from Moody and two from an accredited liberal arts college could return for an Institute degree by taking six additional hours of Bible.

The decision preserved most of the Institute's historic curriculum, yet also changed the original course plan, which dated to the founding of the school, to a system of majors. This gave students more flexibility in choice of subjects.

William Culbertson, educator, had been largely responsible for patiently guiding the

1969: Culbertson Hall rises on the corner of Chicago and Wells. It will top out at nineteen stories with rooms for more than five hundred men students. Behind stands Houghton Hall, and six blocks beyond can be seen the top of Chicago's new 100-story John Hancock Center.

Dr. Culbertson and other prominent scholars work for more than a decade on the revision of the Scofield Reference Bible.

degree controversy to a wise decision.

Other ministries of Moody Bible Institute would make great strides during the Culbertson era—among them its radio outreach, its music program, its publishing operations, and the Moody Institute of Science.

Dr. Culbertson also served with other distinguished scholars on the revision committee of the Scofield Bible, a project that took many years. When he retired as president in 1971, he became the school's first chancellor.

Only a few days after he had conducted the inauguration of his presidential successor, George Sweeting, he entered Chicago's Swedish Covenant Hospital. He was diagnosed once more with cancer, a disease from which he had recovered eight years earlier.

On November 16, 1971, he met the Savior he had served so well.

Chapter 8

THE GEORGE
SWEETING YEARS

William Culbertson, newly appointed dean of education, walked into one of his first classes at Moody Bible Institute in 1942. In the room sat a promising young freshman from Haledon, New Jersey, who had already demonstrated his gifts for evangelism by leading forty high school classmates to the Lord.

Neither the professor nor the student could have guessed that twenty-nine years later, Dr. Culbertson would handpick this man to be his successor as the president of Moody Bible Institute.

For a time during his student days, the chances of an illustrious career in the Lord's service would have seemed dim for George Sweeting. At age twenty-one he became afflicted with cancer and had two major operations.

"My doctor said I probably wouldn't see the year out," he recalls. "And even if I did, he said, 'you'll never have children.' My operations were followed by thirty radiation treatments. My weight went down to 128 pounds.

"While I was in the hospital, I said, 'Lord, this bed is my altar. I want to serve You, any way You want me to serve You. I'd like to be a living sacrifice, Lord. I know You can correct physical maladies, and yet, I want Your will. I want nothing more, nothing less—nothing but the will of God.'

"Soon after, someone sent me a booklet on the power of God's love as a source of His power.

"The first phrase of 1 Corinthians 14 says, 'Follow after love. . . .' So I determined that I would pray for love, that I would cultivate the love of God in my own experience. I said, 'Lord this will be my lifetime goal.'

"In His mercy and grace the Lord corrected the problem. I now have four healthy sons. I get an annual checkup, and my doctor tells me I'm the healthiest preacher he knows! That fills my heart with gratitude and praise."[1]

The girl George Sweeting would marry followed him to Moody Bible Institute. They had met during high school—at a toboggan party. "And we've been on a toboggan ride ever since," she says today, laughing.

Both were offspring of emigrants from Europe, and from Christian stock.

George Sweeting (standing, upper left) as a student at Moody Bible Institute in the 1940s. One of his professors is Dr. William Culbertson, whom he will one day succeed as president.

"My Scottish father," says Sweeting, "was converted and influenced through Bethany Hall in Glasgow, a ministry that resulted from the D. L. Moody evangelistic meetings of the late 1800s.

1. George Sweeting, "Love Is the Greatest," *Moody Monthly* (February 1982).

Mother was reached through the Wishaw Baptist Church in Scotland. In 1922, they immigrated to America.

"That same year, my wife's parents arrived from Germany and settled in the same part of New Jersey. They, too, were godly people, committed to His will.

"During a seven-week evangelistic series, conducted in the spring of 1941 by George T. Stevens, Hilda and I sensed the Lord's working in our lives. In a special service on August 16, 1941, I felt a specific call to the Gospel ministry. After the meeting I spent time talking with the pastor about God's will for my life.

"Getting home meant a ten-mile bus ride and then a three-mile walk. But the ride and walk that night were special. I felt carried along by the thrill and excitement of my decision.

"My mother was the kind of person who never retired until all of her six children were home and in bed. That night she discerned something very important and beautiful had taken place in my life. She shared warmly about the things of God and then we knelt to pray.

"My upstairs bedroom was a small, unheated room that once had been the attic. That night as I prayed alone, I wrote down four goals. Over the years these goals have remained unchanged.

1. Seek, above everything else, to bring glory to God (1 Corinthians 10:31).
2. Cultivate the inner life (2 Peter 3:18).
3. Disciple as many people as possible (Matthew 28:19-20).
4. Win as many people to Jesus Christ as possible (Proverbs 11:30).

"For me the experience was unforgettable. Frankly, I've never gotten over it."[2]

The Sweetings still look back on their rich days at Moody. "Both of us," he says, "feel a great debt to the school that D. L. Moody founded." The two were married during George's senior year at Gordon College in 1947.

The Moody graduation class of 1945, to no one's surprise, chose George Sweeting as its men's speaker. At Gordon College, in Massachusetts, he graduated the president of his class. Later, Azuza Pacific College, Gordon-Conwell Divinity School, and Tennessee Temple College, and John Brown University all awarded him honorary doctorate degrees.

In the quarter century between the time George Sweeting left Moody and then returned to assume the presidency, he had left an impressive mark on the Christian scene, both at home and abroad.

For a decade as a traveling evangelist and chalk artist, he spoke not only in churches and youth rallies in this country, but also to thousands of servicemen on bases around the world. As head of Sweeting Crusades, his message echoed the theme, "Christ is the answer," in many of Germany's refugee camps and in West Berlin's high schools during the postwar years.

When the oldest of his four sons became a teenager, Dr. Sweeting took the pastorate of the inner-city Madison Avenue Baptist Church of Paterson, New Jersey. He had already served two New Jersey churches early in his career, one as associate pastor of his home church—the long-respected Hawthorne Gospel Church. Five years in the heart of Paterson seasoned George Sweeting for the most challenging assignment of all: Senior Pastor of the 4,000-seat Moody Memorial Church of Chicago.

When he accepted the call in 1966, the church, then at low ebb, had been without a pastor for three years. He would have to rebuild and also follow in the steps of men like Harry Ironside and Alan Redpath. The hard-to-reach neighborhood around the church ranged from the modern high-rise "cliff dwellers" of Sandburg Village on the church's south side to the counter-culture of Old Town just two blocks west. But George Sweeting went to work on his goals and long-range plan. Before long the church began to turn around, and attendance climbed.

Before evening services, Sweeting often mingled with the crowd, getting to know each individually. The warmth of his personality would soon penetrate to every part of the large auditorium.

2. George Sweeting, "Thirty Five Years to the Glory of God," *Moody Monthly* (April 1976).

The interior of Chicago's 4,000-seat Moody Memorial Church, which Dr. Sweeting pastors before his call to the presidency of Moody Bible Institute. Situated a mile north of the Institute on the edge of Lincoln Park, Moody Church has no organic connection to the Moody Bible Institute itself, though the two institutions enjoy a warm relationship and a common founder.

"Got the joy?" he would ask, bouncing into the church office. And because enthusiasm is contagious, it soon reflected in others.[3]

It was a natural move for Moody Bible Institute to put George Sweeting on its board of trustees—as alumni representative—once he arrived in Chicago. Then with Dr. Culbertson's approaching retirement from the presidency, the board began to look for his successor: a pastor, an administrator, an evangelist, an educator, one who would not forsake the heritage of Moody Bible Institute.

They found him in their midst. Dr. Culbertson personally spoke to Sweeting about becoming president. The trustees made the request official in April 1971. Upon his installation on August 1 of that same year, an event covered by all four of Chicago's major newspapers, Dr. Culbertson became the school's first chancellor.

Already Dr. Sweeting had plunged into plans for growth. A man of vision, he challenged his employees to "dream dreams" of what God might do through them, and through the Institute, in the years ahead. He and his associates

immediately went to work on a fifteen-year plan that would culminate with Moody Bible Institute's centennial in 1986.

A nationwide radio broadcast rested near the top of his priority list—one that would present the gospel and at the same time familiarize new people with the Moody Bible Institute of Chicago. He soon went on the air with a weekly half-hour program, "Moody Presents." It is now heard on more than 200 stations.

With the 1972 Olympics around the corner, the Institute sent fifty student counselors to Munich to join forces with the Moody Institute of Science in an outreach to the crowds. Thousands attended their daily film showings on Petershoff Square. Tragedy struck when terrorists stormed the quarters of Israeli athletes, but even this opened unexpected doors for the gospel.

Some 262 graduates received their diplomas at the 1973 Commencement. Also honored during the ceremonies that year were the Stanley Kresges of the S. S. Kresge department

3. Oliver.

Dr. Sweeting leads the march of the graduating class though the Arch.

store chain, whose Kresge Foundation helped provide funds to complete Houghton Hall and establish Moody Institute of Science's educational film division.

Late in 1973, Dr. Sweeting and the Moody Chorale retraced the steps of Dwight L. Moody through his British Isles crusades exactly one hundred years earlier. In England, Scotland, and Ireland, they packed churches, school assemblies, and civic auditoriums.

The next year students and employees turned to their own Jerusalem: Chicago itself. Using the medium of direct mail, a personal letter from Dr. Sweeting went to 400,000 homes on the city's North Side. The letter outlined the plan of salvation and offered a free Moody correspondence lesson, *The Good Life*. In follow up, staff and students joined teams from thirty churches and called personally in many homes. A large rally at Chicago's Medinah Temple climaxed the 1974 Chicago Evangelism Outreach. (Similar campaigns reached the West and South Sides of the city in 1975 and 1977, respectively).

A nationwide pastors' conference, also one of Dr. Sweeting's dreams, in 1973 brought more than 600 pastors to the campus from thirty-seven states, Puerto Rico, Canada, and Scotland. No more than 300 had been anticipated. In following years attendance spiraled to more than fifteen hundred. The annual event has sent thousands of pastors back to churches with new vision, enthusiasm, and spiritual commitment.

The educational division also moved ahead. The new Advanced Studies Program brought college graduates to the campus for thirty hours of post-baccalaureate work in an intensive one-year study. University students, often converted through one of the vigorous campus movements, took advantage of this program to ground themselves in the Scriptures enroute to the mission field.

Enrollment in the Evening School

The annual Pastors' Conference, originated by Dr. Sweeting, draws more than 1,500 pastors to hear prominent pastors speak and engage in edifying seminars.

climbed as the Institute planted evening extension schools in places like Joliet and Akron. Inner city turmoil in the late sixties had hurt enrollment on the main campus, as people hesitated to come into the city at night. As the national mood stabilized, enrollment bounced back.

Radio also expanded in the early Sweeting years. The Institute opened WMBW in Chattanooga, KMBI AM-FM in Spokane, WRMB in Boynton Beach, and WKES in St. Petersburg.

Moody Monthly magazine more than doubled its circulation in the early 70s, climbing to a quarter-million subscribers. At a time when many religious publications declined and in some cases even folded, the *Chicago Tribune* cited *Moody Monthly* as a striking exception. The Evangelical Press Association in 1976 named *Moody Monthly* "Periodical of the Year."

Moody Press, already with more than a thousand titles in its line, took a major step in these same years when it launched into Bible publishing, a major investment. It became a distributor of the *New American Standard Bible*, along with only four other distributors in the nation. The *Wycliffe Bible Encyclopedia*, another major project, was released in 1975. Soon to follow would be the *Ryrie Study Bible*, now a best-selling flagship product. The purchase of a large distribution center in Northbrook has greatly aided Moody Press's service efficiency.

In 1973, as the new inner campus and plaza emerged, Chicago Mayor Daley presented

1969: Construction workers complete Culbertson Hall and now develop Alumni Plaza.

MBI a Chicago Beautiful Award in recognition of "significant contributions to beautification of the City."

The miraculous growth of the MBI campus is without doubt one of the extraordinary accomplishments of the Sweeting years. This involved great vision and careful planning and perseverance as Vice-President Marvin Beckman negotiated seemingly endlessly with neighbors and city officials for property that has been valued well over four million dollars. The campus now includes the equivalent of over eight full city blocks.

1976: Moody Bible Institute celebrates the nation's Bicentennial with a Founder's Week rally in Chicago's Amphitheatre. Twelve thousand people brave near zero-degree weather for the memorable event.

As the nation geared up to celebrate its 1976 bicentennial, so did Moody Bible Institute. Moody broadcasting developed an impressive variety of bicentennial programming. Moody Press published a colorful coffee-table type book, *America: God Shed His Grace on Thee*, and sent it to all members of Congress and other selected government leaders. The Institute distributed more than 100,000 colorful bicentennial calendars.

But a gigantic religious and patriotic rally in Chicago's Amphitheatre on the closing Sunday afternoon of Founder's Week left the more than 12,000 who jammed the stadium with an experience they will never forget. Wesley Hartzell, reporter for the *Chicago Tribune*, called it an incredible event in an age when the words "God" and "patriot" were being scorned.[4] Backdropped by a flag measuring forty by sixty feet and the massed banners of the fifty states, Dr. Sweeting warned that the nation was drifting disastrously away from God and the Bible, whose laws lay at the very roots of the country's founding.

"We of the Moody Bible Institute are not prophets of gloom and doom," he declared. "Neither are we gullible optimists.

"The nation," he said, "could have no greater birthday gift than that the regular reading of the Bible be restored to the public schools."

Instead of the Bible, he observed, the nation is reading obscenity. "There are thirteen million filthy magazines sold each month. We protest them. Rome traveled this road and died. America is speeding along the same highway."

Dr. Sweeting called for renewal on three fronts:

To first and foremost, Jesus Christ. To magnify righteousness and restigmatize sin.

To be the right kind of citizens—to be what Jesus called the salt and light of the earth.

To build healthy, good, moral, godly families.[5]

Congressman John Conlan spoke. George Beverly Shea, Myrtle Hall, and Moody alumnus Clair Hess sang. "Patriotic music," wrote reporter Hartzell, "stirred long-forgotten scenes in the minds of older persons who may have remembered

singing the great songs of America in Independence Day parades and rallies in the small towns where they grew up." The Moody Bible Institute's combined choruses and band closed the rally with a heart-thumping rendition of the *Battle Hymn of the Republic*.

George W. Dunne, president of the Cook County board of commissioners, wrote later: "What a wonderful afternoon! I know that there will be many bicentennial activities throughout the year, but none will be more thrilling or inspirational than the affair at the Amphitheatre."

4. Wesley Hartzell, "Bicentennial Rally Stirs Chicago," *Moody Monthly* (April 1976).

5. Ibid.

D. L. Moody, too, would have been pleased. Just a few months before his death following a Kansas City campaign he said:

> There is nothing I am more concerned about just now than that God should revive His church in America. I believe it is the only hope for our republic, for I don't believe a republican form of government can last without righteousness. It seems to me that every patriot, every man who loves his country, ought to be anxious that the church of God be quickened and revived.[6]

In 1978, when a neo-Nazi group threatened to march in the heavily-Jewish populated Chicago suburb of Skokie, Moody Bible

Deep in Mexico in 1972, Dr. Sweeting sketches ruins of the ancient Mayan civilization during the filming of Empty Cities. *The thesis of the film—that much of civilization has spiraled down, not up—offers impressive challenge to the theory on evolution.*

Institute ran ads in both the *Chicago Tribune* and the *Chicago Sun-Times* outlining its support for the people of Israel and its position against the march. In the open letter, the Institute pledged to stand with the Jewish community against propaganda of hatred.

When near the close of 1978 an associate editor of Moody's *Alumni News* interviewed Dr. Sweeting on his goals for the coming year, the president reiterated his pursuit of excellence. "To me *excellence* is a characteristic of God," he said. "The Scripture says His name is excellent. His loving kindness is excellent, His salvation is excellent, His way is excellent, His work is excellent, and His will is excellent. I look at excellence not as a fleshly characteristic at all, but as a reflection of *all* that God is and all that He does and all that He represents. Excellence has been the recurring theme of the Sweeting years.

"Right now we are training three to four hundred more students (per year) than we were eight years ago," Dr. Sweeting noted, but even then he foresaw the potential financial problems facing private schools in the decade to follow. "I hope this will not come about," he said, "but in the days ahead we may have to charge a partial tuition. Some day we may have to charge a full tuition if there is a real financial crunch, especially for private Christian schools." But Moody Bible Institute at the outset of its centennial celebrations still remained tuition free, thanks to the faithful giving of tens of thousands of Christian people.[7]

As Dr. Sweeting succeeded Irwin Moon as the voice and figure of Moody Institute of Science films, his identity grew not only nationally, but also abroad. Periodic trips to the mission fields of the world have helped to establish Moody's current president as an international figure.

In 1983, for example, Korean Christians invited him to help them celebrate the centennial of Protestant missionary influence in that land. His eight days there took him to some of Korea's largest evangelical churches, including the Young Nak Church in Seoul, which has 60,000

6. Ibid.
7. "Dr. Sweeting Talks to Alumni," *Alumni News* (Winter 1978-79).

members, far more than any of the largest churches in America. Sweeting spoke at two of the five Sunday morning services and preached the gospel to 30,000 people live and via closed-circuit television. That same evening, he preached at the Kwang Lim Church in Seoul, which has 12,000 members and three morning worship services. A church-growth seminar at Kwang Lim drew a thousand pastors.[8]

8. Lisa Livingston, "Celebrating a Centennial in Korea," *Moody Monthly* (September 1983).

A segment of the Institute's international students pose with Dr. Sweeting. Many will go back to their own nations to spread the gospel. From its outset Moody Bible Institute has drawn students from many nations. Because of Dwight L. Moody's campaigns, many of the earliest students came from England.

1983: Evangelicals in Korea invite Dr. Sweeting to help them celebrate the centennial of Christianity in their land. There he preaches to churches of up to 60,000 members, far larger than any single church in the United States. With him as interpreter is Korean evangelist Billy Kim.

After his 1983 visit to Korea, Dr. Sweeting wrote:

"Korea has potential to evangelize all of Asia, maybe even the world, as it spearheads a new east-west spread of the gospel.

"Unlike other Asian countries, missions work in Korea did not ride the coattails of colonialism. In fact, Western missionaries have suffered with Korean Christians, who have seen their country overrun several times in the last century.

"Japan occupied Korea from 1910 to 1945. The war-era Japanese repressed Christianity. In one brutal incident, a Japanese official allowed a closed church to reopen for Sunday worship. When the church was filled to capacity, he ordered doors and windows barred and burned the church to the ground.

"The testimony of these and other martyrs instilled respect and acceptance for Christianity in the Korean mind. As people who had suffered often, Koreans were open to a suffering Savior who conquered death to give hope.[9]

The trip culminated with a four-evening evangelistic crusade in Inchon. A thousand people made decisions to receive Christ during the crusade.[10]

George Sweeting is known around the world. For more than thirteen years he has proven to be an invaluable asset to the Institute in his abilities as an orator, motivator, and administrator. His continued leadership will guide Moody Bible Institute boldly into its second century.

9. George Sweeting, "Land of the Morning Calm," *Moody Monthly* (September 1983).
10. Livingston.

Chapter 9

OASIS IN THE CITY

Accents of green interrupt the concrete, and Moody's own buildings wall out much of the city noise in the Institute's plaza.

An estimated 100,000 people a day pass the busy intersection of Chicago Avenue and LaSalle Drive, less than a mile north of Chicago's Loop. Many must wonder just what the Moody Bible Institute complex on the northwest corner is all about.

By its name, it is obviously a "religious" institution. That point is also confirmed by the Scripture verse, changed periodically, which can be seen on the marquee of Houghton Hall, just above the Moody bookstore.

At the top of twelve-story Crowell Hall loom the large neon letters WMBI, giving evidence of radio studios inside.

The campus stretches several blocks north on LaSalle Drive and in some places two blocks to the west. But what really takes place behind those massive brick walls? Is it some kind of monastery? Do they make Bibles in there? Is it a church? A denomination?

Most of the thousands who pass by will probably never step through the main entrance archway to see the real Moody Bible Institute. But the many salesmen who call upon the Institute—to sell everything from printing equipment to paint supplies—are usually amazed at what they see the first time they step onto the premises.

"I never dreamed all of this was here," is a typical response. Nearly three thousand visitors tour the campus each year.

At the other end of the archway on LaSalle, past two plate glass doors at each end, is a beautifully-landscaped courtyard that won a city beautification award. Trees seem to rise from concrete, which is interrupted by numerous raised grassy areas, accented with flowers and shrubbery. Benches and stylized lamps add to the effect.

The scene is a far cry from just twenty-five years ago, when the only grass on campus was confined to a small planter in front of the Institute's old "Sweet Shop." When pranksters made off with the planter one night, word went out that someone had "stolen the campus."

Between classes, hundreds of students stroll, socialize, or read in the plaza. Tall brick buildings on three sides of the plaza shut out much of the noise of the city. Carillon chimes ring out each day at noon, sending old hymns of the faith reverberating even several blocks away.

The campus has been transformed from its appearance just seventeen years ago, when the original building of the Moody Bible Institute still stood on what is now the heart of the plaza. Many alumni would barely recognize it.

Another symbol of Moody Bible Institute's mission catches the eyes of visitors who enter the lobby of Crowell Hall, just off the main archway. A large stained glass window depicting a man spreading seed backdrops the information desk. Taken from the parable of the sower, it is a reminder that there can be no higher call than to spread the Word of God.

One impression strikes you almost immediately as you step into the buildings of Moody Bible Institute. The premises are immaculate, the halls and offices are modern, the atmosphere is bright. Despite its hundred years of heritage, Moody doesn't show its age.

Only a few steps down the hall from the visitor's lounge on the first floor of Smith Hall is a startling figure of D. L. Moody himself,

A replica of the original 153 Building's frontage with the original railings and lampposts, constructed in the lobby of Smith Hall, recalls nostalgic memories for Moody's older alumni (the actual building was razed in 1969). Left to right, on its front steps, stand Executive Vice-President Donald Hescott, President Sweeting, and Vice-President and Dean of Education Ken Hanna.

preaching from the actual pulpit he used on many of his evangelistic tours. The life-size display, made of fiberglass and resin, stands as big as life—five feet, six inches tall and 280 pounds.[1]

On the opposite side of the lobby, a photographic blow-up of the Institute's original 153 Building, complete with three-dimensional effects, again takes you into the past. When the building was razed in 1969, it had become so nostalgic to thousands of alumni that some vigorously protested its destruction.

As it was demolished, brick by brick, two alumni stood watching. One said, "What would Mr. Moody say if he could see this?"

"He would say," the other replied, " 'This should have been done twenty-five years ago!' "[2] Moody was no sentimentalist. He was a man of prayer and of action.

The original Moody campus, in actuality, did rise out of prayer. One night in 1889, before a service at his church on Chicago and LaSalle (now the site of the school's Houghton Hall), Moody stepped out the back door for a breath of fresh air.

"Morrison," he called to his partner, "do you see that lot over there? Let's pray the Lord to

1. *Moody Alumni* (Summer 1983).
2. *Quarterly Fellowship Letter.*

100

The renovated North Hall houses MBI's brand-new athletic facilities, practice rooms for the Men's and Women's Glee Clubs, and many student organization offices.

give it to us for a school. Right now."

Within eight months the historic 153 Building was built. A plaque still marks the place where Moody and Morrison knelt.

Also in Smith Hall, the Moodyana Museum displays some of D. L. Moody's personal furniture. Along another wall stands his chest of drawers, an old umbrella stand, bureau, and folding bed.

Chicago Tribune reporter Ridgely Hunt described the bed as "a sort of forerunner of the Murphy bed; it folds up into a carved oak cabinet. And its springs sag greatly after years of supporting their rotund burden.

"Nobody sleeps in that bed now, of course," concluded Hunt. "It wouldn't fit anyone but old D. L. Moody."[3]

Also a part of the furniture exhibit in Moodyana is the 1893 Estey organ at which Moody's daughter in law, May Whittle Moody, wrote the hymn "Moment by Moment."

A series of more than a dozen dioramas take you through highlights in the life of D. L. Moody and the history of Moody Bible Institute. The large, lighted shadow boxes, each with miniature scenery and figures to scale, are beautifully done in meticulous detail.

Moving from Moody's birthplace in Northfield, Massachusetts (1837), to his conversion in a Boston shoestore (1855), the dioramas depict his move to Chicago, where he is shown riding the streets of Chicago on a pony, rounding up street urchins for his Sunday school. In time the class drew such notoriety that it attracted a visit from President-elect Abraham Lincoln, on his way to Washington for the inauguration.

Another diorama recreates a scene from 1862—Moody is on the Civil War battlefield, as a volunteer chaplain, the morning after the Battle of Shiloh. Still another scene—the Chicago fire of 1871—leaves you almost feeling the heat of the flames. Moody lost both his home and his church in the fire, and the devastation only prodded him to a greater commitment on behalf of the gospel.

Long rows of newspaper front pages mounted on the walls in Smith Hall date back to the days of Moody's evangelistic campaigns.

3. Ridgely Hunt, "Moody Through a Reporter's Eyes," *Chicago Tribune* (14 April 1975), p. 1.

Protected under glass, publications like the *New York Times,* the *Chicago Tribune,* and the *Saturday Evening Post* headline Moody's great meetings and, finally, his death in 1899.

A high point of your tour will be a fifteen-minute multi-media extravaganza developed for Moody's Centenary Celebration. The visual story unfolds with Chicago's first settlement of Potawatomi Indians in the 1600s and parallels the history of Chicago and the development of Moody Bible Institute to the present day.

Comparable in quality to the multi-media, "Here's Chicago," only blocks away in North Michigan Avenue's historic old waterworks plant, it is expected to attract over one-half million new visitors to MBI during the Institute's centenary celebration. The lobby of Torrey-Gray Auditorium has been modified for this presentation, which will require forty-nine projectors and a unique arrangement of twenty-three hexagonal screens.

In the lobby of Torrey-Gray Auditorium is a wall size roster with a seemingly endless list of names. They represent more than five thousand missionaries, trained at Moody, who have served in foreign fields. One of every fifteen Protestant missionaries from North America got his or her start at Moody.

The auditorium itself was named for two early leaders of the school: Dr. R. A. Torrey, who designed the Institute's basic course of study, and Dr. James M. Gray, who followed him as president.

Row upon row of individual seats slope toward a wide platform with a man-sized pulpit. The walls are brick with high gothic windows that point like fingers toward the vaulted ceiling. A balcony overhangs on three sides. The woodwork is blonde, the atmosphere light, cheery. Behind and above the platform the huge decorative pipes of a Möller four-manual organ, one of the largest in Chicago, backdrop a spacious choir loft. The organ has 3,700 pipes—the majority being out of view.

Torrey-Gray Auditorium is used for chapel, student assemblies, conferences, concerts, and other special events. It is the scene of many public Christian events—among them Founder's Week in February (a week-long Bible conference),

the traditional presentation of Handel's *Messiah* just before Christmas, graduation concerts, Friday Night Sings, and the popular "Candlelight Carols" at Christmas.

Across the platform of Torrey-Gray over the years has paraded a "who's who" in evangelicalism. Its walls have echoed the voices of the world's greatest Bible expositors, its most prominent evangelists, its top missionary

statesmen. It has also hosted congressmen, astronauts, and concert artists.

As the Moody Bible Institute student body has grown in recent years, however, Torrey-Gray is no longer adequate for some public events. For several years now, for instance, the Institute has held its closing session of Founder's Week at Moody Church, which holds more than four thousand. In 1984, it closed Founder's Week

Torrey-Gray Auditorium seats more than 2,000, but many events have outgrown its capacity. The four-story Doane Memorial Music Building is at the rear of Torrey-Gray.

in the Chicago area's new Horizon stadium near O'Hare airport. With the approach of the 1986 Centenary year, the Institute envisions a new auditorium complex.

Torrey-Gray connects to the Doane Memorial Music Building through a door at the front of the auditorium. It is a busy place. Four stories high, it has thirty-four practice rooms, eighteen studios, and three classrooms. In this building alone are seventy pianos and six organs! Dedicated in 1955, the building was made possible by a gift from the family of William Howard Doane, who wrote the music for many hymns.

The entire main block of the Moody campus is underlaid by a system of tunnels (some call them the Christian catacombs). Students can move from building to building without going out into the sub-freezing temperatures of a Chicago winter.

The underground dining room is amazingly large and roomy, carpeted in gold with soft lights and tables for small groups. With seating for nearly 750, it stretches more than a half block beneath the plaza. Meals are served cafeteria style and are prepared by Moody service personnel. Another cafeteria, the Coffee Cove, cares for faculty and the more than 300 campus employees. Serving more than three thousand meals a day is no small task, and Moody's operation has earned high respect within the National Association of College and University Food Services.

During construction of the dining hall in 1972, students watched some seventy men hard at work on the project over a period of several months. Shortly before the job was done, the students gave the men a dinner in their honor. They arranged a full buffet meal, planned a program that included a showing of a Moody science film, and closed with words of testimony of what Jesus meant to them.

At the end of one of the poster-lined long tunnels is Fitzwater Hall, named for the late Dr. P. B. Fitzwater, former faculty member who at one time wrote one of the nation's most popular newspaper columns. Everything is modern, well-lighted, comfortable. The building includes classrooms, faculty offices, and an impressive fully-equipped and well-stocked audio-visual center and video studio on the top floor.

The nineteen-story Culbertson Hall stands at the south, facing north. Some 550 men live on its floors in double and single rooms (single students are required to live on campus). A spacious second-floor area provides a lounge, recreation room, snack shop, and TV room. Adjacent is the girls' dormitory, Houghton Hall.

At street level, on the corner of Chicago and LaSalle, is the Moody Bookstore, which also has a lower level. Nearby in the same building is the 400-seat Alumni Auditorium.

Crowell Hall is Moody's main administrative building, named after Henry Parsons Crowell, founder of Quaker Oats and chairman of MBI's board of trustees for more than forty years. On the tenth and eleventh floors, radio stations WMBI and WMBI-FM send out gospel broadcasts twenty-four hours a day to the Chicago area.

This is also the nerve center of the Moody Broadcasting Network, with MBI-owned stations in six other cities and a fast-growing expansion of its programming to hundreds of other cities and towns via translators and satellite (see chapter 16).

The other nine stories of Crowell Hall house the personnel and service departments (adjacent to the main lobby), classrooms (floors two and three), Accounting Operations and Student Admissions (fourth floor), Moody's 100,000-volume library (floors five to seven), and Administrative offices (floors eight and nine).

Moody's flight school is in Tennessee (see chapter 17), and the Moody Institute of Science is in California (see chapter 18). The Publishing Division, Correspondence School, Information Systems, Constituency Services, and radio tape distribution are in another building ten miles to the north. The Moody Press warehouse is in suburban Northbrook, and another bookstore is located on Chicago's south side. A year-round

In this panorama the photographer captures Crowell Hall, Houghton Hall, Culbertson Hall, and Fitzwater Hall in one click of the camera.

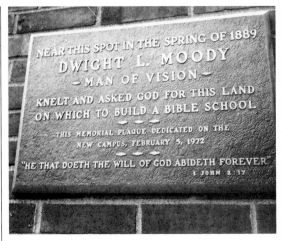

A plaque near the historic spot where Dwight L. Moody knelt to pray for the land on which to build a Bible school.

conference grounds and K-12 Christian day school (Moody Keswick) are situated in St. Petersburg, Florida. Moody-owned radio stations are in such cities as Cleveland, Spokane, Chattanooga, Moline (Illinois), and Boynton Beach and St. Petersburg, Florida. In all, Moody Bible Institute employs more than seven hundred people.

In 1974, when the A. C. Nielsen Co. moved its TV ratings and research firm from the north edge of Chicago, it donated its five-story headquarters building to Moody Bible Institute. For years Henry Coleman Crowell, son of the Quaker Oats founder—and also a longtime Moody trustee—had been a neighbor to Mr. Nielsen. Such was the respect Nielsen held for his neighbor that Moody was at the top of his list when he decided to offer the building to a charitable institution.

The Moody campus has continued to expand as the Institute approaches its centenary year. One recent acquisition, a block of land at Walton and Wells, will soon accommodate an athletic field. Moody does not overly emphasize sports, but recognizes the need for the physical fitness of nearly 1,400 students, most of whom live nine months of the year on three city blocks.

Soccer holds special promise at Moody, not only because of its growing popularity in America, but also because many missionary kids who grow up in foreign lands know and play the sport well. Moody has its share of such talent and has shown well in national competition.

No one has been happier about the development of Moody Bible Institute's campus over the past two decades than officials of the city of Chicago itself. They have encouraged and aided almost every new acquisition. The city does not hide the fact that it sees Moody Bible Institute as a key factor in its urban renewal thrust on the city's near northwest side. Moody's acquisitions and improvements have significantly upgraded property values in the adjacent neighborhood.

Moody is located just five short blocks west of Michigan Avenue and Chicago's "Magnificent Mile." The 100-story John Hancock Building, Chicago's second largest skyscraper, looks almost directly down onto the Moody campus from several blocks away.

One mile south from the Institute on LaSalle Drive is the heart of Chicago's Loop and the Chicago Board of Trade building, focus of the city's financial district. One mile north is Lincoln Park, with its impressive zoo, yacht harbor, and recreational facilities.

The tallest building in the world, Sears Tower, rises about a mile and a half to the south of the Institute. On the north side of its observation deck, directional arrows identifying major buildings and landmarks include Moody Bible Institute.

From the top of the world's tallest building the Institute may seem no different from other buildings in the area. But those who have had any contact with Moody Bible Institute know that it is an oasis in the city.

Chapter 10

PEOPLE: THE LIFEBLOOD OF THE INSTITUTE

It is evening rush hour again. The traffic lights flash to yellow. A weary Harvard-trained executive on his way home from Chicago's LaSalle Street financial district stops at Chicago Avenue. He glances, with only half interest, at the buildings of Moody Bible Institute—simply because they dominate his view. He reads the verse of the week on the marquee above the Moody Bookstore: "In Jesus Christ are hid all the treasures of wisdom and knowledge" (Colossians 2:3).

The light turns green. He drives on by, still not quite sure what Moody Bible Institute is all about. To him neither the school, nor the people behind its brick facade, seem quite real.

What he may have also missed is his own Ivy League heritage.

Harvard College's first presidents and tutors insisted that there could be no true knowledge or wisdom without Jesus Christ. Its "Rules and Precepts" adopted in 1646 included the following:

"Every one shall consider the main end of his life and studies to know God and Jesus Christ which is eternal life."[1]

When Harvard began to drift from its original foundations, evangelical Christians founded Yale as an alternative in 1701. Princeton sprang up, in part, from the First Great Awakening. A strong missionary thrust to the Indians launched Dartmouth. Devout Anglicans founded William and Mary. Baptists planted Brown University.

These were the schools, in colonial times, that turned out the nation's evangelical pastors

1. Robert Flood, *America, God Shed His Grace on Thee,* p. 78-79.

Inside the walls of Moody Bible Institute are real people—more than 1,200 full-time students, most of them on-campus residents, and more than five hundred employees.

All the students and campus employees gather in Torrey-Gray Auditorium for Monday morning chapel. Dr. Sweeting leads this weekly time when the Institute join as a family.

and preachers—until the schools secularized.

Other Christian schools emerged as the nation expanded west, but one by one the majority of these also drifted from their spiritual roots.

In time, schools like Moody Bible Institute, Wheaton College, and others emerged

to fill the vacuum left by those illustrious institutions.

Moody Bible Institute is a real school. And its people are real.

The employees of the Institute number in excess of five hundred in Chicago alone. While some are Bible professors and theologians, the majority would not fall into categories traditionally viewed by the public as "religious" occupations. They are carpenters, painters, electricians, groundsmen, cooks. They are journalists, editors, marketing specialists. They are radio announcers, secretaries, warehouse workers. But all are evangelical Christians.

Some have given up more lucrative positions with prominent firms and name corporations to work at Moody. They have felt called of God there—perhaps as much as any missionary—and have found new purpose and fulfillment in their work.

The majority of employees are typical commuters, who brave the crowds each day on expressways, trains, and buses. Some put this time to good use. Kenneth N. Taylor paraphrased the entire New Testament while commuting between the western suburbs and his job as director of Moody Press during the 1950s. He later founded Tyndale House and published the

Students enjoy light-hearted fun around the piano in the student lounge on Culbertson Hall's second floor.

work as *The Living Bible.*

MBI teachers may grade papers, ponder syllabi, or read. Some memorize Scripture. One Moody commuter read ninety-one books on the train in one year, besides reading through the entire Bible. A voice teacher practices her scales on the busy Eisenhower Expressway. One car pool has a running chess game. Some use this time to pray (drivers with eyes open, of course). An especially energetic car pool signed up for a Moody Correspondence School course on Hebrews. Each night on the expressway, one of the passengers would teach the lesson. At home, these industrious souls completed their exams for credit.

Moody has the paraphernalia of a typical campus: sweatshirts, pennants, and other such emblems of school spirit. It has sports, and it has cheerleaders. It has not made big-time college athletics a priority, but because Moody has its share of missionary kids raised abroad, its soccer team has shown well in national competition.

The students laugh, joke, play, and throw footballs and pillows. They get excited—and sometimes discouraged. They fall in love. Some might even view "Welcome Week," when hundreds of new students arrive on campus, as "the week to meet your mate." Many couples do meet at Moody, and eventually they spend their lifetimes together serving the Lord.

Romance was there even in Moody's day. Once a young man from Ireland became interested in a German girl. She discouraged all of his advances. Disappointed, the man went to Dwight L. Moody himself and laid the matter before him. Moody sent for the girl and had a talk with her. It brought results. The couple soon became engaged. They married when they had completed the Moody program.

In the early days students played tennis on courts nearby. More recently two courts were built adjacent to LaSalle, north of Torrey-Gray.

Two Moody students were once batting around a tennis ball at the beginning of morning rush hour when a big Cadillac pulled up near the courts. The driver peered intently at the game.

Apparently the owner was impressed with the sportsmen, but unimpressed with their equipment. He drove away, soon returning to pitch six brand-new tennis balls across the fence.

He then sped off without awaiting a thank you.

One cannot put all Moody students in the same mold. The school's minimum age policy once restricted enrollees to twenty or older. In 1949 it was dropped to eighteen. Yet the junior college boom, the Advanced Studies Program (ASP), and a higher percentage of married students today all tend to raise the average age and maturity level.

These are real students—a cross-section of young America's best. They hustle at times to a nearby MacDonald's or Burger King, window shop on Chicago's Magnificent Mile, or stroll with a date to the shores of Lake Michigan. They are required to meet a curfew, however. (Legend has it that when the neon letters of WMBI light up on top of twelve-story Crowell Hall, it means "Women Must Be In." In the earlier years of revered dean Franklin Broman, some said it meant "Will Mr. Broman Investigate?").

Classes today, on the average, are much smaller than they used to be. The professor who lectured in yesteryear to large classes may have awed his audience, but it was not always easy to get to know him. Today's Moody instructor

At the heart of Moody Bible Institute is the school itself. All other ministries link to Moody's educational roots. Students and faculty develop a close bond, and the student-faculty ratio is low, as in this popular church history class with Academic Dean Howard Whaley.

maintains student respect, but his spirituality must reflect beyond his academic expertise. Combine the human dimension with godly character, a love for students, a deep grasp of the Scriptures, and the power of the Holy Spirit, and you have a teacher who can communicate to today's generation.

Those who come to Moody learn, sooner or later, that as great as the atmosphere may be, they cannot expect simply to absorb the surroundings and automatically put down deep spiritual roots. They must cultivate their own spritual lives—in the quietness of their own hearts.

The resources around them are superb: a well-rounded curriculum, a quality faculty, a modern library, excellent visual aids, and many potential friends. But add to that the special events that attract a literal parade of evangelical figures to the campus each year. Among them are Founder's Week, a week-long missionary conference, and regular chapel guests throughout the year.

In one Founder's Week alone, for instance, the students heard men like Dr. Francis Schaeffer, Dr. Charles Swindoll, Josh McDowell, Luis Palau, John Haggai, Dr. Warren Wiersbe, David Howard, Dr. Stephen Olford—to name only a few. Moody's location at the crossroads of America, its prestige, its heritage, the convenient presence of its radio station for interviews, all help attract the very best in the evangelical world.

Among the American Association of Bible Colleges (AABC), which is the recognized accrediting agency for Bible institutes and Bible colleges in the US and Canada, Moody Bible Institute has led the way from the start. Dr. Culbertson was one of the founders of AABC in 1947. Today the association accredits more than seventy schools.

Moody students enjoy a unique privilege in that their tuition is free—provided by

Torrey-Gray Auditorium fills to capacity for nearly every session of Founder's Week. In recent years students have been exposed to the wisdom of men like James Dobson, Francis Schaeffer, Josh McDowell, Vance Havner, Charles Colson, and Luis Palau, to name only a few.

thousands of donors across America and abroad. Without that, many thousands on the mission field today, or in other fields of Christian service, could never have afforded an education at Moody Bible Institute—and for that they remain grateful throughout their lives. But there are still expenses: room and board, textbooks, clothing, and other necessities. It is almost routine for a Moody student to open his campus mailbox and find a check from some Christian friend or relative (sometimes from other students!) who suddenly felt led of God to send some financial help.

The size of the Moody Bible Institute's own employee force, and its city location, offers a better-than-average chance that a student can find a part-time job nearby, if not on the campus itself. Moody students earn one million dollars a year from their own part-time employment. Because of their track records as hard-working young men and women who can be trusted, firms like Montgomery Ward and Carson Pirie & Scott put Moody students at the top of their part-time wanted list.

In some cases the Institute can even tie in with the student's field of study and give him some on-the-job training. Students in the communications major, for example, may land part-time jobs in the publishing division, or with Moody broadcasting.

But even if a part-time job doesn't push a student into the workaday world, where he must exercise his faith in the conflict, a weekly Practical Christian Ministries assignment will. One such assignment is required each semester. It may take the young man or woman to a hospital, a home, a church, a Bible club, a campus, a rescue mission, a jail, an inner-city housing project. In such off-campus surroundings, he tries to put what he has learned into action.

Becky Clark of Wheaton, Illinois, elected to befriend twenty-two fun-loving, undisciplined but beautiful little Puerto Rican girls in Chicago's Humboldt Park district, where 6,000 grade school children live within a five-block radius.

Becky went beyond her duties with the required Tuesday Awana club program. As the weeks went by, she says, "I was able to spend time with the kids in their homes and with their

Ministry at Awana clubs is a big part of the Practical Christian Ministries outreach.

families. I was interested in meeting their friends and visiting their schools. We went on shopping sprees in their stores and I ate their food, swallowing it whole with lots of liquid.

"Frustrated, I listened to their jesting in an uninterpreted foreign language. For me the fear and danger that had so painted my first impression lost its vigor. In its place, I was beginning to look past the inevitable ugliness and love beyond my own capacity."

One day Becky asked Maritza Gardia, one of her little friends, what she thought of having the Moody students come to work with her. In her Hispanic ten-year-old accent she repeated, "I am very, very, very—happy. I like 'em—I love 'em!"[2]

Repeat this kind of story more than a thousand times a semester, throughout the Chicago area, and you have the real dynamic of Moody Bible Institute.

Moody students, on their own initiative, decided one year to tutor black children in Chicago's dangerous Cabrini Green housing

2. *Arch,* 1983, p. 63.

Moody's outreach to black children in Chicago's Cabrini Green housing project earns the Humanitarian Award from Montgomery Ward & Co.

project, where disorder and sniper attacks once prompted former Chicago Mayor Jane Byrne to move into the project herself to restore calm.

Twenty-five Moody students worked with children in basic reading, writing, and arithmetic. For their efforts, Montgomery Ward & Co. in Chicago, which sponsored the project, gave MBI students their 1973-74 Humanitarian Award. That was more than a decade ago, but the students have been involved there ever since.

"The best thing about Moody is that it is in the heart of the real world," says student Robyn Wells. "We have created a little Christian society, but fortunately we have kept ourselves open to what is around us."[3]

From its very outset, the Institute has had the reputation of producing shoe leather Christians—those not afraid to get out into the thick of the conflict, often in obscure or seemingly unpleasant arenas that the more highly cultured might see as less than glamourous. But it was D. L. Moody himself who set the example, and who also set the pace.

Chicago knows the presence of Moody Bible Institute.

A Chicago fireman kills time in the firehouse awaiting the alarm that will send him to the next blaze. He pulls a leaflet from a rack on the wall and settles back to read. The rack is stocked with gospel tracts. The racks have been put into almost every Chicago firehouse, at no charge, by the Moody Literature Ministries.

Employees of one of Chicago's largest banks, and passersby gather for a series of Easter

season devotional messages by Moody Bible Institute professors. The first series a few years ago went over so well that this outreach has become an annual event.

This real school, with its real people, sits in the midst of a real world. Even plush Michigan Avenue close by, becoming more plush each year, mirrors the times. Two decades ago students looked out at night to the majestic Palmolive Building, its airline beacon rotating so that, on a clear night, it was said the beacon could be seen by pilots up to 500 miles away. When the towering 100-story Hancock Building rose alongside, the beacon had to be shut off—because it shone into the windows of Hancock's fiftieth floor. But there came an even more significant change. The neon letters of Palmolive came down, and in its place went even larger letters which read, "Playboy." The building had been bought by Hugh Hefner.

Like any other college campus, Moody has its clubs. Along the many underground corridors

3. *Arch,* p. 155.

Moody students work with young neighborhood children in such basics as reading, writing, and arithmetic. In the process, natural opportunities arise for sharing the gospel in a climate of genuine interest and love.

that connect the buildings of the main campus, scores of posters and burlap-backed bulletin boards evidence how much is going on beyond the formal classroom. There's the typical array of sports: volleyball, basketball, soccer, tennis, intramurals. But they are out-numbered by the posters that reflect a concern for outreach and prayer: Europe, Africa, Asia, Latin America, the Muslim World, and more.

There's the Pulpit Club, Student Missionary Fellowship, the Epic Club (Every Person In Communications). A Black Student Fellowship, with more than forty members, keeps black students in touch with one another and with their culture—both Afro-American and African. The Friday Night Challenge (FNC), another student-initiated group, provides a regular forum for student exposure to the many arenas of evangelism both in the US and around the world.

In a typical Friday night session, a young Iranian woman in her national dress, a Christian studying in this country, comes to speak on behalf of her fellow Iranian students in the U.S. She speaks with reality and cries with a sympathy for her own people. "If we reach the students here in America," she says, "they will go back to their home country and reach many more people than we could ever reach."[4]

Internationals enrolled at Moody from nearly twenty nations add excitement to the student body. From Europe, Asia, Africa, Latin America, Australia, they bring a cross-cultural atmosphere to the campus—even before Moody students reach the mission field.

From its beginnings, Moody Bible Institute has had a particular interest in the Jewish people. Its Jewish Missions course introduced in 1923 had turned out by 1936 what

4. *Arch*, p. 64.

Moody Bible Institute does not major in sports, but missionary kids help the school field a highly respected soccer team.

some documented as "half the Jewish workers in the United States" at that time.[5] These workers laid much of the foundation for today's burgeoning Hebrew Christian movement. Three-fourths of the students in today's program, directed by Dr. Louis Goldberg, are themselves Hebrew Christians.

When most regular day school students leave Moody in June, the campus remains active through at least the first half of the summer months. Summer school enrollment generally tops 600. For the most part, it is a different mix: pastors, missionaries, public and Christian school teachers, foreign students, American collegians, homemakers—who may decide to enroll in classes like Moody's annual "Write-to-Publish" workshop.

One man employed with Trans World

5. *MBI Bulletin* (January 1936), p. 15.

Students, faculty, parents, and friends assemble in Torrey-Gray to send another class into the harvest. Every graduate embodies the potential to influence thousands of people in a lifetime—to disciple those who in turn will disciple others.

Radio came from Norway for a special radio course. Another traveled from South Africa to learn outdoor evangelism under Open Air Campaigners. A Wisconsin high school teacher enrolled simply to take some Bible courses so he would be better qualified for work in his own church.

Meanwhile, many of the regular day school students may be busy at work for the Lord in wilderness summer camps, or in child

evangelism, or in their home churches. Some are even abroad. In 1980, twenty-seven students spent the summer in West Africa. In the summer of 1983, fifteen served in Zimbabwe. In 1984, the students evangelized Asia, including Hong Kong, Malaysia, and Thailand.

The Moody Bible Institute Day School enrollment is expected to reach 1,400 by 1986, and the granting of a master's degree seems just around the corner.

At the heart of Moody, however, is the Bible—and the Lord to whom the Bible points. The students and professors at Moody trust it wholly, as the school's official statement of educational philosophy attests. Each decade archaeologists turn up further evidence of the Bible's authenticity. Unearthed ancient scrolls reveal the accuracy of the manuscripts. Fragments of stone document the existence of cities and kings once dismissed by liberal theologians as only legends. To those at Moody, such discoveries come as no surprise. It has never occurred to them that they should hesitate in the Lord's work because some insist that the Bible is half myth, or a "theologian" announces that "God is dead." They have seen far too much evidence to the contrary.

Moody officials have stressed many times that Moody Bible Institute is "first and foremost a school," and that "Bible" is its middle name. The word *institute* has always denoted a specialized training school. Great technological institutes in America specialize in training for science and industry. Moody specializes in the Word of God. Then it puts the Bible into action.

Chapter 11

SHAPING THE CHURCH
IN AMERICA

Moody Bible Institute's annual Pastors' Conference draws more than fifteen hundred registrants.

A television commercial for a nationally-known investment firm says that when it speaks, people listen.

When a pastor speaks, people listen. That is, if he says it well, lives it, speaks from the authority of the Scriptures, and allows the Holy Spirit to do His work. He can influence lives week after week, from small congregations to crowds that may number in the thousands.

Moody Bible Institute has been training pastors for nearly one hundred years, and the majority of those have given the church and pulpit their very lives for the cause of Christ. Their combined congregations would number in the millions.

When congregations across America stand next Sunday morning to sing a hymn like "Great Is Thy Faithfulness, O God My Father," or "Only a Sinner, Saved by Grace" they will be absorbing some of the heritage of Moody Bible Institute— for that is where those songs were written.

The church with a Moody pastor may be large or small. Two graduates and one of its former presidents all have pastored the prestigious Calvary Baptist Church of New York City. When Will Houghton left the pulpit there to become president of Moody Bible Institute, William Ward Ayer succeeded him. Ayer eventually gained the title "God's Man in Manhattan" from a book about him by that name. In 1947, a radio poll conducted in New York City listed Ayer as its third most influential citizen, behind only Francis Cardinal Spellman and Eleanor Roosevelt.[1] John Wimbish, another Moody graduate, followed Ayer

1. William R. DePlata, *Tell It from Calvary,* p. 78.

Students enrolled in the pastors' course from an earlier era built and influenced congregations in their own time. Whether in city, town, or wilderness, the churches they nourished helped lay the foundations for today's evangelical movement.

and gave the church a global outreach.

But other Moody graduates have tackled their pastorates with no church at all! They have been called to obscure areas of need—in city, town, suburbia, or wilderness. They have gathered around them handfuls of families, met for a time in homes or in rented quarters, perhaps struggled through modest building programs. In time they have planted flourishing churches. Most of America's greatest churches had humble beginnings.

Chances are you can step into the majority of evangelical churches across America and find at least someone—sometimes many—whose life has been shaped in some way by the Moody Bible Institute. If not the pastor, it may be his wife, the choir director, the Christian education director, a Sunday school teacher. Or it may be the church secretary, a board member, or perhaps an active layman who is holding Bible studies on the job or in his home.

Moody's impact upon the pulpits of

America is augmented by such events as its annual week-long pastors' conference in early June, which draws 1,500 registrants from up to forty states. It has been estimated that the combined congregations of that pastoral delegation would probably represent more than a quarter-million people. Registrations come from a broad cross-section of evangelical denominations—as many as forty.

Sunday by Sunday Moody graduates proclaim the gospel in large churches like the Colonial Hills Baptist Church of East Point, Georgia, near Atlanta, the Baptist Temple of Brooklyn, New York, and the First Baptist Church of Tucson, Arizona. The majority of churches Moody grads serve are not nationally known—few churches are. Yet, in their own communities or local regions, the influence can be great.

In some cases a pastor may have reached far beyond just his own congregation—through radio, television, or books. Dr. J. Allen Blair

('38), former minister of Calvary Presbyterian Church in Charlotte, North Carolina, reached out for nearly thirty years with his broadcast, "Glad Tidings." In 1979, when he celebrated forty years in the gospel ministry, hundreds turned out for a banquet in his honor, and Charlotte's mayor proclaimed "Dr. J. Allen Blair Day."

The late William E. Kuhnle ('35), who pastored in Milwaukee for nearly thirty years, originated "The Gospel Hour," which at one time was the oldest continuous religious broadcast in the United States.[2] (Kuhnle also composed songs and established Shepherd's, Inc., a home and school for the mentally retarded.)

Harlin J. Roper ('22), who pastored the historic Scofield Memorial Church of Dallas for forty-four years, produced as early as 1973 a series of twenty-six thirty-minute TV programs for the cable television market. As host of "Probe," he shaped a program that brought Christian views to bear on issues of the day.

Moody Bible Institute's influence on the church in America has never been geographically confined. Yet the fact that Dwight L. Moody planted his school in the midst of a city, where it has remained for one hundred years, inevitably has helped shape the sensitivities of its graduates. The city has been the school's training ground, even for students who come from rural or small-town America and are happy to return there. Wherever a Moody graduate may eventually serve, be it even in the African bush, he has tasted at least for a time the American metropolis—and its masses in need of the gospel.

One aspect of this metropolitan heritage has been the city rescue mission. In 1961, a survey revealed that of the 130 rescue missions coast to coast that comprised the roster of the International Union of Gospel Missions at that time, no fewer than forty were headed by Moody-trained superintendents. One large rescue mission employed thirteen MBI-trained men and women.[3]

Chicago's Pacific Garden Mission, perhaps the most famous, saw Moody graduate Harry Saulnier build its staff from a handful to more than seventy in two decades. In one recent winter month the mission gave free lodging to nearly 300 a night and served more than 22,000 free meals. Meanwhile, its long-standing radio drama,

"Unshackled," continued to air on nearly 500 stations worldwide.

William Dillon, Jr., ('68) founded Inner City Impact, a ministry to the youth of Chicago's west side Humboldt Park area, where a mix of Latino, black, and Appalachian white families raise the second highest concentration of children in the city. The Dillon family history of inner-city ministry goes back three generations. Bill's grandfather, Michael Dillon ('06), was the first superintendent of Chicago's Sunshine Gospel Mission.[4]

William Dillon, Jr.'s family history of inner city work goes back three generations. His father and grandfather were also graduates of Moody.

When Grace Willet, a "guardian angel" for thousands of wayward women, retired from her work at Chicago's Central Police headquarters after twenty-eight years, a *Chicago Tribune* feature on her quoted an admiring public defender in Women's Court: "She has helped so many women—I don't know how they will ever find anyone to replace her."[5]

One of the Institute's most colorful pastoral graduates, Dr. William J. McCarrell, took a church in the western Chicago suburb of Cicero about the time Al Capone and his gang moved in on the town. They set up headquarters at an inn just down the street from McCarrell's

2. *Moody Alumni* (Winter 1981).
3. "Soldiers on the Homefront," *Moody Monthly* (April 1961).
4. "Three Generations of Alumni Serve Christ," *Moody Monthly* (Summer 1979).
5. David Gilbert, "Jailed Women to Lose a Pal," *Chicago Tribune* (25 August 1969).

In the 1920s William McCarrell turns the tide of vice in Al Capone's Cicero with a spiritual assault. He later founds the Independent Fundamental Churches of America (IFCA).

set out to shape its environment, not be shaped by it.

Charles A. McIlhenny ('73), pastor of The First Orthodox Presbyterian Church of San Francisco, had to face that conflict head-on. In an incident a few years ago that attracted national publicity, McIlhenny and his church had to defend themselves in an expensive lawsuit brought by the church organist, whom the church had fired when he was discovered to be a homosexual. In what turned out to be a landmark case, McIlhenny stood his ground and the church won. Had it been otherwise, the implications for the evangelical church at large could have been disastrous. Yet as the price of his courage, he and his family have had to endure ongoing harrassment.

In San Francisco in the 1970s, Charles McIlhenny boldly stands firm on a landmark homosexuality case, despite a lawsuit against his church and persecution that continues.

church. Capone soon controlled the city's police and politicians, plus a hundred or more gambling dens, countless brothels, saloons, and speakeasies.

Violence reigned. Cars with armed gangsters cruised the town and shotgunned voters who had marked their ballots to Capone's dislike. Capone's men manhandled the mayor himself as the town stood by. It was Capone's town, but McCarrell didn't let him keep it. Instead, he turned the town around with a task force of evangelistically-fervent laymen (The Fishermen's Club), who included the jails as a part of their evangelistic beat. Among the converts were some of Capone's own henchmen.[6]

McCarrell built what later became the Cicero Bible Church into a congregation of more than a thousand. In protest of denominational apostasy, he founded in 1930 the Independent Fundamental Churches of America (now with more than 100,000 in its member churches). McCarrell still preached vigorously into his nineties, shortly before he died in 1979.

If a pastor is to do his job, his biblical convictions must run deep, and his church must

What of Moody Bible Institute's influence upon ethnic groups?

Its greatest impact upon the black community in the Chicago area has probably been the Moody Evening School. Thousands of blacks—both pastors and laymen—have long taken advantage of the night school curriculum, which is designed primarily to train men and women for more effectiveness in their local churches.

In Three Rivers, Michigan, George Joseph felt God's call into the ministry. But he

6. Dorothy Martin, *The Story of Billy McCarrell*, pp. 92-97.

knew he would need a biblical education. One night a week for six years, he and his wife, Ruby, traveled 135 miles each way to attend the Moody evening school.

"My wife and I had worked extensively with white church camps," Joseph explains in a newspaper interview in the *South Bend* (Indiana) *Tribune.* "We looked around and realized no one was working with blacks; we decided we'd better work with our own people. Black churches are very religious," says George, "but few are well-grounded on the Bible."

The Josephs started a black church with six children meeting in a basement. Today attendance reaches 150. In more recent years they also started a Bible institute. It has now turned out more than fifty graduates. Moody correspondence courses supplement courses in Bible, hermeneutics, homiletics, church history. "We also teach black church history," says Joseph. "We try to teach the cultural aspect of evangelism to blacks, and we make application from the Bible in light of our own culture. Eventually, we hope to become an accredited school."[7]

WMBI radio, a flourishing black-managed bookstore on Chicago's south side, and the weekly ministry of Moody students to the inner city all help to build bridges to the black community. The latter has included a long-standing tutoring program among children in Chicago's Cabrini Green housing project.

The percentage of blacks in the day school in years past has been small, but numbers are growing (with forty-one enrolled for the 1984-85 school year.) Among black Moody day school graduates have been Russell Knight, Jr., national director of Youth For Christ's black ministries, and Ralph Bell, associate evangelist with the Billy Graham Evangelistic Association.

The shift of WMBI-AM to Spanish programming all day on Saturdays (see chapter 16) has established Moody's earnestness in reaching Chicago's growing Hispanic populace. Student outreach, such as in Humboldt Park, helps reinforce that determination.

Rafael Maldonado ('81) enrolled at Moody for evening classes in 1978 to study the synoptic gospels. Just one course. But within months he quit his job with Illinois Bell Telephone Company to become a full-time day school student. Now he directs the Ayuda Family Center, a ministry to Chicago Hispanics. "The biggest problem we have to overcome with our people," he says, "is lack of self-esteem." He credits Moody for "equipping me to use my Bible."[8]

But across the country at large, one of Moody's greatest contributions to the Hispanic outreach—and, for that matter, to other ethnic groups—are its missionaries who return from the foreign field. With years of experience and a command of the language, many come back to the states, sometimes in semi-retirement, to throw themselves into a gospel outreach stateside with the ethnic people they have come to love.

A few issues of the *Moody Alumni News* show the pattern:

Paul and Charlotte (Hall) Sheetz retire from missionary service in Latin America to work with Hispanics in Atlanta—including Cuban

7. "Joseph's Tailor Ministry to Black Americans," *Moody Alumni* (Fall 1981).
8. *Moody Alumni* (Summer 1982).

Ralph Bell, associate evangelist with Billy Graham, reaches out to both black and white audiences with the clear gospel of salvation.

detainees in the federal penitentiary there.[9]

Roger and Joyce (Ahlgrim) Kenny return from Bolivia on an extended medical and educational furlough and become excited about a Spanish ministry in West Palm Beach. "Thousands around us," they write, "do not speak any English. We have a wide-open field."[10]

Others return to work among Hispanics and migrants in such places as Dallas, Tampa, El Paso, and Southern California.

For Roy and Fern (Huser) Tillotson, however, the pattern worked in reverse. For seventeen years they ministered among Puerto Ricans in Gary, Indiana. Then in 1979 they moved to Puerto Rico to work with three congregations that had resulted from their work in Gary.[11]

Bennie and Dottie (Simon) Benson retire from more than three decades in Japan and start a Japanese congregation in Southfield, Michigan. Albert and Mary (Lee) Bobby return from Brazil and work with a Brazilian congregation in Georgetown, near Washington, D. C.

Lillian Chipley retires from India and then plunges into a work with Indians and other internationals in the Philadelphia and New York area. John and Cora Wilkins move to Yuba City, California, to work with East Indian migrants. Bernice Balzer retires from Nigeria to reach Nigerian students in the U.S.

The Chinese in the United States offer another field. Victor and Irma (Mangels) Frank spent thirty-three years on the foreign mission field. When the Communists drove them out of China's Kwantung Province in 1949, they were reassigned to Hong Kong. While a professor at Hong Kong Baptist Seminary in Kowloon, Victor recorded Chinese dialogue with musical backgrounds for Christian films to be used in schools, churches, and hospitals. Irma taught religious education at the seminary, wrote seven storybooks for children, and served as editor and translator for the Baptist Press in Hong Kong.

The Franks were married while students at Moody in 1939. They have taken an orphan girl, Betty, to Hong Kong for teacher training. "We have ten foster children and four foster grandchildren," says Irma.

"Our hearts are still in Hong Kong," Victor adds, "but we hope now to help with Chinese work in this country [in the Pacific Northwest]. There's no retirement in the Lord's work," he says. "Recycling is much better."[12]

Dwight L. Moody passed on a spiritual enthusiasm for the city, but he also left another legacy: Go where the people are!

Terry Lytle ('47) and his wife took that advice to heart more than thirty years ago when they started Drive-In-Churches, Inc. When the lure of the summer outdoors shriveled his crowds at two small churches he pastored in Devil's Lake, Michigan, Lytle decided "if they wouldn't go to church, I'd come to them."

Terry Lytle, with wife Olive, started Drive-In Churches, Inc., to reach resort crowds in Florida and the Great Lakes region. In the tradition of Dwight L. Moody, they go where the people are.

He started with a platform in the middle of a cornfield, then found other creative approaches that eventually led to a beautiful drive-in theater at Pinellas Park in the midst of the St. Petersburg-Tampa-Clearwater resort area, with a capacity for 285 cars. Christian films help attract the crowds, but also a glassed-in performance area accommodates weekly dramas and musicals, using the latest multi-media equipment.

"This is really a 'beginners' church,' " says

9. Ibid.
10. *Moody Alumni* (Fall 1980).
11. *Alumni News* (May-June 1974).
12. "Alumni Who Served in China Retire to Work Among Chinese in Washington," *Alumni News* (Fall 1980).

Lytle. "As soon as people are won to the Lord, we urge them to move out into local churches." Lytle operates a church referral service for converts. "It's important," he stresses, "that their Christian growth begin right away." The program is effective. One woman came to a service, accepted the Lord, and over the next three years was instrumental in the lives of one hundred other people who received Christ at the theater.[13]

Lytle's drive-in ministry is not limited to Pinellas Park. There is another theater in Michigan, two theaters on wheels, and a borrowed yacht that cruises the Great Lakes!

Open Air Campaigners, which uses vans for outdoor evangelism, also takes a go-where-the-people-are approach. A modern-day version of Moody Bible Institute's early gospel wagon, OAC vans have been used extensively by Moody students in Chicago—on streetcorners, in parks, on the beaches. It is little wonder, then, that much of the OAC outreach both in the United States and overseas is in the hands of Moody graduates.

Max Ward ('54) of Seamen International is another go-where-the-people-are specialist. When he steps aboard a Dutch freighter unloading cargo in the port of Chicago, he has one goal in mind: to reach the sailors with the gospel of Jesus Christ. Those on the next ship to arrive may be Portuguese, but Ward is always prepared. No, he is not multi-lingual, but he comes aboard with a supply of Bibles, books, and tracts—in the languages to fit the occasion. He knows how to convey the love of Jesus when he hands them out—even through the language barrier.

Such areas of specialized ministry are examples of arenas into which most churches either cannot go, or choose not to go. Yet this is all a part of Moody's shaping of the church in America.

Senior citizens are another home mission field. Many semi-retired Moody missionaries and pastors serve as chaplains in hospitals and nursing homes. Others are making that their lifetime ministry. Joe Smith ('60) directs Evangelical Hospital Chaplaincy, Inc., which serves eight hospitals and sixteen nursing homes in west central Michigan. Still others are managing major Christian retirement centers.

There have been few pockets of rural America, over the past century, that have not been touched by a graduate of Moody Bible Institute. Some of the earliest pastors rode on horseback to cover their circuits. Not a few served with the historic American Sunday School Union, which organized Sunday schools across the western frontier. They held Sunday schools in boxcars, schools, wigwams, hotels, and even in a saloon. That organization is now known as the American Missionary Fellowship.

Others serve in the mountains of Appalachia with such faith groups as the Scripture Memory Mountain Mission (hidden in the obscure village of Emmalena, Kentucky), the Cumberland Mountain Mission to the east in Martin, the Dessie Scott Children's Home in Pine Ridge, the Kentucky Mountain Mission in Beattyville, and others. Combined, they reached thousands in the back country with the gospel—through Bible camps, VBS, country chapels, Bible study classes, visitation, radio programming, and literature.

A half century ago, home missionary Edith Shaw ('34) maneuvered her truck along the creek beds to a promised cabin in Cowhead Holler near Yeaddis, Kentucky, only to find the cabin had burned! But she stayed anyway, traveling on foot to visit families, nurse the sick, and work in the school. She eventually saw the embryonic Cutshin Bible Mission grow to include a clinic, log cabin lodge, store, garage, and rustic chapel. Today this outreach to isolated mountain people is entirely self-supporting.[14]

Literally thousands of rural churches have been planted by Moody graduates in the past century—from the Northwoods of Minnesota and the upper Michigan peninsula to the Arkansas Ozarks, from the hills of New England and the mountains of West Virginia to the plains of Montana and the rain forests of the Pacific Northwest. The church planting still goes on. In addition to denominational affiliations, alumni

---

13. "Alumni Couple Build Drive-In Ministry," *Alumni News* (Spring 1979).
14. "Soldiers on the Home Front."

Moody-trained Bible translators reach out to American Indian tribes like the Navajo, the Apache, the Mohawk, and the Chippewa.

serve under organizations like Rural Bible Crusade, Rural Home Missions Association, and Village Missions.

One of the most significant aspects of rural work, historically, has been its impact on foreign missionary outreach. Though nobody seems to be able to come up with a documented figure, it is accepted that a high percentage of those going to the foreign field today still come from rural areas. Many of them have been won to Christ through home missions. And enroute to the mission fields of the world they have come for training at places like Moody Bible Institute. Some observers strongly believe that neglect of the rural field can only bring devastating harm to the future of foreign missions.[15]

Over more than a half century, a stream of Moody-trained missionaries has brought the gospel to the American Indian, concentrating heavily among the Navajos in the Pacific Southwest. They can also be found working

15. Robert Flood, "They're Still Pioneering the Rural Frontier" (July-August 1966).

Many graduates pastor in the rural and small-town churches of America. Such churches supply a high percentage of the evangelical missionary force sent from the US.

among the Pueblo, the Sioux, the Tahlequal tribe in Oklahoma, and with Wyoming's Cheyenne Indians, where Wayne Leman and his wife, under the Wycliffe Bible Translators, are giving the Cheyenne tribe the New Testament in their own language. The late Faye Edgerton gave eight years to translating the New Testament into Navajo under Wycliffe, then plunged into the same task with the Apache. Meanwhile, workers in Canada serve among such tribes as the Chippewa, the Cree, and the Mohawk.

On the remote Canadian west coast, Don McNaughton lands his Cessna 185 floatplane on a mountain-rimmed lake and climbs out to unload an assortment of gospel films. He and his wife, Kathy, are missionaries in the isolated logging camps and fishing communities of the Northwest Territory, where the weather can be brutal and unpredictable. For these loggers, who live in roughly-made shanties, religion is not exactly a hot item. It is not an easy mission field, but the McNaughtons press forward with enthusiasm.

Few nooks and crannies have been overlooked by Moody alumni—not even the floor of the Grand Canyon. There workers once labored among the Havasupai Indians, 3,500 feet below the canyon's main rim in a little irrigated mile-square valley walled-in by towering cliffs. Few white men had set foot in the valley until the turn of the century. Access is eight miles down a winding mule trail from the canyon rim. When the John Greenfields, former missionaries to New Guinea, took up the canyon work in 1964, they regarded it as every bit as challenging as the jungles of Indonesia.

Moody-trained migrant missionaries can be found among the Mexican braceros in California's Salinas and San Joaquin Valleys (Al

Galen Call (left), Minnesota pastor, says the "theology, Bible, and Greek background" he acquired at Moody has been "vital" to his ministry. Gene Getz (center), prominent Christian educator, author, and Texas pastor. Evangelist Michael Guido (right), one-time nightclub bandleader. Guido's crusades have brought thousands to Jesus Christ and his column appears in 1,200 newspapers.

Larry Powell (left), successful Chicago pastor, came to Moody from rural Michigan with two hundred dollars in each shoe. "I hid it there," he recalls today, "so the gangsters wouldn't find it." Eric Crichton (center), has enjoyed a highly successful pastoral ministry in Lancaster, PA, after ten years in the business world. Vern Van Hovel (right), minister of music at a large California church, also used his MBI music training to spend "ten wonderful years with HCJB's 'Voice of the Andes' in Equador."

Kantor has worked among them for forty-five years) or among the Cubans, Jamaicans, and Puerto Ricans harvesting winter crops in Florida. Often unable to speak English, constantly on the move, generally underprivileged, they would not make very good prospects for the local church rolls. But they constitute one of the nation's most needy mission fields. [16]

Some have felt called as full-time evangelists, ministering not simply to one church, but to many (Ephesians 4:11). Sometimes these men form their own evangelistic associations. The late evangelist Elton Crowell held more than 700 campaigns in the U.S. and twenty-four other countries during his career. Carl Johnson has traveled throughout the eastern U.S. for more than two decades. As a specialist in the study of revival, however, perhaps no single person has better credentials than William W. Orr, who has been greatly used in revivals worldwide, and whose books on revival are circulated in many languages.

The prisons of America were always a part of Dwight L. Moody's heartbeat. One past Alumnus of the Year, Axel Bolin, is the chaplain at New Mexico State Penitentiary. Gordon Loux joined the work of Charles Colson almost at the outset of the Prison Fellowship ministry and is now executive vice-president of that growing outreach.

In still another special mission field, Phil and Nancy Smick, among others, reach out in Chicago to touch the lives of international students with the gospel. Directing the Chicago work of International Students, Inc., they are befriending hundreds, even thousands, some of whom will eventually return to their homelands to evangelize.

Or who can number the Christian colleges and Bible institutes in the U.S. who owe their existence, at least in part, to the example and pattern of Moody Bible Institute? Many alumni are on their faculties, while others serve as professors and deans at the seminary level. Moody graduate Howard Ferrin founded Barrington College in Rhode Island many years ago and is today its chancellor. The chancellor of Kings College in Briarcliffe Manor, New York, and the president of Calvary Bible College in Kansas City, are graduates of Moody Bible Institute. So also is the founder of Grace College of the Bible in Omaha.

Whether in rural America, the city, or suburbia, the outreach of Moody radio broadcasts, *Moody Monthly* magazine, Moody Press books, and correspondence courses have contributed to shaping the church in America. Yet it has always been the Institute's conviction that Christian media and evangelical para-church institutions, in the final analysis, must build up the local church. George Sweeting has said: "World evangelism is our commission, establishing and building local churches is our method, and the media is an instrument given to us by God to carry out the Great Commission." [17]

From almost its very beginning, churches across America have looked to Moody Bible Institute as a sort of spiritual anchor in the middle of the continent, a champion of the faith, a defender of historic Christianity. It is not the only such bastion, to be sure. But it would be difficult to dispute Moody Bible Institute's unique role, over the past century, in shaping the churches of America.

16. Ibid.
17. "Dr. Sweeting Challenges Fellow Broadcasters," *Moody Alumni* (Summer 1981).

Chapter 12

DISCIPLING YOUNG AMERICA

In Chicago's Marriot, teenagers at a Moody Sonlife-sponsored Christmas conference learn the principles of Christian discipleship.

When Dwight L. Moody first came to Chicago, it did not take him long to assemble a Sunday school. He rode the Chicago streets on a pony, handing out candy apples, and the children flocked around him. They enjoyed the sweets, but they saw in Moody more than a handout. They saw love. They saw attention. And the street urchins Moody rounded up were starved for it.

Who is shaping today's young generation? In some cases, the dope peddlers, the pornographers, the liquor distillers, radical educators, the cultists, the purveyors of hedonism.

But there is another side to young America. These are the millions of youth whose lives are being shaped by earnest Christian parents, by evangelical churches, by youth pastors, by Christians who care. Among these are the thousands of Moody graduates who teach Sunday school, reach out through clubs, win young hearts through child evangelism, and share the gospel in high schools and on the college campus.

While much of this influence goes on within the churches, it also spills over into arenas where the church sometimes cannot, or will not, extend itself. Thousands of youth workers serve under para-church labels like Campus Crusade, Youth For Christ, Young Life. The collective impact may yet decide the course of the nation.

Meanwhile, at elementary and high school levels, the Christian school movement is flourishing, and Moody Bible Institute feeds its share of graduates into those schools—as administrators and teachers.

Between 1965 and 1975, the number of

students in private schools in the United States (outside of the Catholic parochial system) more than doubled. It is estimated that independent schools, most of them evangelical, are currently being founded "at a rate of about three a day, or one every seven hours."[1]

One of those with a special heart for today's youth is Dann Spader, who directs Moody Bible Institute's Sonlife Ministries.

A few years ago Spader was a young, discouraged youth pastor on Chicago's Near West Side, ready to quit.

Then suddenly things turned around. He saw the work thrive and moved on to serve four years as youth pastor at Judson Baptist Church in suburban Oak Park. There he saw even greater things happen with youth, though in that same period he also observed three other neighborhood youth pastors throw in the towel.

What made the difference? In early 1972, at Chicago's Carter Memorial Presbyterian Church, Spader had tried one thing, then another. They were good ideas, but several months showed few results. So he began to retreat on weekends to study Scripture and seek direction.

Like many youth pastors, Spader had been groping for the right program. Using a harmony of the gospels, he discovered that not much happened outwardly in the first year and a half of Christ's public ministry. During that time Jesus performed only two miracles: he healed a nobleman's son and turned water into wine.

But behind the scenes He built close relationships with a few men, established trust, taught them who He was, and urged them to follow Him.

Only after Jesus solidified this core did He finally say, "I will make you fishers of men." Then they moved out as a group.

Spader went back to the Chicago church and began to concentrate on the handful of young people who seemed ready to grow spiritually. Those became the catalysts who gave the group a new dynamic, attracting newcomers from the neighborhood and encouraging regulars who might have otherwise become dropouts. After two years, more than fifty young people attended regularly, close to half the size of the church.

When Spader took his next youth pastorate in Oak Park, the church expected great things to happen. They didn't—at least at first—and the church became impatient. Spader knew it would take time—at least a year or more. He continued to focus on those who were ready for serious discipleship. As individuals responded, he poured himself into their spiritual lives. That small group developed a spiritual oneness and were finally ready to reach out.

Stressing the study of the Word is important for setting strong spiritual behavior patterns.

In four years the group expanded to seven times its original size.

Soon God broadened Spader's horizon. One night when he couldn't sleep, specifics of a plan unfolded. The bottom line—10,000 youth groups involved in discipleship within the next ten years.

In 1979, Spader launched Sonlife and, after a few months, brought it to Moody Bible Institute under the auspices of the extension department. Though still a relatively young program, scores of Midwest churches have adopted its bedrock discipleship principles and are beginning to see results.

A youth pastor in Beloit, Wisconsin, says it has helped him "dream big dreams" and "set definite goals."

1. M. Stanton Evans, "The Private School Boom," *National Review*, 16 May 1960.

Joining as a spiritual community to pray for the needs of others is also a basic that is emphasized in youth ministries.

"It's not a gimmick," says another. "It's God's principles in real life. That's powerful."

At Sonlife youth discipleship institutes held from Iowa to Ontario, Spader and his associates stress such basic principles as:

Love your kids. Put people first, not programs.

Commit yourself to growth. Set specific goals.

Move with the movers. Single out ones open for spiritual growth (you may have to be patient) and begin to disciple them.

Create a strong atmosphere of love. This is the catalyst. That's what they're longing for the most.

Undergird what you are doing with strong Bible teaching.

Spend part of your time on their turf—on campuses (if permitted), in homes, or wherever they meet.

Train them to reach out. Many church youth groups are cliquish.

Show them a confident faith and discipline. Model your life before them.[2]

Each year Sonlife conducts two major

conferences. One for youth pastors is held in May, immediately following Memorial Day, in conjunction with the Institute's annual Pastors' Conferences.

For high school students, Sonlife sponsors an annual three-day Christmas conference at a major Chicago hotel during the Christmas vacation. Registration usually exceeds six hundred.

Scores of Moody graduates serve youth pastorates across the nation—a job that can have great rewards, though the role is not always easy. Surveys reveal that the average youth pastor remains at a church only sixteen months, hardly long enough to see significant results. Sometimes he gets discouraged, or restless, or wants "a real pastorate." The job becomes a stepping stone. Spader would like to see youth pastors as a whole take a higher view of their calling.

Not to be overlooked is the impact the church pastor himself can make on the young people in his congregation. In some cases, he is the key influence in Christian vocational guidance. Over the years, a few churches have sent as many as one hundred young people to the Moody Bible Institute.

Today's Youth For Christ movement, which reaches out to tens of thousands of teenagers through its Campus Life clubs across the nation, traces its roots to Chicago, where evangelist Torrey Johnson and his associates held gigantic youth rallies in Soldier Field during World War II. Moody has supplied YFC with several vice-presidents, including Robert A. Cook ('30), Mel Johnson ('39), Gary Dausey ('59), and Clayton Baumann ('58). Dausey today serves as YFC's executive vice-president.

While director of Chicago Youth for Christ in the early 50s, Mel Johnson initiated on WMBI a thirty-minute Saturday afternoon program for youth called "Tips for Teens." When Johnson moved to Minneapolis in 1955 to direct the YFC work in that city, "Tips for Teens" followed him, but changed to a daily fifteen-minute program. The international broadcast is

2. Robert Flood, "Who's Helping the Youth Pastor?" *Moody Monthly* (October 1980).

Youth pastors gather for a Sonlife conference. Many of Moody's own graduates begin their ministries working with youth—some in the church and others with such campus para-church ministries as Youth For Christ, The Navigators, and Campus Crusade.

now heard over more than 100 stations. Over the years Mel Johnson has influenced thousands of young people for Jesus Christ, and he still speaks personally to audiences about 200 times a year. Bruce Love ('52) helped develop Youth For Christ's outstanding Lifeline delinquent rehabilitation program, which has been praised by officials from governors on down. Ron Hutchcraft ('65) serves as New York area director of Youth

For Christ, and extends his outreach by radio.

No man is more dedicated to youth, and to his Lord, than Harvey Russell ('50), who runs a class "A" program at the Joliet (Illinois) Christian Youth Center, a non-denominational work, supported financially by the people of Joliet. Russell helped found the center more than thirty years ago. Now in his fifties, with graying hair that adds to his look of wisdom and

Gary Dausey, executive vice president of Youth For Christ, trained at Moody Bible Institute.

Mel Johnson has influenced tens of thousands of young people for Jesus Christ over nearly a half century.

Bruce Love, executive director of Metro-Chicago Youth For Christ, cites the value of the "one-on-one" evangelism that he learned at Moody.

sincerity, Russell continues a timeless appeal to teens in that city. To hundreds he has been a second father. Says Doug Carlen, a former student at Moody Bible Institute, "I don't know how I would have gone through high school without the influence of Harv Russell."[3]

Moody graduates can also be found on the university campus, working with such movements as Campus Crusade, InterVarsity Christian Fellowship, The Navigators, and lesser known groups. At the University of Minnesota, Jennifer (Grant) Board disciples collegians under The Navigators. In the East, Barbara (Roembke) Koch and her husband coordinate the Campus Crusade work in the Pennsylvania/Delaware area. In Portland, Oregon, Randy Haglune ('77) works by arrangement with his denomination (Conservative Baptist) as a campus ambassador to Lewis and Clark College. But Donald Dosedio ('70) and his wife, also headquartered in Portland, have founded their own campus movement: Christian Discipleship on Campus.

Among those shaping the lives of even younger people are those with such movements as the Christian Service Brigade, Pioneer Clubs, and Awana, the latter a movement co-founded by Lance (Doc) Latham ('18), now age 91, who for forty years pastored Chicago's North Side Gospel Center. And as churches reach out in these programs, they also build bridges to parents.

Who could count the hundreds who involve themselves each year, especially in summer months, in the nation's Christian camps? Such ministries reach one million children each year.

Of the more than seven hundred such sites which belong to the Christian Camps and Conference Association (there are a hundred in California alone), some like Sky Ranch near Dallas, have been founded by Moody graduates.

Sonlife's Christmastime Chicago seminars always receive a huge response. Over six hundred teenagers enroll in this well-rounded holiday program.

The Institute has also fed many of its graduates into the ranks of Child Evangelism Fellowship. Some direct the work statewide, as in Missouri and Ohio. Others may coordinate a metropolitan area—like Oklahoma City or Greater Chattanooga. Still others are county directors, skilled at mobilizing volunteers.

Hundreds of others have felt called into the public school systems of America as teachers,

3. Doug Carlen, "The Person and Work of Harv Russell," unpublished paper.

Moody feeds some of its graduates into the country's burgeoning Christian schools movement (three new Christian schools open each day). Moody also owns a school in St. Petersburg, Florida. Associated with Moody Keswick, it has seven hundred students grades K-12.

guidance counselors, administrators. They are people like Peter Derzipilski, who retired in 1981 as school administrator for San Diego City Schools, and David Schulert, who spent thirty-nine years in public education, the last twelve (before his retirement) as director of curriculum for the Lansing (Michigan) Public Schools. They are educators like Jim Bernero, principal of an all-black elementary school of more than seven hundred on Chicago's south side.

Where it has been allowed, some graduates have taught the Bible in public schools for years, especially in the South. In many cases, release-time classes have been the open door.

Moody's own school historically has centered on higher education, but in the mid 70s when the Institute acquired a facility in St.

Petersburg, Florida, that had long been known as Southern Keswick (later re-named Moody Keswick), the package included not only one of the South's finest Bible conferences and a Christian radio station, but also a Christian school, grades K-12, with nearly 700 students. To direct this ministry, the Institute hired as the school's headmaster Don Barber, who had spent twenty years as assistant superintendent at Flossmoor District #161 in the Chicago area. Keswick Christian School is a self-sustaining private institution that employs forty-one teachers and three administrators.

Whatever direction God may lead, Moody Bible Institute and those it trains will continue to look for ways to shape the youth of America with the Christian gospel.

Bruce Hanks (Class of 51), a Baptist pastor in Milaca, Minnesota, is a distant cousin of Abraham Lincoln (a descendent of the family of Lincoln's mother, Nancy Hanks). In black frock coat, black bow tie, and stovepipe hat, said People *magazine in 1976, "He's a dead ringer for Abe Lincoln." Hanks is the same height as Lincoln (6'4"), and he even has a wart on his cheek where the sixteenth president had his. Hanks left the pastorate for a time during the bicentennial years to travel the country in the role of Abraham Lincoln. He still has opportunity to share the gospel and the nation's Christian heritage with schools, churches, and farm groups throughout the Midwest.*

"Nevada Steve" Homoki was once a Hollywood stunt man, old-time western actor, and rope and whip artist on the rodeo circuit. In 1929, he rode the famous bucking horse Five Minutes to Midnight—few have ever done so. But before he could get off, the horse twisted in midair and came down on him, breaking his back, neck, and twelve bones. Miraculously, he lived. Later "Nevada Steve" trusted Jesus Christ as Savior and entered Moody Bible Institute, then worked as a missionary among the Navajo Indians. But for more than twenty years until his sudden death in late 1984, he spent his summers entertaining teenagers at the evangelical River Valley Ranch in Maryland.

Thousands of Moody alumni daily sow and reap in the secular world around them.

Chapter 13

SALT IN SOCIETY

While the majority of those trained at Moody Bible Institute enter full-time Christian work, the school has also turned out hundreds, even thousands, of what D. L. Moody called "gap men," those whose occupations are not church-related, but who nonetheless are advancing the cause of Christ. They are computer specialists, engineers, salesmen, business people, policemen— just about any job you can name that does not contradict Christian conscience. They are people who sometimes even win golf tournaments, or who are named to the Outstanding Young Men and Women of America, or who are honored as "Mother of the Year."

They are people like Judy Marr, a receptionist for Delta Airlines; or Richard Newell, a tool and production planner in Boeing 747 division, and David Landis, vice-president of a Jackson, Wyoming, bank. They are Frank Everett, Canadian potato farmer; Jim Broman, Englewood, Colorado, fire chief (son of former Dean Franklin Broman), and Paul Vick, former Wichita, Kansas, police officer and now an FBI agent in Southern California.

Vick was elected president of Wichita's Fellowship of Christian Peace Officers, a group formed in 1978 after a demoralizing police strike. Wichita's chief of police and the police chaplain felt it could be a positive, healing force between people. Although they were accused of being formed as a union-busting vehicle, the Wichita police chief told the local press, "Whoever started those rumors, or believes the rumors, has never been to one of the meetings or knows what we are all about. I encourage them to come and join us."[1]

Some alumni have combined law with the pastorate. An adult probation officer for the state of Iowa also serves interim pastorates. A retired pastor in Everett, Washington, serves as a police department chaplain, on call night or day. Another helps coordinate public information for the Michigan State Police.

Daryle Doden is the thirty-nine-year-old president of Ambassador Steel in Butler, Indiana, one of the nation's largest companies dealing in steel reinforcing rods—a company he founded. Each new customer gets a letter explaining Ambassador Steel's philosophy:

"From the beginning, the management was determined to make God the Senior Partner of the firm. We also strive to ask Him for guidance regarding every decision. . . . If you are troubled or perplexed and looking for answers, may we invite you to look to God and ask Him to be your Savior, for God loves you."

Doden admits to being "a bit apprehensive" when he first sent out the letters a few years ago. Though it took courage, he wanted to make it clear that "our goal in business is to present Jesus Christ as the answer to all of man's needs."

"Making money," he says, "is secondary." When he meets other businessmen, "They find it hard to comprehend that the dollar isn't your first goal in business . . . they have trouble believing it."

Still, Ambassador has done quite well in the money department, recording over one million dollars per month in sales. Not bad for a company

1. "Vick Heads Wichita Fellowship of Christian Police Officers," *Moody Alumni* (Winter 1981-82).

Daryle Doden, founder and president of Ambassador Steel, builds a strong Christian witness into the fabric of his business.

personal effort to talk about Christ to everyone who comes through the door." Many would consider it a waste of important time. Doden points out that his business is successful anyway.

"You can't lose," Doden says of his way of doing business based on Christian principles. Clients aren't afraid to deal with him because they respect his integrity. Ambassador Steel does not attempt to use Christianity as a wedge to get business deals. Nor does the firm claim to be perfect—it only pledges to try. And "just because we're Christians," says Doden, "doesn't mean we're going to be financially successful. The rain falls on the just and the unjust."[2]

Many former students run their own businesses. A scan of past issues of the *Alumni News* turns up such examples as a floor coverings firm, an auto exchange, a photography studio, and a dog grooming business.

Other Moody alumni are accountants, computer programmers and analysts, marketing managers. One can even find a pharmacist and an assistant postmaster. They are also in public

2. "Alumnus Conducts Business for Christ," *Alumni News* (Summer 1979).

that began through what most would call a lucky break, although, because of his faith, Doden doesn't see it as mere luck. Ambassador began in late 1973 when Doden was working as a remodeling contractor. In a conversation with a concrete dealer, Doden learned that there was a severe shortage of steel reinforcing rods for concrete. That brought to mind a businessman he had met at an Osceola, Indiana, church where Doden had been minister of music.

Doden and his contracting partner were able to come up with five tons of steel rods from the Osceola factory owner. They started in business from a pay phone in a shopping center, calling concrete companies that might be interested. Today the heart of Ambassador Steel's operation is in warehouses in Kokomo, Chicago, and Cleveland.

"If the company doesn't look over-wealthy," said a feature article in the Auburn, Indiana, *Evening Star*, "perhaps it's because a large amount of the profit is donated to Christian causes. . . . but more important to Doden is his

Real estate broker Michael Warren takes with him into the business world the spiritual skills he learned at Moody.

relations, insurance, microelectronics.

Numerous graduates are clinical psychologists, in some cases combining their Moody training with schooling at the Narramore Foundation's Rosemead Graduate School of Psychology in Rosemead, California, or elsewhere. Some are social workers—in places like Detroit, Chicago, and Tulsa. Lowell Routley of Davenport, Iowa, directs the Quad City Counseling Service, a non-profit Christian mental health agency. Hazel Goddard, a one-time editor with *Moody Monthly*, is president of Christian Counseling Ministries in Buena Vista, Colorado, with a branch in Daytona, Florida. Roger Cantril is director and pastoral psychotherapist for the Counseling Institute of Kansas City, and has formed a holistic health care enrichment center called the Cantril CARE Corporation. Some join counseling staffs of larger churches. Joanne Hedgepeth in 1982 joined the Air Force as a clinical psychologist, with a captain's rank.

While the vast majority of missionary aviation students wind up on the mission field, it is not true in every case. David Wiley is a pilot for United Airlines. Jack Stowers has been an aircraft mechanic with Western Airlines in San Francisco. Rod Collier is a mechanic at the Indianapolis airport, but also serves as a youth pastor. Others are corporation pilots.

Among former students one can find architects, industrial engineers, automotive researchers, electronic engineers. But you can almost be guaranteed that each one, along with his wife, is also active in a local church. David Chizum, for example, works with the Department of Defense, but also serves the Columbia, Maryland, Presbyterian Church as missions coordinator. Doug Hamilton of Lansing, Michigan, works as a cobol programmer for Oldsmobile, but teaches Sunday school and sings in the choir at his inner city church. Former pastor Clifford Curtis worked twenty years with the DuPont company in Wilmington, Delaware, but during that same time he also helped start several new churches.

Evening school graduates, of course, who often are already in secular occupations, find that their Moody training undergirds them to be salt

Dr. Richard Jensen, Ohio State University professor, pursues research to computerize cockpits. He is a graduate of Moody's missionary aviation program.

in their society. Wendell Goad II, for example, is an attorney in Merrillville, Indiana. But he is also involved with Prison Fellowship, a Gary, Indiana, rescue mission, and a flourishing Southlake businessmen's fellowship.

On the rural scene, one can find farmers, agricultural extension agents, conservationists, dairymen. A. Hayden Porter became a full-time Wyoming cattle rancher, after retiring as academic dean of Big Sky Bible College in Montana. At Big Sky his wife, the former Nancy Alexander, served as school nurse.

Some have gone on from Moody to pursue the field of medicine—among them Keith Goeking, chief in the Department of Obstetrics and Gynecology at Dyess Air Force Base Hospital in Abilene, Texas. Many are nurses—some working in hospitals after service on the mission field, or while home on furlough.

The late Benson Hitchcock served for two decades as director of the Senior Citizens Fund of Kalamazoo, Michigan, helping build and maintain a complex of nursing homes. He was president of the Michigan Nursing Home Association, and in 1972 attended the Ninth International Congress on Gerontology in Kiev, USSR. Benson credits Moody Bible Institute for laying the groundwork for his ministry over the years, which has included prominent pastorates and organizational positions of stature. "Under the teaching of men like P. B. Fitzwater and Wilbur Smith," he says, "I found a love for the Word of God and a

knowledge of how to study it. I worked under Wendell P. Loveless as a student announcer on WMBI. Franklin Broman made a major impact on my life."[3]

3. "Hitchcock Retires as Nursing Home Director," *Moody Alumni* (Spring 1982).

Jack Houston, general assignment reporter for the Chicago Tribune, *has also been its education editor and its religion editor. He has initiated lunchbreak Bible studies with work associates.*

MBI alumni who work as secretaries can be found in firms like Eastman Kodak, Sears Roebuck, and E. F. Hutton. Diane Hacket, an executive secretary for an oil company in Denver, wrote of her excitement about "the many opportunities to witness at the seventh largest oil company in the world."

At the *Chicago Tribune*, where he has served as religion editor, education editor, and general reporter, Jack Houston ('58) soon found he was not alone as a believer. Among colleagues he discovered Dave Nystrom, an award-winning photographer and also a former Moody student. The two of them began to meet for Bible study with Casey Banas, then assistant to the editor, and editorial cartoonist Wayne Stayskal. Such times strengthened their sense of God's calling to their professions and sensitized them to their potential witness among the people they worked with.[4]

Meanwhile, Jonathan Peterson ('76) has been named religion news editor for the United Press International Radio Network and Broadcast Wire. From his former position as news/program director of an FM station in Minnesota, he moves to UPI's new offices in Washington, D. C.

Tim Walberg won election to the Michigan House of Representatives. When he announced his candidacy, Walberg concluded his speech by saying, "Our nation, and our state, were founded upon traditional values, values that recognized God as the ultimate authority and His Word as the guide for liberty. John Witherspoon, the only minister to sign the Declaration of Independence, recognized that when he said, 'A republic once equally poised must either preserve its virtue or lose its liberty.' Can we afford to go on supporting politicians who disregard such admonitions? I think not!

"Yes, I believe there is a place for a minister of the gospel in the House of Representatives," concluded Walberg. "I will not exploit religion, yet I will not hide my faith. It is my desire as it was said of King David of old, that I will have served my generation according to the purposes of God."[5]

Whether in the political arena, business, medicine, or a countless number of other occupations, Moody Bible Institute produces many who stand in Christian courage to be the salt of the earth.

4. Calvin Biddle, "Bible Study in the Newsroom," *Moody Monthly* (February 1973).
5. *Moody Alumni* (Winter 1982-83).

Chapter 14

OVER LAND
AND SEA

The *SS Dorchester*, packed with troops of World War II, cut its way through icy waters off the coast of Greenland in February 1943. Suddenly it was struck by German torpedo fire. Hundreds stood all but paralyzed by the fear of evacuating into icy waters.

Four chaplains were aboard—one of them Lieutenant George Fox, a 1923 graduate of Moody Bible Institute and one-time New England pastor. A War Department report describes the scene:

"Fear of the icy water had made many aboard almost helpless. The chaplains calmed their fears and are given credit for saving many men by persuading them to go overboard where there was a chance of rescue."

The chaplains encouraged men, prayed with them, helped them into lifeboats and life belts, and at last, in the supreme sacrifice, gave up their own life jackets.

As the ship was sinking bow-first, men in the water and in lifeboats saw the chaplains link arms and heard them raise their voices in prayer. They were still praying together on the deck when the ship made its final plunge."[1] A United States postage stamp issued in 1948 honored their heroic martyrdom.

1. DeRemer, pp. 91-92.

George Fox in far left.

Chaplain Harold Voelkel preaches to prisoners of war behind communist lines in North Korea (see page 167).

Over the years, Moody Bible Institute has continued to have a part in the training of those who minister in the armed services. From Moody they have gone on to seminary, then earned appointment to the chaplaincy after rigorous screening both by the government and their denominations.

The late Chester R. Lindsey, class of '41, served as a U.S. Army chaplain for thirty years and rose to United States Chief of Army Chaplains, retiring as a general. He was commandant of the U.S. Army Chaplaincy School in New York state for his last five years of duty.

Chaplain (Capt.) Jerry Moritz is now the deputy chaplain of the United States Marine Corps. In a previous assignment, he served as the assistant force chaplain, Commander Naval Forces Pacific, where he helped direct the work of the Pacific Fleet's sixty-five chaplains and reported through his chain of command to a three-star admiral. When not docked at San Diego or in one of the other ports rimming the Pacific, his men served in the millions of square miles of ocean expanse, looking after the spiritual needs of some 50,000 men.

Jerry Moritz at one time planned to be a missionary in South America, until God redirected

Chaplain Jerry Moritz, now the second-ranking chaplain in the United States Marine Corps. At one time he served the US Navy Pacific fleet.

his steps. His appointment to the chaplaincy at first seemed unlikely. He had been diagnosed with "flat feet, a broken nose, and bronchial asthma" and classified 4-F. But he persuaded the authorities to reclassify him, and in 1962 he applied for a chaplain's appointment. Three years later, the Office of the Chief of Chaplains called him on the same day his church board had voted to more than double his fifty dollars per week salary.

On his first duty aboard a destroyer out of Norfolk, Virginia, Moritz promptly established group Bible study as one of his strengths. And the best place to hold these studies, he found, was in the ship's mess decks just before the evening movie. Men would come early to get good seats—and hear the gospel.

When Moritz volunteered in 1970 for combat duty in Viet Nam, he was assigned to the 1st Marine Division and positioned twenty miles northwest of Da Nang. Each morning he checked the map at Combat Operations Center for the position of the troops, then headed out by foot, jeep, helicopter, or boat to spend time with the men. Most of the time he walked—often over territory riddled with traps and mines. "At our firebases up those mountains," Moritz remembers, "there wasn't much room for anyone to stray far, and I could really get close to the men."

There were some close calls—like the time he spotted an explosive less than two feet away. Or the helicopter ride he missed one night, which suffered a fatal crash. One man, well aware of the risks Moritz took to reach his group, said Jerry's preaching was like "a home-cooked meal."

"I wouldn't have exchanged those meetings with other men up on those ridges and hillsides," Moritz says today, "for the fanciest cathedrals in the world."[2]

Through more than two decades now in the chaplaincy, Moritz has relied heavily on Moody science films, Moody Press books, tracts, and especially Moody correspondence courses. While a chaplain at Great Lakes Naval Training Station, north of Chicago, Moritz saw unusual response to the gospel. With up to 2,500 boot camp recruits in chapel on Sunday mornings, he

2. *Moody Monthly* (September 1966), p. 93.

rarely saw fewer than fifty make decisions for Christ. Moritz started many of these men on Moody correspondence courses to help with follow-up. Wherever he has been, he has left behind a string of Bible study groups designed to nourish believers and to reach non-Christians.

Interestingly, the SS *Dwight L. Moody*, named in honor of the famous evangelist, sailed the Atlantic and the Pacific during the latter half of World War II. In deference to Moody and his followers, it was launched, say reports, not by a bottle of champagne, but by a bottle of water! It transported both military and commercial cargo. The ship was eventually retired to the national

The SS Dwight L. Moody, *which transported troops and cargo during World War II. After several years in the defense reserve fleet at Beaumont, Texas, it was finally sent to its grave.*

defense reserve fleet at Beaumont, Texas, and then later sent to its grave.[3]

Former MBI president Will Houghton served as a chaplain on the East Coast for a time, ministering to troops leaving for the World War I battlefield. Houghton brought the legendary "Defender of Malta," General Sir William Dobbie, and Lady Dobbie to the United States under the auspices of Moody Bible Institute. They ministered to thousands across the country—among them Eleanor Roosevelt.

General Sir William Dobbie, legendary "Defender of Malta," whom Moody Bible Institute sponsored in a 1945 cross-country tour (see page 76).

Dr. George Sweeting, as an evangelist, preached to thousands of military men in West Germany following World War II, using as the motto of his crusades "Christ is the Answer."

Dwight Moody knew how to relate to men, yet not compromise the gospel. It is still this kind of man who makes the greatest impact in the chaplaincy.

Guns were booming in Korea when Alfred Brough was a student at Moody Bible Institute. Vietnam was little known. But a few years later he found himself an Army chaplain in the Mekong delta. Soon after his arrival, some of the men came to him and said they were tired of kicking beer cans out of their way in the theater where they were holding services. They wanted a chapel of their own and didn't want to wait until the Defense Department put one up.

So Chaplain Brough began receiving funds contributed by the men of the battalion, and soon their chapel took shape. Its 200 seats were filled every Sunday. Each Sunday Brough risked traveling by helicopter to six other jungle locations, taking news of eternal life to men who lived on the threshold of death. The Army named him chaplain of the year.[4]

The late Herman L. Driskell ('14) was one of the few who served as chaplain in both world wars. As some retire from this ministry and perhaps assume a pastorate, others of the younger Moody generation take their places.

The Moody witness within the armed services, however, goes far beyond the chaplain. Hundreds have served in times of both war and peace. The 1945 *Arch* yearbook listed almost five hundred former students and employees who

3. DeRemer, p. 92.
4. Robert Flood, "Jerry Moritz: Navy Chaplain," *Moody Monthly* (November 1980).

Bill Tollberg, whom the US Navy honored by launching the USS Tollberg *after his extraordinary heroism near Guadacanal.*

served in World War II. Fifteen were killed.[5]

One was Bill Tollberg. He and his wife, who had both attended evening school during the 1930s, worked together in jails, hospitals, and a Chicago mission. When the war broke out, Tollberg's education did not qualify him for the chaplaincy, so he enlisted in the Navy. Aboard ship, he bore a faithful and fruitful witness.

Then one day, off Guadalcanal, a Japanese torpedo hit Tollberg's ship, and a shattering explosion released high pressure steam, killing everybody in the engine room but Tollberg. Severely scalded, partly blinded, he groped over the bodies of dead comrades, and with his fast-ebbing strength, closed an oil valve, saving the lives of other trapped shipmates before he himself died. For extraordinary heroism, the Navy Cross was awarded posthumously. But even more precious was this letter from a shipmate: "Even since his death there have been some who have accepted Christ because of his testimony. He being dead yet speaketh." Later, the Navy further honored him by launching the USS *Tollberg*.[6]

Twenty-five years later, William Hellyer was a civilian worker at Guantanamo Naval Base. He had led a number of men to the Lord and established several Bible classes. Intent on the mission field, Hellyer eventually became a medic in Vietnam. In the Central Highlands, while aiding wounded comrades, he was killed by enemy fire. He was buried in Illinois with full military honors.

Hellyer's parents were sent their son's medals, along with his personal effects. These included his Greek New Testament, his pocket Greek lexicon, his pocket Bible, and numerous tracts. Also enclosed was his bloodstained *Moody Monthly* Daily Reminder, which contained a lengthy prayer list. On a tape to a friend he had alluded to God's sovereignty in life and death: "The circumstances of my death," he said, recognizing his vulnerability, "are as present with the Lord as the circumstances of my birth. With God all things are Now. That's why Christ said, 'before Abraham was, I AM.' "[7]

Moody alumni reach out to the military in endless ways. Carol Ruhf Tokatioglou and her husband travel all over the world for Officers Christian Fellowship. Though they minister primarily to the American military, they reach out also to the many international officers who come to the U.S.A. Hundreds, if not thousands, of servicemen can point to the impact of Frank Hooper upon their lives. Hooper for years has operated a Christian servicemen's center in Puerto Rico, and his proteges have streamed to Moody Bible Institute, then to the mission field or into other ministries.

This kind of story can be repeated in servicemen's centers around the world. Tom Hash ('55) and his wife, the former Dotty Keeler, founded the Overseas Christian Serviceman's Center thirty years ago. Today its twenty-nine ministries spread from Asia to Europe—from Korea and the Philippines to Panama, and from coast to coast in the U.S., reaching thousands each year.

It would be impossible to calculate the total impact of Moody Institute of Science films in the military. A few years ago six hundred Army, Navy, and Air Force chaplains gathered in Chicago for their national convention. Dr. Irwin Moon addressed the chaplain's presidential banquet after a concert by the Moody Chorale. The chaplains viewed a kaleidoscope of Moody services available to the military, including a super-eight movie projection concept MIS had just released. Its compactness was ideally suited to space-limited submarines. Even at that time all MIS films had been produced in the super-eight cartridge and were being premiered on Polaris submarines and at three air bases.

The chaplains viewed a special pre-release of *Empty Cities*. Said Chief of Navy Chaplains RADM James W. Kelly to Dr. Moon: "I've shown your films hundreds of times. I know them so well I could quote them by heart. You and your people have done us a great service."[8]

When Dwight Moody first conceived the inexpensive religious paperback, those in the military were among his special targets. Over the

5. DeRemer, p. 93.
6. Ibid., pp. 92-93.
7. *Quarterly Fellowship Letter* (June 1968).
8. "Dr. Irwin Moon Speaks to Military Chaplains," *Moody Monthly* (July 1949).

In Vietnam, Chaplain Doman unpacks Moody Press books he had just received from the Moody Literature Mission. Military chaplains call on Moody both for printed matter and gospel science films. Some graduates enter the chaplaincy. Others minister at Christian servicemen's centers around the world.

years Moody Literature Ministries has supplied tens of thousands of dollars in books, tracts, films, and correspondence courses to help chaplains do their job.

One could wish that war, and the threat of war, might disappear, but those who know the Scriptures also know it will not happen—until the return of Jesus Christ. On one occasion a few years ago, William D. Stewart, then a Moody Bible Institute extension representative, spoke on prophecy in a Washington, D. C., church. An Army colonel in the congregation felt his associates were missing something, so he invited Stewart for breakfast at the Pentagon. There Stewart had the privilege of opening the Word of God in the Military Strategy Room for all who would come.[9]

Doors sometimes open in strange places and in strange ways. The outreach of Moody Alumni to those in military service still goes on—in air, over land and sea.

9. "MBI Graduates Make Impact in Chaplaincy," *Moody Monthly* (April 1968).

Dwight Hartzler with wife, Margaret, and their translation helper study fine points of the Sentani language as they work in Indonesia with Wycliffe Bible Translators.

Chapter 15

TO EVERY
NATION

Northfield, Massachusetts, in the late 1880s was the best known village in the world, outside of Bethlehem. It was the birthplace and home of Dwight L. Moody, the site of his two Northfield schools, and the scene of gigantic summer conferences that drew thousands.

It was also the site that gave great thrust to the world missionary movement, even before the existence of Moody Bible Institute. University students gathered to hear Moody and others deliver the challenge of the Great Commission. At Northfield, in those days of spiritual fervor, the missionary phrase was coined, "Our supreme task is world evangelization in this generation."[1]

On the Northfield grounds stands an impressive monument with this inscription:

> Here in July, 1886, to the Glory of God and to the advancement of His Kingdom, Dwight L. Moody and the Intercollegiate YMCA of the United States and Canada called together a conference of students from 27 states and many lands beyond the seas.
>
> From the spiritual impulse here given, 100 men offered their lives for foreign missionary service.

In later years, after Moody's death, Northfield's spiritual thrust faded as documented in *So Much to Learn*, by Burnham Carter (1976). But fortunately, Moody's Chicago school soon picked up the torch of world missions. Now, one hundred years later, because of Moody's world vision, no continent is the same.

The names of nearly 6,000 missionaries posted today in the foyer of Torrey-Gray auditorium attest to the scope of Moody's missionary involvement. And the roster has to be continually updated.

Wycliffe Bible Translators, now the largest missionary agency in the world, reports that Moody Bible Institute leads all other Bible schools and colleges in alumni serving with the mission. They are staked out in various parts of the world, carefully rehearsing unpenned languages, reducing sounds to phonetic symbols, tediously siphoning them into new translations of the Word of God.

"For years MBI graduates have served with Wycliffe," observes Dr. Sweeting. "Currently more than 400 alumni are active in the work. 'Uncle Cam' Townsend claimed God's promise that people from 'every tribe and tongue and people and nation' would gather at heaven's throne' (Rev. 5:9).

"It now takes an average of 12 years to translate a New Testament. If the current pace of translation holds, every language could have a New Testament by the time my grandson, Chris, retires.

"Cameron Townsend's motto was 'Pioneer, always pioneer.' Before his death in 1982, he sought young people who were willing to dare the outer limits of challenge for God. He told his co-workers to 'stay close to Moody Bible Institute' because he believed it would yield pioneers in world evangelism."[2]

The Evangelical Alliance Mission, with more than one thousand missionaries, also finds Moody Bible Institute its number one source of supply among all schools. Moody Bible Institute

1. George Sweeting, "Northfield's Reminder," *Moody Monthly* (November 1979).
2. George Sweeting, "Pioneer for Our Grandson's Grandsons," *Moody Monthly* (May 1984).

This listing of names in the old original building of Moody Bible Institute is now outdated by several decades. A similar board, though much larger, now rings the foyer of Torrey-Gray Auditorium.

supplies more than half the world's missionary pilots.

J. Herbert Kane, who is one of the world's foremost missionary strategists, said as late as 1981, "There is no doubt in my mind that Moody Bible Institute is in a class by itself. When it comes to world missions, Moody has chalked up a record second to none. No other school in the world has produced so many missionaries. It is a staggering thought that one out of every fifteen career missionaries from North America is an alumnus of Moody Bible Institute!"[3]

Out of Moody Bible Institute have also come many of the world's top missionary statesmen, including two whose work in Africa earned them Moody "Alumnus of the Year" awards. Under the leadership of Moody-trained men, the Sudan Interior Mission grew into what was for many years the largest faith mission in the world. When its founder and head, R. V. Bingham, died in 1944, Guy Playfair became its general director. Playfair had gone to Africa under SIM in 1910, when it had only seventeen missionaries. It expanded into an organization with more than one thousand missionaries. Dr. Raymond J. Davis, whom God used to design the Association of Evangelical Churches of West Africa, was SIM's general director from 1962-1975.

Dr. David H. Johnson, late general director of The Evangelical Alliance Mission, took TEAM's missionary force from 228 in 1946 to 820 in 1961, and expanded its fields of service from seven to seventeen countries. Dr. Vernon Mortenson, also a Moody alumnus, succeeded Johnson as general director, and by 1974 the missionary force had topped 1,000. As Mortenson continued to stress church planting, TEAM-founded churches on the mission fields tripled and membership quadrupled. Mortenson's far-flung responsibilities took him to all the mission fields—a total of twenty-seven overseas trips.[4]

Dr. Wendell W. Kempton ('54) is president of the Association of Baptists for World Evangelism, Inc., involved in church planting, Bible translation, and hospital work throughout the world. William H. Taylor served as general secretary of the Central American Mission for many years. Phillip Armstrong helped found the Far Eastern Gospel Crusade (now Send International) in 1945, the result of a need he and other Christian servicemen had seen while serving in the Pacific during World War II.

Shortly after he had turned his position as general director of the mission over to a successor

3. "Herbert Kane: Alumnus of the Year," *Moody Alumni* (Spring 1981).
4. The Evangelical Alliance Mission, news release, 3 October 1974.

in 1980, Armstrong, with four others, was killed in a plane that went down in the waters above Cape Yakatag on the southern coast of Alaska. Armstrong was returning from a fact-finding tour of a new radio station site of the Central Alaskan Mission, a new division of Far Eastern Gospel Crusade at that time.

John Gration directs the world missions graduate program at Wheaton College. Dr. J. Herbert Kane, former professor of missions in the School of World Missions and Evangelism at Trinity Evangelical Divinity School has exercised great influence as a missionary strategist and author of missions textbooks. His outreach extends to the university campus. A few years ago, Kane helped spearhead a three-day missions conference at Ohio's Miami University which drew four hundred registrants. Said Kane in an interview afterwards, "The students were very

keen. They stayed after the meetings. They gathered around. They asked questions. They invited me to their dorms. And that was a secular university!"[5]

Yet the greatest heroes may be those who have labored for years, unnoticed, in obscure corners of the world, patiently laying the groundwork for a vital Christianity that will someday explode into prominence. And when it does, most of the world will not even understand why it happened.

No man can fully appreciate what these men and women are doing, Dr. Culbertson once said, until they see it firsthand, as he did in his tours of the mission field in 1957 and 1960. The following pages offer a whirlwind tour of five continents, only a taste of the action from a century of world impact.

5. "Herbert Kane."

Under the direction of Dr. David H. Johnson (left) and Dr. Vernon Mortenson, both graduates of Moody Bible Institute, The Evangelical Alliance Mission grows in three decades from 228 missionaries to more than a thousand.

AFRICA

This painting by missionary/artist Phil Lasse (see page 158) captures the beauty of Kenya's wildlife.

More than a century has passed since David Livingstone pioneered the heart of Africa and earned such world reknown that he was buried in Westminster Abbey. The image of the missionary in a pith helmet, hacking his way through the jungles with a machete, hangs on in the minds of some, but a new Africa has emerged—one that *U.S. World and News Report* says will be largely Christianized by the end of the century.

The earliest missionaries Dwight Moody motivated at Northfield looked toward Africa more than any other continent, and so also did the first half century of missions emphasis at Moody Bible Institute.

Five Moody-trained missionaries have given their lives for the gospel in Africa.

Ella Schenck, class of 1896, was the first. As a United Brethren missionary, she helped run a girls' home in Sierra Leone, Africa, when the British imposed an unpopular "hut tax" of one dollar to two dollars a year to pay for police protection. In the resulting May 1898 rebellion, Ella, thirty-two, and seven other missionaries were clubbed to death.

A degenerate was blamed for the death of Hulda Stumpf ('07), murdered on a January night in 1930 in her little house in Kijabe, Kenya. She was sixty-three and had served under Africa Inland Mission.

Lucia Cozzens ('15) served in the Cameroons, Africa, as official hostess for the United Presbyterian mission home there. One October night in 1949, typical of her mercy, she got up several times to give a sick girl medicine. But before morning an intruder broke into her home and beat her to death.

At the end of World War II, Walter Ohman ('27) could hardly wait to get back into Ethiopia, where he had planted the gospel more than a decade earlier. What would he discover? In 1938, when Italian armies forced Ethiopia's pioneer missionaries—including Ohman—to leave the work they had started, he left behind a handful of believers. How many would there be now? Had they stood up under trial?

Ohman headed for Soddu. He was astounded! In that area there were now some ten thousand Christians! That was in 1945. By 1960, Ethiopia had an estimated 160,000 baptized believers.

It had all started when, in 1933, at Soddu, Ohman and the Sudan Interior Mission's E. E. Lewis baptized ten Walamo converts. By 1937, those had increased to about a hundred. Ohman had learned the Walamo language, reduced it to writing, and translated the gospels of Mark and John.

But Mussolini's soldiers were on the way. Hastily Ohman prepared his converts, further grounding them in the Bible. For nine months bombs rained on Soddu. Ohman was cut off from all supplies. Forced to evacuate, he was finally flown out in an Anglo-Egyptian bomber and sent to pioneer a new field in the Sudan.

For the Ohmans the terror of war was not over. Returning to Africa on the *Zam Zam* after furlough in the United States, they were shelled by the Germans. The ship and all their possessions went down in the Atlantic, and they were taken prisoners of war.

Ethiopians today are thankful for Ohman. Among the Walamos, thousands know his name.

Like Ohman, the Ethiopian church believes strongly in the Bible. Their hymns reveal how firmly they are convinced that Jesus is all the Bible claims Him to be. This seems to reflect Ohman's groundwork among the original converts. Ohman also taught them organization. Today they have their own well-organized churches, councils, and annual conferences. They even send out their own missionaries.[6]

As trouble brewed in the Congo (now Zaire), the prospect of dying at the hands of guerrillas was very real as two women missionaries talked on the veranda one October evening in 1964.

"We died to self years ago," said Mary Baker, "or else we would never have come to the Congo in the first place. Any subsequent death will be only physical." She reminded her friend of

SEPTEMBER · 1961

Moody MONTHLY

From the Citadel for Christ · · · Volunteers on Foreign Fields

Walter Ohman, featured on this 1961 cover of Moody Monthly, *helps open Ethiopia to the gospel before World War II. Margaret Nichols Laird, pioneer missionary to the Central African Republic, is portrayed at upper left.*

2 Corinthians 1:9: "But we had the sentence of death in ourselves."

About a month later, Mary, fifty, in her fourth term with Unevangelized Fields Mission, and nearly thirty other missionaries and their children were shot by Simba rebels at a ferry landing in the Congo, their bodies thrown in a river.[7]

As recently as November 1984, Canadian-born missionary pilot Stanley Ridgway ('75) was killed in Zaire when rebels based in bordering Tanzania commandeered his plane. The rebels forced Ridgway and two Zairian Army officers to fly them from Manonro to Moba, on the shores of Lake Tanganyika. After the plane landed, the three were shot. Ridgway was Moody Bible Institute's twentieth martyr.

World attention focused on the Congo when medical missionary Paul Carlson (not a Moody alumnus), a colleague of Baker who was also martyred, made headlines around the globe. Carlson did not die in vain. Thousands of others around the world committed themselves anew to the cause of world evangelism.

Dr. Titus Johnson, pioneer medical missionary ('18), also narrowly escaped a few years earlier, but survived to write a first person account of the drama for *Moody Monthly* called "Storm in the Congo."[8]

James Luckman ('31) built Ethiopia's first hospital for lepers, began the first radio gospel broadcast and opened numerous mission stations.

Most who pioneered in Africa have retired or died. Until her death in August 1984, at 103 Carrie (Schonheit) Raynor ('07) was the Africa Inland Mission's oldest living missionary. Born on a farm outside of Detroit, Michigan, in 1881, Carrie was challenged to missionary service in Africa by Charles Hurlbert, then general director of AIM. After graduation she sailed for British East Africa (Kenya) on November 2, 1907. Twenty-two other missionaries were on the boat,

6. "Volunteers on the Foreign Field," *Moody Monthly* (September 1961).
7. Jeanne Doering, "They Were Willing to Die," *Moody Monthly* (June 1981).
8. Titus Johnson, "Storm in the Congo," *Moody Monthly* (March 1961).

including Jesse E. Raynor, whom she married a year later.

The Raynors spent seventeen years in Africa. Carrie taught school, training African Gikukyu men to become teachers and women to read as they became believers. She started a girls' school, supervised a dormitory, and cared for abandoned babies. As a result of her teaching skills, many Gikukyu people learned to read and write their own language as well as English. In 1924, the Raynors returned to the United States. During the depression she managed apartment houses, then took her exam, and became a real estate broker.

At age 101 she still read books, worked crossword puzzles, watched television, and kept up on world news. In November 1982 she had become a finalist in the *Los Angeles Times* tangle towns contest after correctly unscrambling each of fifty names of towns. She was then entering the play-offs, which would determine a first-place $15,000 winner.[9]

The late Margaret Nicholl Laird spent fifty years as a missionary to the Central African Republic, as linguist, nurse, homesteader, missionary to cannibals, and planter of schools and hospitals. She and associates translated the New Testament into the native Santo language by 1935, with the entire Bible completed in 1962. Mission schools provided the base of the republic's education.

In the 1960s, a contingent of priests from Paris imposed upon the state legislature to make the Central African Republic's official language French—a move that would have undermined both the educational and the spiritual base missionaries had invested so many years to build.

On the day the republic was to decide the issue in the state legislature, a state official with high personal regard for Margaret Laird and the work of evangelical missions stepped in to defend the missionary point of view.

"Mr. President," he said, "I've been thinking. There are one hundred men in this assembly. I think it would be interesting to hear where we first learned to read and write and where we got our hunger for knowledge."

The contingent from Paris protested, but the president obliged.

Ninety-one of the men had learned to read at Protestant mission stations. Eight had learned at government schools. One had learned at the Catholic mission.

The secretary of state asked, "Do we need to discuss this any further?"

The French delegation went back to Paris defeated. God had answered prayer. The Central African Republic had preserved its native language. "I remembered how forty years ago," reminisces Laird in her book, *They Called Me Mama,* "I had thought it would be impossible to make Santo the state language. Yet 90 percent of that legislative body's leaders had started by studying at a Protestant mission. It had taken me forty years to realize what a privilege had been mine."

From almost the very outset of her arrival in the Central African Republic, Margaret Laird

9. *Moody Alumni* (Winter 1981-82).

1983: A group of young people in Zimbabwe gather to hear students from Moody Bible Institute (who are out of picture at left). The school takes some fifty students abroad each summer.

saw God work miracles in answer to prayer. With a big heart and enormous physical stamina, she enveloped the Africans in her love and taught them to love and trust Christ. In 1959, the Central African Republic awarded this alumnus of Moody Bible Institute the "Knight of the Order of Merit," highest honor of the republic.[10]

Pioneer work still goes on, though it takes many different forms. Translation work, of course, tends to be primitive. A. Keene Spitler and his wife, Helen, have been at work for more than thirty years among the Somalis in Ethiopia and Kenya. They have translated the entire New Testament into Somali as well as parts of the Old Testament, a dictionary, tracts, and Bible correspondence courses.

Van Smith and wife Nancy (Ross), with Helimission in Nairobi, fly missionaries to various parts of Kenya. The Meru tribe lives just east of Mt. Kenya. When nearly one thousand people were baptized at one service, the leader of another

religious group offered nearly three month's pay to anyone who would destroy the mission helicopter. No one accepted. With much starvation just across the border in Uganda, Van has assisted relief organizations with the helicopter because trucks bringing food supplies by land were often held up and looted.

John Heath and his wife serve in a tiny country in Africa called Lesotho, surrounded by the Republic of South Africa. The government of Lesotho asked Missionary Aviation Fellowship to provide their flying medical service with transportation to the remote villages hidden over 7,000 feet in the mountains. Heath promptly set up a radio shop and organized a communications network of radios into a system that would provide rapid transfer of medical information and flight tracking for the safety of two MAF pilots. Although Lesotho is 70 percent Christian, these interior areas are still relatively untouched by the gospel.

The technology of modern missions takes another form at places like Liberia, West Africa, where Ron Shope and others work with missionary radio station ELWA. In the studios of the Liberian Broadcasting System, Shope produces a half-hour weekly program called "Christofest," which features music by the Liberia Youth for Christ singing group, interviews, testimonies, and gospel challenge.

Moody alumnus Phil Lasse has brought other skills to the African scene as a missionary, graphic designer, and wildlife artist *par excellence.* Phil and his wife (Shirley Deanne Smith) have spent more than twenty years as missionaries in Africa. He served first as a graphic artist for the Africa Inland Mission Press, where he helped produce two Christian magazines, while Shirley taught at nearby Rift Valley Academy. In 1977, they began a new work in Nairobi, with Shirley working with evangelistic luncheons and city-wide Bible studies among women. The family is now on extended furlough Stateside.

The son of African missionaries, Phil Lasse has spent most of his life in Africa and was taken on his first safari at age one. Familiar with the ways of the wilderness, he made wildlife art

10. Margaret Nicholl Laird, *They Called Me Mama*, pp. 153-157.

his specialty, and from his own gallery he has released several series of limited-edition lithographs. The late Joy Adamson, author of *Born Free*, once said that "Philip Lasse is unmistakably bound for the top in wildlife art," and thousands who have enjoyed his work agree.

Kenya, where there is a strong cluster of Moody alumni, is perhaps the strongest Christian nation on the African continent. At Kijabe, a major mission station and site of Rift Valley Academy (a large school for missionary children), missionaries were encouraged recently by an official visit from the Kenyan president.

Africans are gradually taking over the leadership of their own churches. This is a healthy trend, especially if the leaders are well grounded theologically. Tom Chandler ('67), who has worked with Christian Nationals Evangelism Commission since March 1983, has just helped to bring the Nairobi Evangelical Graduate School into existence, while at the same time he works on a Ph.D. in cultural anthropology at Stanford University.

Political unrest continues to disrupt the mission work in Rhodesia, where the Norman Everswicks had to close a 150-bed mission hospital, and in Swaziland, where all foreign teachers have to be out by 1985. But in Africa such scenarios are not new.

Weeks after the Congo shockwave a quarter century ago, missionary Dr. Titus Johnson made his way back to his hospital in Kibunzi. "Not a white man could be seen anywhere along the long stretches of road," he wrote. "Empty mission stations, Protestant and Catholic, empty factories, empty farms, empty establishments. Congo had lost 80,000 of its 125,000 white people."

But within days of his return, a handful of the same soldiers who had cried for vengeance and death as Johnson lay hugging the ground in a roadside ditch, walked into his services. Rapport built until the soldiers, who had only weeks before been enemies, invited him into their camp to conduct regular services. "I have a conviction that what happened in this limited experience,"

Phil Lasse (right) examines one of the paintings that prompted the late Joy Adamson, author of Born Free, *to cite him as "unmistakeably bound for the top in wildlife art." Yet Lasse, now on furlough stateside, considers himself first a missionary who just also happens to be an artist.*

wrote Dr. Johnson in *Moody Monthly* "will be the answer to Congo's tragic upheaval—a greater and better opportunity than ever to preach Christ by invitation. The gospel they now think they can get along without will some day be the object of their ardent desire."[11]

The missionary doors eventually opened again, the nation has stabilized, and the gospel goes forth, with the Africans themselves assuming more of their own church leadership year by year.

In Florida, both the Sudan Interior Mission and the Africa Inland Mission have impressive retirement homes, where those who once served the Lord together on a far-away continent still fellowship together.

The pioneer missionary to Africa, working against what seemed overwhelming odds, kept at the task, confident that God would someday raise up a continent of Christians.

That is exactly what is happening.

11. Johnson.

EUROPE

The Eiffel Tower, one of Europe's most famous landmarks. The light of the gospel has long faded in much of the continent, but there are signs of revival.

In the eyes of the general public, Europe does not carry the image of a mission field. It is the land of the Reformation, a land of cathedrals.

It is a continent with culture, education, rich heritage. It supplied the settlers of early America, many of religious fervor.

Yet today Europe is also a continent at low spiritual ebb, with few churchgoers. In the last few decades missionaries scattered around the countries of Europe have been trying to reverse the tide, and there is evidence they may be succeeding. The spiritual skid, in the eyes of some, has bottomed out, the young generation is showing new interest in spiritual things, and revival may be on the horizon.

In the British Isles, of course, the name of Moody left its impression more than a century ago, when the Moody-Sankey team moved the continent with three campaigns. The results can still be seen throughout England and Scotland.

In 1974, on the one hundredth anniversary of Moody's arrival there, Dr. George Sweeting, the Moody Chorale, and a few of Moody's faculty and staff retraced Moody's steps in an intensive, three-week itinerary of concerts and evangelism. They took the gospel to the great auditoriums of Britain, to schools, to factories, to street corners, and places of government. They sang in great churches such as St. Giles Cathedral in Edinburgh, Scotland, where John Knox, adversary of Mary Queen of Scots, once ministered. And along the way they also sang in churches that Moody's campaign had helped establish, and they heard everywhere the

1972: Moody sends an evangelistic team to the Summer Olympics in Munich. Just behind this outdoor cafe setting in the heart of the city Moody science films (Naturwissenschaftliche) show every hour.

testimony of D. L. Moody's ministry a century earlier.[12]

At Dublin, an elderly lady told how her father had accepted Christ under Moody's ministry. But the story did not end there. Her father went on to write a number of religious books that have had international impact. He raised a Christian family that continued to spread the gospel, and so his daughter, Clara Stewart Watt, lived to see another Moody team retrace Moody's historic steps.

The warmth of the Christians they met, now a decade ago, may have signaled what lay ahead. God could still revive Europe. It was Dwight Moody's spark that sent William T. Grenfell to a far-reaching work among the Labrador fishermen. What might a new generation of young evangelists yet accomplish?

Ian B. Leitch of Balerno, Scotland, a young evangelist who travels throughout Europe for Heralds Trust, was a struggling young Christian in 1954. He and his parents attended a concert by the Moody Chorale (their first European tour) at the Carrubbers Close Mission in Edinburgh, Scotland. That very church, one that has enjoyed a strong ministry in Scotland for more than a century, was founded by D. L. Moody.

"That night the Lord spoke to my heart," says Leitch. "The singing was beautiful and really

ministered to me. The young people gave their testimonies. That night I was challenged to the reality of Christianity and to service for my Lord. From that time on I began dreaming about attending the Institute." Later, with his wife, Leitch came to America and attended Moody, then went back to proclaim the gospel across his land.[13]

The fervent ministry of George Verwer and the hundreds of young evangelists with Operation Mobilization has left its mark upon Europe. His 2,300-ton ship, Logos, and also the Doulos, have docked in ports all over Europe, and teams have distributed tons of gospel literature.

Greater Europe Mission, founded after World War II, has established a network of Bible institutes throughout Europe, and many Moody alumni are involved. They are scattered throughout the countries of Europe, working among many different subcultures. In West Germany, the Robert Ehles serve under Campus Crusade for Christ, reaching business executives and political leaders. Another alumnus directs a hospitality house. Ruth Bruckner, with The Navigators, disciples university students. The John Peters,

12. Calvin Biddle, "British Campaign Over but Outreach Goes On," *Moody Monthly* (April 1974).
13. *Quarterly Fellowship Letter* (March 1967).

George Verwer, founder of Operation Mobilization, exhorts listeners to a single-minded commitment to Jesus Christ and the evangelization of the world.

moving from a pastorate in San Mateo, California, work with the Pocket Testament League in the distribution of Scriptures. Eberhard Guting pastors a Presbyterian congregation in Osnabruck.

In neighboring Italy, workers follow up opportunities opened by Christian radio. In France, the Ken Beckwiths are helping to *build* radio stations. Steve Niles pastors a church in Lyons, and the family also directs a youth camp. Jan Lee (Richards) Starring and her husband in Caluire work not primarily with the French people, but with Cambodians!

Over the border in Spain, Bible correspondence courses seem to be the key to evangelistic strategy in cities like Barcelona and Malaga. But Linda Earl Miller and her husband have felt God's call to the Basque culture, rapidly gaining prominence in Spain. Presently there are no Basque-speaking evangelical churches. In neighboring Portugal, Majorie Hawes works in part with gypsies. Meanwhile, Dale Chappel reaches out through Portugal's Youth for Christ movement.

In Vienna, couples like the Dick Wardens and Don and Barbara Silvis reach out to children through tent evangelism, to teenagers through mountain retreats, and to young professionals through home Bible studies. As a result, new evangelical churches have begun to emerge.

Other Moody alumni can be found in the tiny kingdom of Monaco, at Monte Carlo, on the Mediterranean—where the powerful transmitters of Trans World Radio beam the gospel over all of Europe and beyond. Like artillery power, going out day and night, it softens the terrain for missionary ground troops everywhere. Yet its signal does not stop at the borders of the Iron Curtain, but penetrates into vast reaches where the missionary cannot go.

Europe is also one base for outreach to the Muslim world. Islam is the second largest religion in France, and in England churches are being turned into mosques. In Marseilles, France, Ken McBride directs Radio School of the Bible, the mass media arm of North Africa Mission, which ministers to Muslims. Numerous Moody alumni specialize in an outreach to Muslims under Gospel Missionary Union, with bases in Malaga, Spain, and Brussels, Belgium, where the Fred Plastows report that often more than a hundred calls a day come into a telephone ministry to hear a three-minute gospel message in Arabic.

AUSTRALIA

Sydney, Australia, in the "land down under." Moody graduates serve both in its cities and in its "Outback."

While Dwight Moody evangelized a century ago in the British Isles, it was his successor, Reuben A. Torrey, who proclaimed the gospel both in Great Britain *and* Australia. He took with him as song leader and soloist Charles Alexander, also a man with roots at Moody. During the four-and-a-half years Torrey and Alexander labored together, one hundred and fifteen thousand persons made professions of faith in Christ.[14]

In Australia today, the work of Moody alumni spans an extreme of cultures, from the city socialite to the remote aborigine. Some of these alumni are Australians, who crossed the Pacific to study at Moody Bible Institute, then returned to the land down under.

Jim Vine, of Open Air Campaigners has also evangelized aggressively in Australia. There he and his family have performed countless musical concerts, held church crusades, and spent weeks in beach evangelism. Vine has spoken in many high school assemblies and developed a book party ministry. Yet he expresses concern that the society in which workers minister seems spiritually apathetic because of its affluence.

The surroundings of Kathy Barker Glasgow stand in sharp contrast. She and her husband are missionaries with Wycliffe Bible Translators in Australia, working in the northern territory among the aborigines. Bob and Sylvia Peterson, though not living among the aborigines, are based in Darwin where Bob is working to provide Scripture portions and literacy materials for the aboriginal people. Sylvia teaches at Marrara Christian School, and as their lives become intertwined with those around them, they are able to share the gospel of Jesus Christ. While in tribal surroundings in 1980, they reported some aborigines learning to play the guitar and organ, composing their own hymns, and gathering daily to sing and share the gospel.

In Sydney, Nola Randall's mission field are the Laotians, the Vietnamese, the Chinese, and other refugees of Indo-China who settled on Australian shores. She reports on the endless opportunities—"the Lord has brought the mission field to my doorstep."

Meanwhile, Graham Barker and Ian Wells, both Australians, reach Australian youth, Barker as the national campus life training director for Australia Youth For Christ. Wells, a former youth pastor and member of the South Australia State Police, is youth ministry consultant for the South Australian Baptist Union. The Dave Kendalls, under Teen Crusaders, reach out to street kids in Sydney.

And while the Jim Ankneys plant churches in Sydney, on Australia's eastern shores, Ben Bakker is 2,000 miles across the continent at Perth on the west coast, serving under The Evangelical Alliance Mission.

In an innovative program, Dick Innes has reached out across Australia by direct mail. Under Acts International, which he founded after graduation from Moody, he has mailed attractive and colorful gospel literature, customized to reach the non-Christian, to millions of Australian residents. He has seen thousands respond to the gospel.

14. E. O. Sellers, *Evangelism in Sermon and Song,* p. 70.
15. *Alumni News* (Fall 1981).

Asia

Asia spreads across nearly an entire hemisphere, encompassing both the highly cultured and the primitive. Much of it is under communist regime. But all its peoples need the gospel.

It might be difficult to find Moody alumni in Asia.

Not because they are not there, but because so many of them are off the beaten track.

A great many are hidden in the jungles of Irian Jaya or Papua New Guinea. Walter Post, pioneer missionary from the class of '24 (now retired in Salem, Oregon) was the first missionary to the interior of New Guinea. By 1960, he had a Bible school with eighty-five students. Scores of Bible translators, jungle pilots, and support personnel have followed his path. But it would take a veteran missionary pilot who knows his way around that land's mountainous terrain, remote villages, and jungle airstrips to get you to the right tribe and the right missionary.

Others in Asia are no easier to find. You might have to look in the mountainous, land-locked nation of Nepal, or in the jungles of the Philippines, or on one of the tiny islands of Micronesia in the South Pacific, which are barely specks on even the best of maps.

But those who seem to disappear from the mainstream of society for the sake of the gospel have followed a rich heritage of predecessors.

Isobel Kuhn was one of the most popular and talented coeds at the University of British Columbia. That was in 1922. Seven years later she was penetrating the mountain jungles near the China-Burma border. For twenty-five years, far from the society in which she had once moved, she served with the China Inland Mission.

Isobel had graduated with honors and was teaching school in Vancouver, B.C., when she decided to give God first place in her life. She entered Moody Bible Institute in 1925. Then the drive and stamina that had pushed her toward a successful career projected her, instead, into the oblivion of southwest China, home of the remote Lisu tribe.

Biographer Carolyn Canfield, in her book *One Vision Only,* writes that Isobel Kuhn demonstrated one of Christ's greatest paradoxes, " . . . whosoever will lose his life for my sake, shall find it."

Isobel and her husband, John Kuhn, whom she had met at Moody, finally had to leave their work with the Lisu tribe in 1950, the year the communist takeover forced the China Inland Mission to pull out. Isobel and her six-year-old

Walter Post (center), the first missionary to penetrate the interior of New Guinea, chats with Dr. Culbertson (right) on his 1960 tour.

son were hastily ushered over the high Pien Ma Pass—China's back wall—into Burma. Her husband escaped a year and a half later.

When the CIM re-deployed its missionaries into other southeast Asian countries in late 1951, John and Isobel Kuhn pushed into pioneer work in Thailand.

Stricken with cancer, Isobel had to return to the United States in 1954. She died in March 1957. Yet in the last months of her life, confident of what lay ahead, she wrote what critics agree are the best of her several books, including *Ascent to the Tribes* and *By Searching,* books which have inspired countless others to give their lives to the mission field.[16] Beyond this, the gospel that she and her husband planted within the Lisu tribe eventually exploded into such widespread revival that today millions of Lisu Christians can be found throughout Southeast Asia.

In the first half of this century, before Communists closed the doors, the vast majority of Moody-trained missionaries streaming to Asia went to China. It was there, also, that the majority of alumni who have been martyred gave their lives.

The Boxer Rebellion in China in July 1900 claimed the first two of these, both serving under the China Inland Mission. Hattie Rice ('92) was forty-two when beaten to death by Boxer rebels; Josephine Desmond ('84), a nurse, was

thirty-three when killed by rioters outside a city door.

Five years later, in October 1905, China claimed another Moody alumna, Dr. Eleanor Chesnut ('94), a Presbyterian doctor. When some Chinese became irrational during a religious festival, Eleanor and several others at her mission station fled to a mountain cave. When the mob found them, Eleanor pleaded with them for the lives of the new missionaries.

"If we have ever done you harm," she said, "kill us, but don't kill these new missionaries for they have never done anything to you." But Eleanor, thirty-seven, who had spoken earlier of welcoming death at any time for the sake of Christ and China, was shot along with five others.

Swedish Alliance missionary Robert Blomdahl, thirty, from the class of '22, also served in China. He and Filip Malmvall (a Moody graduate) were traveling, when bandits broke into the hostel where they had stopped. As Robert reached into his pocket to surrender his watch, the bandits shot him. Filip was spared.

Robert's widow, Elly, who bore their first child (a son) four-and-a-half months after his death, wrote: "If I would hold him back he would say, 'No, Elly dear, we are not here for pleasure but for Christ's sake, and thus we must be faithful.'"

Gustaf Tornvall, thirty-three, had gone into China under The Evangelical Alliance Mission. He and three others were reportedly robbed and murdered by bandit soldiers in July 1932 while taking famine relief funds to Sian, China. Their bodies were never found.

Two years later, John ('32) and Betty ('31) Stam, missionaries under China Inland Mission, were captured in Tsingteh and held ransom by Communists for $20,000—a high sum in those days.

In a December 6, 1934, letter explaining the rebels' demands, John told mission colleagues: "All our possessions and stores are in their hands, but we praise God for peace in our hearts and a meal tonight. God grant you wisdom in what you

16. "Volunteers on the Foreign Field."

do, and us fortitude, courage, and peace of heart. He is able—and a wonderful Friend in such a time. . . . The Lord bless and guide you—and as for us, may God be glorified whether by life or by death."

That same day the Communists decided to kill the Stams' three-month-old baby, Helen Priscilla, because she kept crying over the noise and rifle fire. But an old farmer they had just released from prison—not a Christian—offered his life in exchange for the baby. In front of the Stams, the Communists chopped the farmer to pieces.

Two days later, John and Betty, aged twenty-seven and twenty-eight, were beheaded in public. But their baby, hidden in a house, was found unharmed thirty hours later by a Chinese Christian and smuggled out of danger.

1932: Communists capture John and Betty Stam (see pages 69-70) of the China Inland Mission, hold them for ransom, then murder them brutally. The Christian world is shocked.

Esther Nordlund ('19) served in China with the Evangelical Covenant Church. In January 1948 the bus she was riding to attend a mission council was halted by bandits believed to have been communist soldiers. They robbed the passengers, shot Esther and two other women missionaries, then sent the bus on its way.[17]

When the Communists closed the door on mission work in China and sealed off its border to the outside world for more than a quarter century,

years of work and sacrifice seemed lost. Did so many die in vain?

As China once more opened its doors, the true picture slowly trickled out. There are now as many as fifty million Christians, it has been said—ten times the estimated number as when the missionaries were forced out. Most of them meet in house churches, not cathedrals, as they walk on egg shells with government authorities. Yet despite persecution, the growth of the church in China has surpassed the wildest imaginings.

In the summer of 1980, the *Alumni News* reported that David Chen, an Evening School graduate of 1946, had been located laboring in a carving factory in China, where he had worked for twenty years. A former theological professor in Nanking, Chen, at seventy, continued to serve the Lord, counting it "a privilege to suffer for Him."

In an interview with *Moody Alumni* magazine, missionary statesman J. Herbert Kane said of his years in China:

"We had the good fortune to work in a very responsive part of China. The churches were growing up almost spontaneously—so rapidly that we could hardly keep track of them—and most of the people who came to Christ came from hearing the testimony of Chinese Christians." Missionaries

17. Doering.

The Stam baby escapes harm when a bystanding farmer asks that he be killed in order to save the young child. The story makes national headlines in the US.

had planted the gospel, but it was the Chinese themselves who spread it. It is best, said Kane, that "a non-Christian hear the gospel for the first time from the lips of his own people."[18]

When China closed, its missionaries had to be reassigned—in many cases to Taiwan, Hong Kong, and other countries of Asia. Meanwhile, people like Ethel Groce Chan took on gigantic tasks almost single-handedly, in her case a ministry to the boat people of Hong Kong, most of whom had never lived outside a small floating houseboat.

As Communism spread into Southeast Asia, it claimed still another Moody alumnus in the 1960s.

Gaspar Makil, like Chet Bitterman, slain in this decade by Colombian rebels, was a member of Wycliffe Bible Translators. Philippine-born Gaspar had become a Christian while studying engineering in the U.S. He met his wife, Josephine (an MBI evening student), while at Moody, and they went to Vietnam with Wycliffe in the spring of 1962.

A year later, in March 1963, the Makils, their four children, and another Wycliffe family with a baby, were driving outside Saigon when stopped by a communist roadblock. Suddenly the guerrillas shot and killed Gaspar, the other man, and one of the Makil children in Gaspar's arms.

Gaspar, thirty-three, had once written: "He who brought all things into being is able also to give meaning to life. His will in my life is good for me. It is acceptable to me. And it is perfect. . . . Whatever may be His leading will be my highest good, and that is in His hands."[19]

Two Moody alumni were martyred in the early 40s as World War II spread into the Philippines. Signe Erickson ('24) and Erle Rounds ('25) both served with the American Baptist Convention. They and a number of other missionaries had fled the Japanese.

For eight months in 1943, they hid in a mountain retreat on the island of Panay, living in grass huts with bamboo floors. Finally discovered in December, they received permission to pray before being executed.

After an hour, they declared, "Now we are ready." Besides Signe and Erle, the Japanese beheaded Erle's wife and nine-year-old son, eight other missionaries, and five other Americans.[20]

But today, Moody-trained missionaries still bring the gospel both to Japan and to the Philippines.

One labors in Nagasaki, the city once devastated by the atomic bomb. Another works among deaf believers in Yamagata. Timothy Pietsch, at the Tokyo Bible Center, is one of two missionaries who came to Japan before World War II and who continues to minister there. His radio broadcast is heard over thirty-four stations and outlets in Japan, and he helps oversee four churches.

Moody missionaries serve under such organizations as The Evangelical Alliance Mission, the Conservative Baptist Foreign Mission Society, Send International, Baptist Mid-Missions, and the Southern Baptist Convention. Together they plant an ever-growing number of evangelical churches.

Laverne Hintz has served in Korea, the Fiji Islands, and Guam; now she reaches out to Philippine professional women, many of whom are government employees. Other missionaries, in far more remote surroundings, bring the gospel to the tribes. Thelma Andress Svelmoe and her husband, Gordon, completed translation of the New Testament for the Mansaka tribe, population 25,000, on the southern island of Mindonao. It was the first New Testament translation released by Wycliffe in the Philippines. The entire New Testament is now available to the 150,000 Blann people in the hills of South Cotabato, also on Mindanao, thanks to years of work by Barbara Blackburn ('50). Having completed her translation in 1981, she has now moved on to a tribe in Australia.

India is not without Moody representation, including the major cities of Bombay, Calcutta, Madras, and New Delhi. Much of the work there is either educational or medical, but always with a gospel witness. James and Joyce Garlow have ministered for more than a quarter century at the Mabunda Christian Leprosy and General Hospital. In 1976, they founded the

18. "Herbert Kane."
19. Doering.
20. Ibid.

Northeast India Baptist College. Margaret Kautz Shishak and her husband founded the Patkai Christian College in Nagaland in 1974, and by 1980 it had a full four-year program and 350 students. Meanwhile, in Ada, Michigan, Torrey Barcanic would hardly seem to be in the right place to help evangelize India. But he is business administrator for Bibles for India, which supplies Bible and correspondence school courses for India's national churches.

Only a handful of Moody alumni can be found in Korea today, because missionaries of an earlier era did their job so well that, for the most part, they are not needed!

Few Americans learned to know Korea and its people better than Harold Voelkel. For more than thirty years he moved among them. As a Presbyterian missionary, he began his Korean service in 1928 after graduating from Moody Bible Institue and Princeton. He could not foresee then that two decades later Korea would become the battleground for the two most powerful military forces of the mid-twentieth century.

Down at Tae Chun Beach on the China Sea, Voelkel and other members of the Presbyterian mission were holding their annual meeting on June 25, 1950. Suddenly the Reds struck with tremendous force and surprise, catapulting the Korean War. Voelkel and other missionaries were evacuated to Japan.

His stay there was brief. Taking a leave of absence from his mission, he became a United Nations chaplain. For a time he served as chaplain to troops. Then, partly because of his knowledge of the Korean language, he was given responsibility for prisoners in North Korea. Day after day, month after month, Voelkel entered the barbed wire compounds to face bitter Communists, bewildered draftees, Koreans with many needs. For them all, he had the message of the gospel. Soon he established a temporary Bible institute. Hundreds, he found, were eager to know the Bible. Of these, no fewer than 642 expressed the desire of entering the Christian ministry upon their release as prisoners!

By the time the war ended in 1953, Voelkel had brought the Christian gospel to thousands of red prisoners formerly indoctrinated with Communism.[21]

Erwin Raetz, another alumnus, answered God's call to Korea and was put in charge of gathering up and supervising the care of 12,000 little ones for the World Vision orphanages.[22]

When George Sweeting visited Korea in 1983, he saw firsthand the fruits of Christian missions in that land. Upon his return he wrote in *Moody Monthly*:

> Korea received its first Protestant missionaries from America in April, 1884. Within 100 years, the country has become a major missions force. More than 1,000 Koreans are now serving on foreign fields. Korea has potential to evangelize all of Asia, maybe even the world, as it spearheads a new east-west spread of the gospel.
>
> Each morning at 4:30, church bells summon more than 500,000 Koreans to an hour of prayer. Sunday services are repeated three to five times at some churches so everyone can participate in worship.
>
> The Judeo-Christian concept of God has been planted in the Korean language. It is one of the few Asian languages with a singular word for God. *Hamman* means "the one God above all others."[23]

While missionaries cannot operate behind the Iron Curtain or in Red China, the powerful transmitters of Christian shortwave radio around the world penetrate this communist air space from almost all angles. The Far East Broadcasting Company, in fact, is now even able to beam the gospel from its transmitter at Belmont, on the San Francisco peninsula, over the North Pole into Russia. Moody alumnus Geoffrey M. Cook is director of programming for the Far East Broadcasting Association. Though based in England, his responsibilities include coordination of studios in Scychelles, India, Pakistan, Lebanon, and Kenya. He is only one of many trained at Moody who staff some of the world's most powerful radio voices, penetrating not only almost the whole of Asia, but also other continents.

21. "Volunteers on the Foreign Field."
22. George Sweeting, "Land of the Morning Calm," *Moody Monthly* (September 1983).
23. Ibid.

LATIN AMERICA

A Hispanic child among symbols of Latin America. The current surge of evangelical Christianity on this continent traces back to those who for years have been laying the missionary foundations for it.

In Quito, Ecuador, high in the Andes mountains, the powerful transmitters of radio HCJB beam the gospel not only throughout Latin America, but around the world. HCJB is a recognized institution in Ecuador. In fact, the Ecuadorian government issued five postage stamps in commemoration of the station's fiftieth anniversary.

It was Moody alumnus Clarence Jones who co-founded HCJB (Heralding Christ Jesus' Blessings) more than a half century ago, and who indeed could be called the pioneer of missionary radio itself. He also founded the World Missionary Radio Fellowship, and today dozens of MBI-trained missionaries serve under its auspices.

In one section of Guatemala, eight couples are involved in a church-planting ministry. Most are MBI graduates. They arrived on the scene in 1975 and in the first four years alone planted 320 evangelical churches. It has been projected that Guatemala will become the first Latin American republic to become predominantly evangelical. Such trends, say some,

could not be overlooked as a factor in the 1983 overthrow of Guatemalan President, Rios Mott, a self-identified evangelical. While newspapers at

Moody alumnus Clarence Jones, co-founder of powerful HCJB in Quito, Ecuador, and "the father of missionary radio worldwide."

the time continued to label Guatemala "90 percent Catholic," others there today see it as already at least 20 percent Protestant evangelical.

Dr. Esther Matteson has been one of Wycliffe Bible Translator's foremost linguistic consultants. Back in 1947, five years out of Moody Bible Institute, she traveled by canoe and raft to an almost inaccessible tribe of Piros in Peru. When the adult Piros rejected her attempts at conversation, she began working with the children. They soon made her their favorite. Gradually the others accepted her.

It took one-and-a-half years to master even simple speech, but by the end of 1948 she had written the first reading primer. In time the Piros, long exploited by outside traders who had taken advantage of their illiteracy, became excited at the prospects of being able to read. As they learned, they quickly taught others. In 1949, the gospel of Mark was translated, and a church began to grow.

Meanwhile, WBT co-workers at nearby Yarinacochia introduced diversified farming, improved varieties of chickens, and sanitation standards. In 1953, six Piros became government-qualified teachers and set up a government-sponsored school system in the tribe. Today the tribe's entire level of living has been raised, and the majority of the tribe are professing Christians who look to the Piro New Testament for their standard of conduct.[24]

In a tour of these mission fields in 1960, Robert Constable, then executive vice-president of Moody Bible Institute, described a typical scene in which MBI alumni were laboring:

"Now we are in Yarinachocha, the jungle base. All around are 240,000 square miles of dense green jungle, through which great muddy rivers meander to the Amazon. The base is on the shore of Yarina Lake, and from here translators go out among the tribes for weeks at a time, learning the languages, reducing them to writing and publishing the Word of God for the people."

Of Esther Matteson he wrote, "She has just told us of going up the river to inoculate a tribe against a smallpox epidemic. After the work was done, one of the women said to her husband, 'Unless she had come we would have just sat here

In the early 1950s, Esther Matteson travels by canoe to reach the remote Piro tribe in Peru. Today she is considered one of Wycliffe Bible Translator's foremost linguists.

and died.' Esther commented to us later, 'Unless I, or some other child of God, was able to get the Word of God to them in their language, they would just sit there and go out into a lost eternity.' "[25]

Later, in a thatched hut without walls and on only a dirt floor, three hundred miles from jungle base, in a pouring rain, Constable wrote:

> Three Indians, two men and a woman, have been standing here watching everything I do. Sometimes they laugh. I don't know why. . . . I cannot communicate anything to them. But Wayne and Betty Snell are in the next hut. They too received their missionary training at Moody Bible Institute. They have learned to speak with these people, have put the Scriptures in their language, and the Word of God has worked in many of their lives. Before the Snells came, these Indians were afraid. All other white men they had seen had come to steal their children and to make them slaves. It took much . . . to gain their confidence. Now this tribe waits on the river bank, with obvious joy, to welcome Wayne and Betty when they arrive.

24. Ann Woodward, "Our Incredible Missionary Translators," *Moody Monthly* (May 1968).
25. *Quarterly Fellowship Letter* (June 1960).

I am humbled in the presence of these missionaries. Loneliness, mud, rain and flies, the torturing problems of saying things so that the people can understand. No playing at Christianity out here, but the grim and stark reality of a constant fight against the devil for the souls of men.[26]

As on other continents, it has cost Moody alumni lives to plant the gospel in Latin America.

In November of 1930, two Moody graduates—Arthur Tylee ('22) and Mildred Kratz ('23)—were among five slain at a station of the South American Indian Mission in the Amazon jungles of Brazil.

Indians of the area, angered that one of their men died after Mildred treated him, staged an unexpected bow-and-arrow attack at breakfast time. Also killed were three Indian Christians and the Tylees' two-year-old daughter. Mrs. Tylee, although severely beaten on the head with a hoe, survived.

Central America was in turmoil fifty years ago when Karl Bregenzer ('28) went to Nicaragua under the Moravian Mission. In March 1931 U.S. Marines came to restore order, and dissidents in the hills broke into guerrilla warfare. Indian friends took the Bregenzer family to safety, but Karl, thirty-seven, stayed to witness to the guerrillas. They killed him on the spot.

Moody aviation graduate Ancel Allen ('56) was air-dropping 7,000 gospels of John over villages in the mountains of Mexico one September day in 1956. Ancel, thirty-three, with 1500 hours flying experience with Air Mail From God Mission, had been shot at before. But this time the bullets brought down his plane, and he died in the crash.[27]

Evangelicalism is spreading rapidly in Colombia today, a turn of events that would have seemed incredible a few decades ago when Moody graduates like the Joe Butts and Elof Andersons pioneered in that land. In those days both Anderson and Butts narrowly escaped death. On one occasion Anderson was arrested by local police, thrown in a filthy cell, and kicked and beaten. Later he was fined for distributing "heretical" Sunday school quarterlies. His home was ransacked, his church and congregation stoned during services. One chapel was burned. One night at a chapel Christmas program, three bullets whistled over his head and thudded into the wall.

Joe Butts also faced terror. After opening an elementary school and inaugurating a Bible conference in the mountain village of El Carmen, he was attacked by a mob with knives. Other missionaries who eventually took over the work at El Carmen fared no better. They had to flee when violence broke out in 1949.

El Carmen saw no missionaries for ten years, but when the Buttses returned there in 1959, they found the town had been transformed. Where once they had been threatened and stoned,

26. Ibid.
27. Doering.

there now were churches of from fifty to 150 believers. Scattered throughout the rural areas were many small congregations. By most El Carmen residents today, missionaries are warmly welcomed.[28]

John Beekman, laboring for years with a bad heart and then a plastic heart valve, planted the gospel among Chol Indians deep in Mexico. In 1950, they were totally pagan. Ten years later when Dr. Irwin Moon visited the tribe on a worldwide filming tour, he saw firsthand what the Christian faith meant to these people. Moon watched thousands of Chols gather for the dedication of their tithe—on this occasion a shipment of corn—as it was loaded onto a cargo plane for export. His full story, and the continued growth of the Chol church, is documented in the

John Beekman (right) recalls to Dr. Irwin Moon the story of the Chol Indians of southern Mexico and the details of his plastic heart valve. Beekman and his wife planted the gospel among the Chols in the early 1950s. When he returned to the tribe after years of absence, he found some 20,000 evangelical Christians.

film, *Survivor Number Three*, produced by the Moody Institute of Science, and the book *The Man with the Noisy Heart*.

Forrest Zander went to Latin America as a missionary pilot with Jungle Radio and Aviation Service (JAARS), the flight arm of Wycliffe Bible Translators. He was the first man to lower a wheel—tied to the end of a rope that twirled from his plane—to the primitive Auca Indians of Ecuador. They had murdered five American missionaries in the Ecuadorian jungles in 1957—an event that made international headlines. Zander eventually came to meet the murderers, by then converted, as brothers in Christ.

Zander later became Wycliffe's chief administrator in Peru, then in Colombia, keeping in close contact with the government leaders of those nations—from presidents and ministers of education on down—on behalf of the Wycliffe work. One day in early 1981, a terrorist set out to kidnap Wycliffe's top man in Colombia. It would have been Zander, but he had left only weeks earlier for furlough in the United States. Instead, they took one of the men Zander had left behind—Chet Bitterman.

Throughout Latin America today, from the cities to the jungles, Moody alumni are planting churches. They serve under such faith missions as the South American Mission, Wycliffe Bible Translators, and the Unevangelized Fields Mission, along with various denominational affiliations—primarily Baptist. Some serve under the Sudan Interior Mission, which sounds like an error in geography until one understands that, a few years ago, the Andes Evangelical Mission merged with the Africa-based SIM.

In Bolivia, missionaries have seen startling church growth, especially in such cities as Santa Cruz, where the South American Mission has had to assign twenty-five missionaries to keep pace. There several Moody alumni work with Wycliffe in tribal translation, among them Becky Burke Ott, who with her husband completed the New Testament in the Ignaciano language, then prepared a book of folk tales, a hymnbook, and a dictionary. In that same country, Marian Lorenz

28. "Volunteers on the Foreign Field."

Prost, with husband Gil, completed the New Testament in the Chacobo language in 1979. Meanwhile, Betsy Wrisley presses toward completion of her work with the Quechua language.

In Brazil, with a land area half the size of the entire continent and a language (Portuguese) that differs from the other countries of Latin America, missionaries report with enthusiasm that nationals are assuming leadership. On-site tribal translation work, however, is restricted. Therefore, national young people have been trained to take over the work.

In Peru, the work of evangelism and church planting presses forward. Again, the strategy is a national church discipled and trained to lead its own way into the future. Wycliffe workers from Moody there include the Floyd Lyons, the Dick Hudsons, the George Woodwards, and Eric Kindberg.

In Colombia, once the scene of violence against Protestants, evangelicalism spreads. Alumnus Eleanor Coddington Stewart and her husband, who recently retired to California after thirty-six years serving the Presbyterian Church of Colombia, reports that during their last eight years there, 250 members grew to 3,000. Wycliffe translators are active there—like Grace Hensarling, who graduated from Moody Bible Institute only in 1977. She has settled into Colombia's northern mountains to learn the Kogi language.

In Ecuador, a large number of Moody-trained missionaries are affiliated with the World Radio Missionary Fellowship, which operates HCJB in Quito. Their assignments are diverse, ranging from station engineers and radio/television programmers to the medical work of those like Dan Swanson, who is the head of anesethesia, surgery, delivery, and central supply at a hospital on the edge of the jungle. Orbra Bliss took four years to design and build a powerful 500,000 watt transmitter for HCJB—an antenna that towers not from the mountains of Ecuador, but from the gentle hills of Elkhart, Indiana.

In Venezuela, Moody alumni serve with The Evangelical Alliance Mission and the Evangelical Free Church, among others, and have

The legendary Cameron Townsend, a Moody evening school alumnus, receives Mexico's distinguished Aztec Eagle (the highest award given to a foreigner) from that country's ambassador to the US. The Wycliffe Bible Translators he founded, with five thousand missionaries, is now the largest mission in the world.

seen the gospel become more firmly planted. Others labor to translate the Scriptures into Sanuma, the language of a remote Venezuelan Indian tribe. Keith Jones directs the Las Delicias Bible Institute.

Moody alumni in Central America include Bob Gunn, who with his wife, Mary (Bower), directs the work of Wycliffe Bible Translators in the narrow isthmus of Panama. Several Moody graduates are associated with them. To the north in Costa Rica, others are affiliated with such organizations as CAM International (formerly the Central American Mission). Further north in Honduras, other alumni can be found in school teaching, church planting, and film evangelizing.

A week-long tour of Mexico by Moody officials in June 1984 documented firsthand the progress of the gospel in that nation, both in the cities and in Mexico's remote outposts. Again, missionaries strive to train the national church and, if possible, work themselves out of a job. Toward that end, William Conard ('63) edits a new magazine in Mexico called *Continente Nuevo* (New Continent), focusing on practical aspects of the ministry for pastors and Christian workers across Latin America. The magazine was founded by international evangelist Luis Palau.

Arthur and Velva Phillips have spent

more than forty years in Latin America, directing the work of Child Evangelism Fellowship on that continent. They were the first CEF missionaries to be sent out from the United States. They have now planted the work in twenty Latin American countries.

More than fifty Moody-trained missionaries serve in the Caribbean. One couple spent two years on the island of Grenada, then moved on to St. Vincent, and then to St. Lucia. In just a few years they had established twelve churches on these islands—more than a decade before Grenada became the scene of international crisis.

In Haiti, under the West Indies mission, Moody alumni helped build Radio Lumier, which now blankets much of Haiti's five million populace, and letters pour in at the rate of three thousand a month. Because 90 percent of Haitians cannot read, many are convinced the future of the gospel in this country, and the future of Haiti itself, is inseparably linked to radio.

On the island of Martinque, known as the Emerald Island for its lush green, Howard and Betty Weyant labor in the shadows of a volcano that in 1925 took the lives of 22,000 inhabitants in five minutes! The lone survivor was a prisoner. Weyant tells of his work pastoring a number of churches in a mountainous area of the island.[29]

In Barbados, easternmost island of the Caribbean, Bernaline Laird enrolls thousands in Bible correspondence courses. She came to those island shores forty years ago. She had enrolled at Moody after a male quartet from the school sang in her home church in East Moline, Illinois.

On the island of Bonaire, the gigantic transmitters of Trans World Radio (TWR) beam the gospel across the Atlantic to Africa and Europe, as well as into South America. The Moody force there at times has been large enough for a small alumni chapter. Tower rigger Denny Hogan works among a complex of some thirty TWR towers (one climbs as high as a seventy-story skyscraper). There would be more alumni

29. "Our Alumni in the Caribbean," *Moody Monthly* (March 1970).

1983: Astronaut Jack Lousma (right) pilots the Columbia space shuttle into orbit. Dave Fisher, producer of the Slavic Gospel Mission's science program, beams Lousma's Christian testimony into communist lands—simultaneously with the flight. Listeners respond and even a former youth editor of Pravda *is impressed.*

there, but they have moved on to new assignments—at Trans World Radio's other superpower stations in Monte Carlo and in Swaziland, Africa.

While serving at Trans World Radio's station in Monte Carlo, Dave Fisher ('60) saw the potential of using science to reach the Soviet mind. The Communists have long promoted the idea that science has disproved the existence of God. One cosmonaut said he "failed to find God" in space. As a result, many Russian people put "holy books" like the Bible into the category of fantasy.

Today Fisher scripts and produces the Slavic Gospel Association's Radio Academy of Science broadcasts, which are beamed into communist lands in six languages. As co-editor of the book *Scientists Who Believe* (Moody Press), he works to interface science and the gospel. When astronaut Jack Lousma took space shuttle Columbia into orbit, Fisher pre-recorded Lousma's Christian testimony and broadcast it into the Soviet Union while the shuttle was in flight.

Mail from listeners reveals the program's growing impact. One letter came from a former editor of the youth edition of *Pravda*, Russia's official newspaper. He labeled Fisher's program "clear and convincing."

Moody Bible Institute has been on the world scene now for one hundred years, and it has been able to sustain a long-term thrust on the

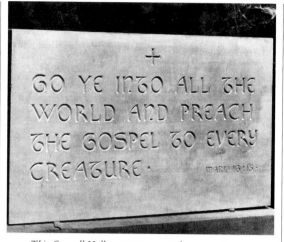

This Crowell Hall cornerstone stands as a continuous reminder of the Institute's commitment to Christ's last commandment.

mission fields of the world. As an older generation passes, another picks up the torch.

It can be seen in these two simple reports buried in the *Alumni News*, both coming out of the same nation:

"Horace D. Murfin, Class of 1932, died March 31, 1983, in Brazil, at age 81. Horace died of a heart attack and was buried on the banks of the Tocatins River in North Brazil. He had served the Lord in Brazil for 50 years."

"Linda Johnson, Class of 1983, left in February 1983, to serve . . . in Brazil."[30]

30. *Moody Alumni* (Summer 1983).

Dr. Sweeting reads the inscription on a monument at Northfield, where the challenges of Dwight Moody sent many to the mission field a century ago.

Wendell P. Loveless, WMBI's first director, gives the
signal and the gospel goes forth on radio.

Chapter 16

ON THE AIR

Calvin Coolidge was in the White House. The Scopes "Monkey Trial" was a year past. Charles Lindbergh's flight to Paris was a year ahead.

It was the midpoint of the Roaring Twenties; the era of twenty-dollar rent, the five-cent trolley, and "listening in."

Early evening, July 28, 1926, found Chicago's radio faithful hunched as usual before their receivers. Their ears were pressed to sweaty headphones or straining to catch the sound released by crackling speakers.

Precisely at seven o'clock a strange new sound was heard: a gospel song. "I want you to know Him," the words declared. A clear and forceful spoken message followed. The speaker: Dr. James M. Gray, respected president of Moody Bible Institute.[1]

That broadcast launched WMBI as one of the first religious radio stations in the country, and established it as a pioneer in Christian broadcasting.

How did Moody Bible Institute break into radio broadcasting only a few years after the nation's first radio station, Pittsburgh's KDKA, went on the air in 1920? And especially when some Christians were inclined to believe that radio might be more "of the devil than of God?"

The pivotal figure was Henry Coleman Crowell, the Yale-educated engineer who had come onto the Moody scene in 1923. The son of Henry Parsons Crowell, MBI's board president, he brought with him not only a knowledge of radio's technology, but also a vision of how it might be linked to the gospel. Crowell and two other men took the matter before God.

With a pledge of $2,600 from friends, the Institute bought a used 500-watt transmitter from the *Detroit Daily News* and installed it in a tiny penthouse atop the women's dormitory (now Smith Hall). For a studio, they hung the ground floor of a men's dormitory with heavy drapes. The Institute applied for a license, but there seemed little hope in the chaotic scramble with the government for wavelengths.

Henry Coleman Crowell, educated in engineering at Yale, sees the link between radio and the gospel become a reality by 1926. This son of the Quaker Oats founder became executive vice-president in 1945, then later assistant to the president.

In the meantime, in a dramatic incident, God opened another channel to put Moody on the airwaves.

Two young Moody students were playing

1. Wayne Christianson, "The Little Station That Went On and On," *Moody Monthly* (July-August 1976).

their cornets at a display booth at an exposition in the Chicago Furniture Mart. Station WGES, broadcasting from the event, suddenly found its scheduled talent delayed by a violent thunderstorm. In the emergency, the WGES program director asked the Moody students to fill in.

A few days later, WGES officials asked Moody to broadcast from their studios each Sunday evening, at no charge, in a special Institute broadcast. The program aired for several months. That led to arrangements with another Chicago station, WENR, to broadcast six times a week—from Moody's own newly refurbished studios on campus.

President James M. Gray took part in the first broadcast, though with considerable skepticism. Having delivered his message, he walked out of the studio, proceeded across Institute Place, and stepped into his office. The phone rang. To Gray's astonishment, it was a call from Florida, reporting that his message had just been received there. More calls and letters followed. Before long, Gray's doubts about the value of radio had been dispelled.[2]

But Moody was still not quite on the air yet with its own station.

Four months later, on July 27, 1926, a wire arrived from Washington. An unexpected shift had opened up a frequency, the only one in Chicago. The Institute could launch a station, WMBI, if it could move in quickly.

The little group worked frantically. T. J. Bittikofer would be the soloist; Dr. Gray would bring a message. Wendell P. Loveless from the Extension Department would read a statement of dedication. The very next day, July 28, 1926, WMBI went on the air.

"We dedicate this broadcasting station tonight," Loveless said, "as a witness that the church is the Body of which Christ is the Head and that its mission is to carry the gospel of salvation to all men, and to every nation under heaven."[3]

Problems arose within hours. The next morning Institute officials learned that WKBA, owned by the Arrow Battery Company, had also been granted a license and had gone on the air the

same evening as WBMI on the same wavelength! Fortunately, the two stations were able to work out a satisfactory division of time.

Simultaneously, Chicago's WGN and WSWS charged WMBI with station interference, and asked Moody to cease broadcasting. Neither had legal grounds, since WMBI's wavelength was fifty kilocycles above or below the frequency of either station. The problem seemed to stem from imperfect receivers and transmittal equipment, common to radio in those days. To help solve the problem, WMBI graciously offered to send an engineer to adjust the radio receivers owned by those people who reported interference from the Moody station.

WMBI faced its next crisis when in 1927 President Coolidge signed into law the Radio Act of 1927. This placed control of radio in the United States in the hands of a Federal Radio Commission, who would issue licenses, designate wavelengths, and decide the power and hours of station operation. The commission admittedly faced a chaotic situation. More than 700 stations had already been licensed, and several hundred more applications to erect news stations were on file. Yet the commission had only eighty-nine wave channels to assign.

It seemed only an outside chance that WMBI could ever stay on the air.

But Henry Crowell had done his homework. He kept abreast of every detail and development in the field of radio broadcasting, complex even then. Public hearings were scheduled in Washington, D. C., and he would be well prepared.

Also, the day after the Radio Act was signed into law, James M. Gray sent a letter to the Institute's entire mailing list—130,000 names. He enclosed a postcard asking friends to stress the fact that WMBI should be granted a license by the new commission. Fifty thousand cards were returned!

In Washington, Crowell made his case on behalf of WMBI and religious and educational stations as a whole. It seemed to go well.

2. Getz, p. 280.
3. Ibid.

"Aunt Theresa" Worman takes charge of the KYB Club in 1933, and it eventually becomes the longest continuous children's program on radio.

But a week later Chicago's WBBM pressed WMBI to give up its station and share time with them. The cost was too high. WBBM lowered its price. Now the hours were too few. The commission in Washington also strongly urged that Moody accept the offer. The Institute said no. Instead, Moody board chairman Henry P. Crowell, his son Henry Coleman, and an Institute attorney rushed back to Washington for a personal hearing. This time they convinced the commission that WMBI should stay on the air.

Meanwhile, Wendell Loveless and his staff had hammered out WMBI's programming—one that had quality, content, variety, balance. Moody Bible Institute became the first school in the United States to offer radio classes in Bible for credit. The KYB Club (Know Your Bible) for children emerged, with "Aunt Theresa" Worman taking the program in 1933. By the time she retired in 1971, hers would be the longest continuous-running children's show in the history of radio.

Early in 1928 WMBI installed a powerful new 5,000-watt transmitter in Addison, west of Chicago, and expanded its schedule to thirty-six hours a week. The future appeared bright.

But with an amendment to the Radio Act, more than half the stations in the Midwest might have to be eliminated. Moody was assigned to share with WOWO in Fort Wayne, Indiana—then WBT in Charlotte, North Carolina! Confusion reigned. WBT had almost full-time rights of its own, including evening hours. Moody would have to take only what time might be left. It was unacceptable.

Then came a new twist. On November 11, 1928, another telegram arrived from Washington: "Your license being withheld temporarily. Last application indicates two alien trustees." Two Moody board members were Canadian. The next day Crowell made his fifth trip to Washington. The solution: WMBI would incorporate separately from the Institute. (This double incorporation was dissolved in 1939, when it was no longer necessary.)

associates kept making in Washington began to pay off. By 1932 WMBI showed strength—even though the radio industry was still in a crisis. It had a good financial base, excellent equipment, and an adequate staff.

There were other factors too. From the outset WMBI took great care not to offend listeners with strong propaganda, financial appeals, or slanderous remarks against other religious viewpoints. Guest speakers were forewarned against careless speech. Had Moody Bible Institute not established such ethics early, it may never have had the chance to make its great impact.

With the completion of twelve-story Crowell Hall in 1939, WMBI moved to its new studios on the building's top three floors. In 1943 it was assigned its current AM frequency of 1110 kilocycles. That same year WMBI acquired a sister FM station, the first non-commercial religious FM station in the country. Its successor, WMBI-FM, now broadcasts around the clock.

In 1958, the Institute purchased its first station outside Chicago—an FM station in Cleveland.

Young George Beverly Shea sings for WMBI radio and later emerges as Billy Graham's soloist.

WMBI continually had to justify its existence, as critics classified religious outlets as propaganda stations of interest only to a small section of the public and advised that they be assigned inferior wavelengths and hours. But the favorable impression Crowell and his Moody

WMBI interviews Chicago Mayor Kennelly. Years later, in 1984, Harold Washington becomes the first Chicago mayor to visit a Moody Bible Institute chapel service.

When WMBI celebrated fifty years of broadcasting in July 1976, nearly ten thousand visitors jammed its studios during the weekend open house, and Mayor Richard J. Daley proclaimed "WMBI Week" in Chicago.

Moody programming has grown from the gospel music-message concept of the early days to include also a multi-faceted offering of Bible teaching, news, Christian drama, call-in-programs, homemakers' features, public service, and education. Yet almost all of it has a distinctive Christian flavor. And no commercials.

Over the last sixty years of broadcasting, thousands have been brought to Christ and millions of letters have streamed into WMBI offices telling of blessings received. Stories are told of dramatic conversions, like that of the suicidal man who switched on the radio to drown out the noise of his revolver. At that moment a WMBI speaker was declaring the gospel, and the man received Christ.[4]

Today thousands of Chicagoans wake up to the music of WMBI radio and the "Morning Clock." Many listeners leave the full range of Christian programming on all day and even into the night.

In cities like Cleveland, Chattanooga, Spokane, and St. Petersburg, other Moody-owned stations nourish the Christian populace. The programming is much the same as WMBI, though localized in part.

Until recently just 11 percent of the nation's population lived within the range of a Moody radio signal. That is, until the wonders of the space age opened a window to all of North America. Moody's greatest years of pioneer radio may have just begun. By the end of the Institute's centennial year, the Moody Broadcasting Network may well be in hundreds of American cities.

How can this be?

Hold on tight for the fastest trip you have ever taken.

The program signal leaves the studios of WMBI, atop twelve-story Crowell Hall on the Moody Bible Institute campus.

It is carried by microwave to Monee, Illinois, southwest of Chicago.

From there the signal is beamed to an RCA Satcom IIIR satellite 22,300 miles above the equator.

From there it bounces back to down-link receivers in the North America coverage area,

1982: This downlink dish is installed on the north side of the campus, and the Moody Broadcasting Network goes satellite.

bringing the signal within reach of anyone with the proper equipment to receive it.

The signal has traveled 45,000 miles from its origin at Moody in only a fraction of a second!

You may or you may not find Moody programming on your dial. If you are not within range of a Moody-owned station or one of its translators, your community first needs a satellator—which receives the satellite signal and converts it to FM for reception by radio in your community.

Or, if your city has an established cable company, your FM radio can be hooked up to receive the audio signal from the satellite.

Already many towns and cities across America have installed the necessary equipment and are enjoying the Moody Broadcasting Network. Hundreds of other applications are in process. In most cases the initiative of a church, or group of churches, brings the station into a community.

Moody Broadcasting Network (MBN) is not trying to compete with other Christian radio stations, says Broadcasting Division's Manager Robert Neff. "In most cases," he says, "it will go

4. Ibid.

where there is no other Christian broadcasting."

Until the development of satellite technology, it would have been impossible for Moody to extend its radio outreach much further. For years the Federal Communications Commission has limited the number of stations owned by any one group to seven AM and seven FM. That FCC restriction has now been removed. The Institute currently owns and operates seven FM and four AM stations.

Without satellite technology, not many communities hungry for Christian radio could have afforded it. It takes hundreds of thousands of dollars to build a station—and $50,000 to $200,000 a year to operate it. And even if Moody could purchase additional stations, the cost these days could be astronomical. A Chicago FM station sold not long ago for eight million dollars.

By contrast, the annual costs of a satellator can be as low as $3,000 to $4,000. Since it is not a regular station, it needs no local staff to operate it. The professional programming, benefitting from more than a half century of expertise in Christian broadcasting, is produced and aired from Moody's Chicago studios.

Stations who join the Moody Broadcasting network via satellite eventually pay their own way through the gifts of new listeners, fees from local user groups, and contributions from the broadcasters whose programs will be transmitted by satellite. But Moody must still absorb heavy start-up costs: to lease space on a satellite, to pay salaries of new personnel to market the program and the service, to purchase new equipment.

With so many stations joining or waiting in line, the investment is sizable. To help finance this new outreach, the Moody Radio Network in 1982 launched its first "Satellite Awareness" campaign with a goal of raising $1,000,000. Mobilizing its network staff on airwaves and telephone, it met more than half of that goal in just two days! The public repeated a similar response in 1983. Moody Vice-President Brandt Gustavson, former president of the National Religious Broadcasters, points out that while one million dollars is no small investment, it is "less than the cost of two minutes of TV commercial time on the Super Bowl!"[5]

The Moody radio signal has also been extended to new communities by "translators," which retransmit the signal on a frequency separate from the one received. By this means it has extended the coverage of Chicago's WMBI-FM to Rockford, Illinois, and East Moline's WDLM-FM to Freeport, Illinois. It has transmitted Moody's Chattanooga station, WMBW, into cities like Atlanta, Knoxville, and Birmingham. Chattanooga's signal is also relayed up to the tri-cites area of eastern Tennessee, including Moody's aviation complex in Elizabethton. Spokane's KMBI, using eleven different translators, now extends its signal to communities throughout Washington, Idaho, Montana, and Oregon. Microwave relay extends Spokane's KMBI signal northward to Edmonton and Calgary.

Initiative comes from those communities who want the coverage and who are within potential signal range of an existing Moody-owned station. People in that area form a committee, raise the money, and lease the land. Moody's coordinator of the translator program helps the local committees place their translators and guides the groups through FCC regulations.

Still other Christian stations—more than sixty-three of them, in fact—joined the Moody Broadcasting Network within the first two satellite years as affiliate stations. These full-power AM and FM stations spread from Alaska to Florida.

Affiliate stations can receive Moody's network programming whenever they desire. The arrangement helps a station cut costs, enhance programming, and remain on the air twenty-four hours a day. Program choices for affiliate status include "Open Line," "Prime Time America," "Sunday Praise," and "Music Through the Night," and International Media Service.

Any town with cable radio/TV can also link up to Moody's satellite network—at a cost as low as $1,500.

The Moody Broadcasting Network is expanding so fast that even the listing of stations in this book, updated at press time, will be incomplete by the time it reaches you.

5. *Quarterly Fellowship Letter* (June 1982).

The expanding outreach of Moody Broadcasting is not likely to stop with North America. Already evangelical Christians are planning to launch three satellites designed to blanket the earth with Christian programming twenty-four hours a day with twenty-four TV and twenty-four radio signals. In 1983, for the first time, Moody's annual Founder's Week was broadcast live to many stations across America. Some day a missionary in the bush country of Kenya will probably be able to listen to this event *live*! What's more, that missionary would be able also to engage in a two-way conversation with Dr. Sweeting, while the world listens in.[6]

Interestingly, there was a day in WMBI's infancy when its signal did reach out across the nation, and sometimes even beyond. During the winter of 1927, when WMBI carried "The Midnight Hour," a special interest broadcast from 12:00 to 1:00 A.M., the station received mail from as far away as the Hawaiian Islands. The next year it heard from every state in the union, and on one occasion even from New Zealand, 9,000 miles from Chicago![7] The right atmospheric conditions, a clear channel, and minimal station interference late at night explains the phenomenon. Today's crowded airwaves restrict most signals to a much smaller geographical area. (Recently, though, a listener in Michigan picked up the signal of Moody-owned WRMB, Boynton Beach, Florida.[8]

Already WMBI's popular call-in program "Open Line," with Moody Radio Pastor Donald Cole and others, has gone national. For years it has been available only to WMBI listeners, but now, because of satellite, it is just as easy for the listener in California to pick up the phone and call in with a question as it has been for those in the Chicago area. Subjects range from questions about the Bible to critical issues of political, moral, ethical, and religious significance. The result has been a more aware and informed Christian public.

Or consider that, because of the satellite, Christians across the nation now have access to a daily Christian-oriented news service. The International Media Service was created by journalist Forrest Boyd who had spent years in network news and felt there was a great amount

Donald Cole, radio pastor of WMBI, fields sometimes difficult questions on "Open Line" and other Moody call-in programs. Meanwhile, satellite technology introduces cross-country participation.

of significant news with a religious, moral, or ethical perspective not being adequately reported. The public was not getting the full picture, because important elements were often left out or distorted.

Boyd had served as news director for several radio and television stations and was White House correspondent for Mutual Radio for eleven years.

Although it can be costly to operate radio stations, not one of Moody's eleven stations has ever sold a minute of advertising time. The stations are licensed non-commercial by the FCC. Funds to operate these stations come mostly from listeners.

WMBI airs such non-Moody-produced programs as Billy Graham's "Hour of Decision," "Back to the Bible," "The Lutheran Hour," the "Back to God Hour," "Radio Bible Class,"

6. *Alumni News* (Summer 1981), p. 9.
7. Getz, pp. 298-99.
8. "Long Distance Broadcasting," *Moody Memo* (7 August 1981).

Jim Warren, with co-hosts, introduces "Prime Time America," mixing Christian music with dialogue and interviews. Moody's wide variety of programming offers excellent choices for nationwide airing.

"Grace to You," "Focus on the Family," and others. It also airs the Pacific Garden Mission's "Unshackled," the longest running radio drama in the history of radio, secular or Christian.

On Moody's "Prime Time America," quality Christian music is mixed with dialogue and interviews. Public service programming ranges from weather news and traffic reports to interviews with Chicago area social agencies and a garden show with Dick Delano, *Chicago Sun-Times* garden editor, himself an evangelical Christian.

One of WMBI's most popular programs is "Morning Clock," one that commuters dial as their cars crawl into the city each day.

Particularly unique is host Bob Murfin's frequent "cup of cold water" initiative. If word reaches him of someone who has been injured or stricken with disease, Murfin responds—and gets his listeners into the act. Based on the words of Jesus in Matthew 10:42, he urges listeners to send cards of encouragement.

One morning Murfin received word of a

family in desperate need. There were ten children, and the father was unemployed. They had no beds, very few clothes, no laundry facilities, and some badly needed medical attention.

After determining the authenticity of the situation, Murfin requested help on "Morning Clock." The results? Twenty beds, free dental work, eye glasses, wiring for their house, a washer, a dryer, baby furniture, a year's supply of vitamins, food, clothes, dishes, and too many other things to mention. Enough came in to supply twelve other needy families. Months later, useful goods from complete strangers continued to arrive.[9]

Or consider the case of the lonely twenty-three-year-old Navy ensign. The young man, Murfin learned, was heartsick when his assignment forced him to trade his Christian friends and family for a tour of duty at sea.

When the ensign's ship pulled into port

9. "A Bucket of Cold Water," *Moody Monthly* (January 1973).

In animated style, Bob Murfin helps wake up Chicago with "Morning Clock." Many of his listeners are in cars on crowded expressways into Chicago.

at Pearl Harbor, the first mail call bounced him out of the blues. The mailman announced, "We must have a celebrity on board!" presenting the ensign with 700 letters from "Morning Clock" friends. For six months, mail followed the ensign from port to port.[10]

In a move that reflects Moody radio's willingness to pioneer, WMBI-AM switched its Saturday programming to all Spanish in 1980. Hispanics account for one of every twelve of Chicago's population. And though census figures in 1980 reported 348,000 Hispanics in Chicago, undocumented aliens may bring that figure closer to one million. WMBI's "Radio Esperanza" reaches out to this audience.

Major cities with significant Hispanic populations usually have one prominent nationality—New York's Puerto Ricans, Los Angeles's Mexicans, and Miami's Cubans. But Chicago is unique—its Hispanics come from every

Jim Shedd pioneers WMBI's Spanish programming, which utilizes WMBI's AM frequency all day on Saturdays. It is estimated Chicago may have up to one million Hispanics.

10. *Moody Memo* (20 April 1973).

nation where Spanish is spoken.

"The Hispanic immigrant is in a new society," says Jim Shedd, who coordinates WMBI's Spanish programming. "He feels lost. The vast majority is first generation Hispanic."

Shedd, a Moody alumnus with an anthropology degree from Wheaton College, has himself pastored Spanish congregations. He keeps in close touch with Chicago's Hispanic pastors to help him zero in on Hispanic needs. His father's parents, both Moody alumni, became missionaries to Bolivia at the turn of the century and ministered there forty-six years.[11] Shedd grew up in South America as an MK.

Moody's stations not only nourish Christians, but also build bridges with the non-Christian public, which in turn softens the ground for all evangelical churches. On reader wrote: "I'm not a Christian. I have; however, been enormously impressed by the simplicity, directness, and astonishing honesty with which you share your faith on the air. It has exercised a powerful influence on me."[12]

Scores of men and women have poured their lives into the ministry of WMBI over the years, some becoming prominent in the evangelical world. Billy Graham soloist George Beverly Shea, for example, once sang regularly on WMBI, before either he or Graham became internationally known.

The voice of recently-retired news director Walter Carlson was a familiar one to WMBI listeners for more than forty years. Before his conversion and his arrival at WMBI in 1942, "Peppy" Carlson had traveled up and down the west coast singing country, pop, and jazz.

But behind the scenes are those who, while their names may not be so well-known, are just as dedicated: engineers, writers, producers, secretaries. A full-time force of ten serves WMBI under station manager Tom Sommerville. The Moody Broadcasting division, under Robert Neff, employs some ninety staff members.

Beyond the outreach of the fast-growing Moody Broadcasting Network itself are the many Moody-produced programs which air on non-Moody stations. More than three hundred stations use at least some Moody programming, with a broad selection of programs.

The Christian radio industry abounds with those who have roots at Moody Bible Institute. The exposition of Martin R. DeHaan II ('74), Radio Bible Class, reaches millions. Melvin Jones ('44), recently retired executive director of Back to the Bible Broadcast in Lincoln, Nebraska, served for decades as Theodore Epp's top associate. Ruth Johnson Jay, also for many years with Back

11. Deanna Finley, "Here's Hope for Saturdays," *Moody Monthly* (July-August 1981).
12. Christianson.

Left: Long-time News Director Walter Calrson (recently retired) grabs the latest incoming stories from the UPI teletypes in 1960. Right: WMBI announces its radio intent, with its antenna half finished at the time this photo was taken. Satellite lies a half century ahead.

to the Bible, founded its youth choir in 1948. Ray Brubaker ('45), commentator for "God's News Behind the News," is heard on more than seven hundred stations. Meanwhile, Moody graduates have been involved in spreading the gospel by radio on stations from Hawaii to Baltimore. Today 50 percent of Moody Broadcasting's own staff are alumni of Moody Bible Institute.

It has been almost sixty years since WMBI began to pioneer the religious radio frontier. The very year Dwight L. Moody died, a young, creative Italian, Guglielmo Marconi, had managed to make practical use of the hertzian waves and had succeeded in reaching all the way across the Atlantic. Moody had no radio then to multiply his audience, nor, for that matter, did he even have a microphone to magnify his voice. Dwight Moody, attuned as he was to the use of mass media even in his day, would surely rejoice.

And with today's technology, the greatest days of pioneer broadcasting may still lie ahead.

Today a single satellite hanging 22,300 miles above the equator brings programming of the Moody Broadcasting Network to the nation. The signal travels round-trip some 45,000 miles in only a fraction of a second!

Chapter 17

MISSIONARIES OF THE SKIES

In the central mountains of Irian Jaya, Indonesia, Charles Bennett ('53) lands a Twin Otter on a remote jungle airstrip and steps out to meet members of the Dani Tribe. Until 1950, these people, only a step removed from the Stone Age, were at constant war with one another. Missionaries entered the isolated area in the 1950s, thanks to the help of jungle pilots. Now there are more than 100,000 Christians, and because of this, peace reigns. The Danis are evangelizing other tribes at a rapid pace. Bennett had come to help thirty Dani pastors set up a major spiritual "crusade." He, until recently, was president of Mission Aviation Fellowship (MAF).

In Africa, Chuck Kunkle ('71) flies food and medical supplies to a missionary outpost in the Cameroons. On the return flight he brings aboard a missionary headed home on furlough and a sick native child bound for major surgery in a distant hospital.

In South America, Duer Smedley ('72) and Ken Debelah ('73) set down in the jungles of Brazil with two translators to scout the potential of a pioneer outreach to an unreached tribe. Without the airplane, it would have taken weeks to reach the site by trail and dugout canoe.

Around the world, Moody-trained pilots take off on an average of every four minutes, around the clock, on missions of love and mercy. More than two hundred of them, who constitute at least half of the world's missionary pilots, fly daily support missions into all kinds of terrain often inaccessible except by air.

Although Moody once trained its pilots in

A pilot flies high over South American mountains. Moody Bible Institute trains more than half of the world's missionary pilots.

the shadows of Chicago's O'Hare Field, heavy air traffic there finally forced a move, and the heart of the operation since the late 1960s has centered in the foothills of the Great Smoky Mountains in the eastern tip of Tennessee.

The Moody Aviation training complex is, in reality, the Moody-operated Elizabethton Municipal Airport, tucked away in a small valley near the base of the Smokies. Because of frequent Moody take-offs, it is one of the busiest airports in Tennessee.

The surrounding terrain is an ideal setting for training jungle pilots. The 4,000-foot runway runs east to west between two mountain ranges. To the north lies a 4,500-foot range, and to the south, 6,000-foot mountains. At the east end of the runway is Forge Hill, a knob of rock jutting 700 feet above the level of the strip. The weather frequently is cloudy and foggy.

But this is luxury compared to the primitive runways these pilots will have to use— or build themselves—on the mission field. So Moody has cleared off a cow pasture not far away and built a nine-hundred-foot strip. It has also constructed a small strip 4,000 feet up on a mountainside in the nearby Smokies. The strip angles uphill and jogs to the left—a tricky challenge for any pilot. Moody floatplanes practice upon the waters of nearby Lake Watauga, engulfed by towering mountain peaks.

The Moody pilot is no ordinary pilot.

When he graduates, he has to know how to take his plane apart, and put it back together again. He has to be his own mechanic, because he won't find a convenient repair shop in the

Students build this primitive runway in the nearby mountains to simulate actual mission field conditions.

jungles, and there simply isn't enough manpower to allow for specialists who are either pilots or mechanics only.

If there is no airstrip, he may have to gather some forces and build one. He often has to be his own weather service, navigator, cargo handler, and control tower.

And he will also have to know some sociology and anthropology. If he were to build an airstrip in the wrong chief's territory, for instance, he could be in big trouble. Or if he should pay national workers too much to help him build an airstrip, he could create runaway inflation within the tribe. Dropping gifts, with the best of intentions, might lead to the worship of airplanes. It has happened in New Guinea.[1]

As manager of a one-man airline, the missionary pilot is also an administrator. He is the missionary's purchasing agent and his advisor on customs and foreign currency. And as a contact man with government officials, he is a man of ambassadorial qualities who can often speak the national language fluently.

These are men with imagination, ingenuity, resourcefulness. But above all, they are men whose lives are committed to Jesus Christ— men who have obeyed God step by step and seen Him undertake.

The missionary pilot's plane becomes ambulance, post office, and grocery store—both for missionaries and for the tribespeople they serve. And one never quite knows what the cargo might turn out to be.

The first day on his own in the Philippines, one pilot saw a woman, two children, and a corpse on the concrete apron—all waiting for him. "I had asked this fellow," he said, "how many wanted to make the flight, and he had said his wife, two small children and his mother. He didn't tell me his mother was dead!"[2]

In Latin America, Forrest Zander loaded a pig that he had been told was well tied down. In flight, he suddenly discovered that his cargo was on four feet, peering over his shoulder.

1. Wesley Pippert, "The Making of a Jungle Pilot," *Moody Monthly* (March 1972).
2. Calvin Biddle, "Moody Pilots—They're More Than Good Flyers," *Moody Monthly* (March 1974).

On the field it takes special skills to drop down over the trees and bring the craft to a halt on short, bumpy airstrips.

Fortunately, the animal did not try to hog the controls.

What kind of individual enrolls in Moody's aviation program?

Only a few start with pilot experience.

Sandy-haired Doug Boyd flew nine hundred hours as a helicopter pilot over Vietnam in 1968 and 1969. Once he was shot down—"I made a turn and they just nailed me." Later he went to Moody to redirect and polish the flying skills he had learned in combat. After serving in Indonesia, he joined the home staff in California.

The majority learn to fly from square one. A story on the Moody aviation program by Wesley Pippert, reporter for United Press International, described this kind of prospect in terms of "an Iowa farm boy who has never flown but could make a corn picker fly if you gave him a monkey wrench and some baling wire."[3]

At least one graduate is even a product of missions itself: Lenardo "Nard" Pugyao ('75), a jungle boy from the northern mountains of the Philippines. When a Wycliffe translator hiked into Nard's village years ago, Pugyao was a ragged, barefoot seven-year-old. "He was the first white man I had ever seen," says Pugyao, who today descends out of the skies to bring the gospel to his own people.[4]

The training of a Moody pilot starts first on the main Moody campus in Chicago, where for two years he grounds himself in the Bible. In addition, he studies theology, anthropology, evangelism, Christian education, music, and missions.

But this does not assure that he will

3. Pippert.
4. Leonard Pugyao as told to Robert Griffin, "Filipino Full Circle," *Beyond* (July-August 1983).

Nard Tugyao is a Moody trained missionary pilot serving his own people in the Philippines.

become a missionary pilot. Upon transfer to Tennessee he must first pass a rigorous week-long Flight Camp. One of four will be gone from the program by the end of that week.

This means a student must want to go to the field first as a missionary and secondly as a pilot. He should be ready to go, he is told, "whether he flies, swims, or crawls." One earnest would-be pilot whose name failed to make the list after flight camp, quipped, "Well, I guess I'd better start swimming."[5]

Moody Aviation's program comes in two parts: the Flight School and the Aviation Maintenance Technicians' School. This assures not only an expert pilot, but also a skilled mechanic.

In his first year in Tennessee, the student earns his private pilot's license. He spends at least nineteen hundred hours in the shop and fifty in the air. As in all Moody Bible Institute programs, his tuition is free. He pays only for flight time and about $1,300 for tools, books, and materials.

That same year the student works toward his FAA licenses in both airframes and powerplants. Power-plant troubleshooting is a must. Aviation electronics prepares a pilot to handle electrical trouble in his plane or fix a generator at some isolated mission station.

The math-physics course is easier to take if students realize that someday they may have to figure how much weight their planes can take without risking structural failure.

Sheet metal work and welding classes are vital. Some pilots have had to almost rebuild a plane from scratch in the middle of nowhere.

A pilot needs a minimum of 200 hours to get his commercial license. The Moody graduate will log between 350 and 400 hours in the air. He has learned to fly in canyons and how to slip over a ridge when the ceiling is low. "There's a safe way to do it and an unsafe way," says Moody's Pre-Aviation Coordinator Bob Rich.

By the end of his third year in Tennessee, the student has earned his FAA commercial pilot's license. But not before he first has successfully completed a demanding advanced cross-country flight to Mexico, California, and back (half the cross-country group reverses the itinerary and heads for California first).

Unforseen circumstances can add to the success of the cross-country experience. A typical scenario includes the deterioration of weather conditions. Students have to change course, decide a new destination, file a new flight plan. Metal particles appear in the oil of a Cessna 185, signaling mechanical problems. Solution: remove the engine, send it back to Elizabethton with an instructor for overhaul, rent another plane from the School of Missionary Aviation in San Diego.

The pilots in the Mexico group, meanwhile, conquer another kind of experience. They navigate over hundreds of miles of jungle terrain. They have to speak to control towers whose language is different. And they have to follow the flight rules of another nation.

Upon return to Tennessee, the students take one weekend to rest. Then they set out in pairs—for three more days of cross-country flight, perhaps to Florida, or to Wisconsin—but this time with no instructor aboard.[6]

Once a pilot passes his FAA exams, he is in the "pro" ranks. But Moody students don't stop there. They spend still another year mastering the techniques of mission-field aviation: low flying, take-offs and landings on short, narrow runways, "dead reckoning" navigation, and the like. They have to go far beyond the requirements for a commercial pilot's certification, even with an instrument rating attached.

Along the way to graduation, the Moody-trained pilot probably has picked up several courses from a list of options that include glider training, multi-engine, seaplanes, and aerobatics.

Glider training? Aerobatics?

That's right. The pilot over a jungle can never be sure that his engine won't quit. If he knows the principles of gliding, he can use the air currents to sustain a flight much longer. Or, a pilot in extreme turbulence can get flopped upside down. A person familiar with aerobatics can make a safe recovery in such critical situations.

Moody also uses a heavy, sluggish seaplane to maneuver around the vicinity of Lake Watauga. There are special techniques for landing

5. Pippert.
6. Bill Crider, "Moody Bible Institute Pilots Train Cross-Country," *Alumni News* (Summer 1979).

on water. It takes special skill, also, to drop over a clump of trees and come to a screeching halt in a few hundred feet.

To train its students, Moody has a fleet of planes that include thirteen Cessnas, two Beechcrafts, and one Schweitzer glider. For a time it also had two helicopters, in anticipation of a full-fledged helicopter flight-training program geared to missions. Helicopters, missionary aviationists reasoned, could drop down onto the spot, eliminating the need to build or maintain remote runways, which tropical rains often make soggy, and which rapidly-growing foilage often tries to reclaim. But helicopters also proved too expensive to operate. It was still more efficient, pilots on the field found, to stick with the conventional plane.

Ken Simmelink, a former executive with MAF, directs the Moody Flight School in Elizabethton.

He is backed-up by a staff of instructors, among them a LeTourneau Tech graduate who was a maintenance man for Capitol Airlines. Another served in Indonesia for several years. One flight instructor flew in the Philippines. Also on the staff is a general aviation engine expert.

The coordinator of development was a manual arts instructor before coming to Moody. He graduated in 1960, became an instructor in technician training, and then moved over to his first love, flying.

The story of how Moody Bible Institute entered the field of missionary aviation revolves primarily around the vision of one man: Paul Robinson.

The former Louisiana State football player turned pastor (Robinson graduated from the Moody pastors' course in 1936) had been sold on world missions when he took a country pastorate and began to preach on the subject. Soon his own preaching hit home. Robinson and his wife, Lillian, felt called to go themselves—specifically to Brazil, a country half the size of the South American continent and covered with millions of square miles of jungle.

Robinson knew that missionaries in this region, and in other parts of the world, often risked long, dangerous treks to reach remote

Paul Robinson (left), here with Wood Dale manager Paul Wertheimer, guides Moody's fledgling aviation program through its earliest days in Chicago.

outposts. Long delays without food and medicine sometimes meant death. Time and energy consumed on mere survival kept missionaries from their primary task: evangelism. So Paul Robinson decided he would learn to fly.

Four days after his first solo, the Japanese bombed Pearl Harbor. The attack grounded all civilian pilots. Mission fields closed. Robinson joined the Civil Air Patrol, where he could continue both to fly and to maintain his pastorate. He earned his commercial pilot's certificate, then gained flight-instructor status.

By the time the war was over and Brazil re-opened to missions, the Robinsons were too old for the field. And they had a growing family. Mission boards refused to send them out. So Robinson turned to the next best option. He would teach potential missionaries to fly.

"I was helping my wife dry dishes one evening," Robinson recalls, "when the whole panorama of a missions training program unfolded in my mind's eye. I dropped the dish towel—no dishes—and went to my desk. I wrote most of the night and all the next day until I felt I had it."[7]

Robinson took his idea to what he considered the "top" and was prepared to work his way down a list of schools. "But I never got off the top," he says. "Moody bought the idea."

During Founder's Week, 1946, Robinson proposed his idea to MBI Vice-President Henry Coleman Crowell, who in turn shared the concept with President Will Houghton. Houghton invited Robinson to come before the executive committee. Next came a presentation to the board of trustees.

"I was a country preacher from the boonies," Robinson says. "They must have sensed how I felt, for I have never been put more at ease then when I was in the presence of those great men of God."

After a few questions, one man rose and said, "If the rest of you feel as I do, and if this young man will help us, I suggest we proceed. And I would like to buy the first two airplanes."[8]

That summer, with three students and a single J-3 Piper Cub, Robinson opened his program at Elmhurst Airport, in a suburb west of Chicago.

At first he taught prospective missionaries to fly. But he discovered most missionaries wanted to use airplanes as they used jeeps. Most cared little about maintenance, nor would they fly enough to keep their touch. The results, Robinson knew, could be disastrous.

"I knew we had two choices: quit or go all the way with a professional maintenance and pilot training school."[9] He chose the latter.

Less than two decades later, an FAA administrator, in a *Chicago Tribune* report, would call Moody's missionary aviation operation one of "the most comprehensive and exacting training programs anywhere." Flight magazines wrote long features about Moody becoming the world's largest source of missionary pilots. Robinson himself was named Moody's 1974 alumnus of the year.

Robinson never planned to head a program so extensive. "I didn't want to do it

7. Kay Oliver, "Paul Robinson: Winging It," *Moody Monthly* (September 1975).
8. Ibid.
9. Ibid.

Students earn their FAA licenses in both airframes and powerplants. A pilot needs a minimum of 200 hours to get his commercial license. The Moody graduate will log between 350 and 400 hours in the air.

myself," he says. "I looked for someone better qualified."[10]

Though he stayed with the program until his retirement in 1974, Robinson found his help in Dirk Van Dam, a former Air Force Academy flight instructor who graduated from Moody in 1954 and returned to take a faculty position after an Air Force tour. When the flight school moved from Chicago to Tennessee in 1967, he became director, but Robinson continued to coordinate the Chicago end of the program and to screen students.

Robinson looked not only for technical skills and strong spiritual commitment, but also for people skills. "The biggest problems you will face on the mission field," he would warn students, "will be people. Some morning six people will need emergency flights—and five are going to be mad at the pilot."[11]

It took only a short while for Robinson's program to outgrow its original facilities at Elmhurst. The operation moved in 1947 to what became known as Moody Wood Dale Airport, a dirt airstrip and hangar in the shadow of O'Hare Field.

By 1954, Robinson had added another facet to what was then the Missionary Technical Course: radio and communications. The radio major trained men in point-to-point two-way communication on isolated mission fields. Later, a broadcast major trained them for the technical aspects of radio broadcasting.

By the 1960s, the skies around O'Hare had become too congested, and Moody began scouring the nation for a better training base. The eastern Tennessee site seemed to stand out among others as a remarkable provision of the Lord. A modern facility, barely used, it was far beyond what the program had earlier enjoyed. And it was in mountainous surroundings that would be much more typical of the mission field than the relative flatness of the land around Chicago.

To those who wondered about paved runways for young pilots who would make most of their landings on remote dirt airstrips, Robinson explained: "We are a training program and we can ill afford, as has been our case during past years, to sit around waiting for a field to dry. Our paved runway will get us off the ground in

all kinds of weather."[12]

As Moody developed its Tennessee complex, young pilots and their families settled into local homes and churches. A crowd of more than one thousand, including congressmen, FAA officials, and local residents, joined MBI personnel for the dedication in April 1970. Fittingly, the new 46,000-square-feet airport structure, which included shops, classrooms, offices, and a lounge, was dedicated in memory of Henry C. Crowell, who had picked up so quickly on Robinson's aviation idea back in 1946.

Meanwhile, in Nashville, then Tennessee Governor Winfield Dunn honored Moody Aviation's Bob Rich with a special maintenance/safety award for his outstanding work in updating the Elizabethton aviation complex. In 1973, the FAA named Moody's Reid Berry "Flight Instructor of the Year" in Tennessee. More recently—in 1980—the FAA gave Moody flight instructor/safety officer Joe Hopkins its Flight Safety Award for the entire southeastern US region.

Upon the move to eastern Tennessee, Moody pilots made every effort to fit into their new surroundings, a principle these pilots would also employ later on distant mission fields. When a severe drought hit eastern Tennessee their first year there, Moody Aviation cooperated with wildlife officials in "Operation Squirrel." The pilots scattered eleven tons of shelled corn, by air, over nearby Holston and Iron Mountains. It was both good local PR and an excellent training exercise.

Dr. Richard Jensen, Ohio State University education professor who pursues research to computerize cockpits, attests to the quality of Moody's Aviation program in an interview with News in Engineering, an Ohio State publication. "Moody runs a first-class operation, from an aviation and safety standpoint," says Jensen, who graduated from the program himself.[13]

10. Ibid.
11. Ibid.
12. "MBI Aviation Complex Rises in Tennessee," Moody Monthly (September 1969).
13. Interview with Richard Jensen in News in Engineering, published by Ohio State University. Excerpted in Moody Alumni (Spring 1983).

Students maneuver this float plane onto the edge of Lake Wautauga high in the Smokies. Some students learn aerobatics, a handy skill if the pilot has to pull his plane out of a dive.

He tells of Moody's ability to produce quality pilots when he recalls a training trip from Elizabethton to Los Angeles. "Out west," he says, "we had no markers on the ground, no radio. We flew low and navigated out the window." Not all training was visual flight, however. He also tells about instrument flights with only radio aids.

Jensen went on from Moody to receive certification as a commercial/instrument pilot and flight instructor. He took a job with an aviation research center at the University of Illinois, where he earned a master's in 1972 and a doctorate in 1979 in engineering psychology. His doctoral dissertation dealt with advanced CRT cockpit displays, intended to replace the use of most gauges. His predictive display screen shows where the craft will be in eight seconds, so the pilot can adjust his steering to stay on course.

A large map covers one whole wall of the lounge area in Moody's Tennessee complex. It is a mass of pins, each representing a Moody-trained pilot somewhere in the world.

Moody supplies well over half of the pilots for the Mission Aviation Fellowship (MAF) and Wycliffe's Jungle Aviation and Radio Service

(JAARS), the world's two largest missionary aerial service organizations. Other Moody graduates go to the Sudan Interior Mission and other independent mission boards, and occasionally one joins a denominational group.

Because of the excellent training—and God's protection—Moody Aviation graduates have received, they have had a remarkable safety record, in view of the terrain in which they have to fly day-in and day-out. Yet there have been losses. MAF flier George Raney died in the Philippines when he suffered a power failure on takeoff from a jungle strip. Another pilot was killed in Mexico while air-dropping Scriptures, but he was found to have been shot out of the air, and is among Moody Bible Institute's twenty missionary martyrs. George Wall died when his plane crashed near Victoria, Cameroon, West Africa, in July 1977.

Daniel "George" Penner ('73) was killed in a 1982 crash while flying for MAF. The accident, apparently weather-related, occurred in the 11,000 foot level in rugged mountain terrain near Huehuetenango, Guatemala. Penner provided virtually the only transportation service to numerous Indian settlements in the jungles and mountains of northwest Guatemala, an area of intense guerrilla activity. He chose to remain in spite of threats to his life in order to identify with the village people who could not leave.

When his field leader questioned him about the risk, Penner replied, "I have searched the Scriptures and I do not find guaranteed personal safety."[14]

At his funeral hundreds of Guatemalans paid their respects to his widow, Esther, including many "poorest of the poor" who walked for miles to do so.

These are the kind of men who make up God's flying task force.

The missionary pilot flies many kinds of individual missions, of course, some of them seemingly glamourous, some rather mundane. But behind his job is really one precisely defined mission: to bring the gospel of salvation to peoples of every tribe and tongue and nation.

And behind this supreme mission is the Lord Jesus Christ. The missionary pilot knows that his sovereign Savior and Lord is One whose "faithfulness reaches unto the clouds" (Psalm 36:5). He knows that this One whom he serves created the heavens in which he flies, and is "Master of oceans, and seas, and skies" (Psalm 135:6).

14. *Moody Alumni* (Summer 1982).

In earlier days missionaries often had to reach remote tribes and peoples by canoe. The airplane can reduce weeks of travel into hours. In this scene from the photo archives, the biplane and the canoe rest side by side.

Irwin Moon runs a million volts through his body.

Chapter 18

SCIENCE AND THE
GOD OF CREATION

A half century ago, the American public did not link God to science. Even many Christians, who should have known better, kept a low profile when it came to the integration of science and faith. Perhaps intimidated by proponents of evolution and the attacks of science-minded critics, they saw no way to reconcile the apparent conflict.

But a young science-oriented pastor, Irwin Moon, saw it otherwise. Science offered all kinds of evidence for the existence of God, he was convinced, yet so many had failed to realize it.

So Irwin Moon began to stage scientific demonstrations in his own church. Young people responded with particular enthusiasm.

The demand for what became known as Moon's "sermons from science" soon exceeded his limited time. He resigned from the pastorate of the Montecito Park Union Church in Los Angeles to give full time to his "laboratory of faith."

Moon's love for science had followed him from his boyhood in Grand Junction, Colorado. His parents and neighbors, long-suffering victims of his scientific pranks, took it for granted he would never be swerved from his dream of becoming a physicist.

In 1939, on a step of faith, and with the help of local businessmen, Dr. Moon built a Sermons from Science auditorium at the San Francisco World's Fair. He saw the opportunity of reaching thousands with convincing evidence that the God of creation revealed in nature was the same God of redemption revealed in the Bible. For nine months, Moon gave eight performances a day, seven days a week, to overflow crowds.

More than two tons of equipment, most of it homemade, went into the production of a spectacle that spanned the whole field of science. Moon fried eggs on a cold stove, lighted lamp bulbs with his bare fingers, altered his voice with whiffs of a helium-oxygen mixture, and unfolded a world of chemical, and physical, and biological wonders. As a climax he let one million volts of electricity smash harmlessly through his body.

The show was a tremendous success. Crowds came to look and to listen quietly to his insistent, thought-provoking refrain: "Can you believe these miracles are the result of chance or accident? Or are they part of a divine pattern? What do you think?"

After the fair, Moon became an ardent amateur moviemaker. He shot color films of a few simple and dramatic scientific demonstrations and wove them into his presentations. The response was terrific.

Soon the upstairs of his two-flat home became a veritable movie studio. The bathroom became a film laboratory, and visitors ducked under lines of drying film all over the house. He was used to making his own equipment, and now he went to work in earnest.

In the bedroom Moon focused a movie camera and a bank of floodlights on a potted camelia shrub. These he connected with an electric timing device of his own invention. As the camelia grew and finally burst into bloom, the timer automatically turned the lights and camera on and off at predetermined intervals.

The result was a gorgeous, smoothly-flowing sequence in full color in which a camellia blossom opens in minutes. It was such a sensation that Moon had to allow time every showing to explain that he hadn't learned the secret of speeding-up plant growth.

During World War II, Moon took his show to the troops abroad. When he saw firsthand what military training films could accomplish, he was more convinced than ever that he would have to put his own material onto film and distribute it far and wide.

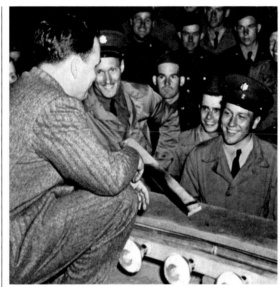

Moon takes his "Sermons from Science" to the troops in Europe. There he decides his material should go onto film.

He found an enthusiastic booster in Dr. Will Houghton, a man of broad vision who wanted the Institute to sponsor the project at once. But Houghton first had to convince the MBI board of directors back in Chicago, who would surely take a dim view of such a radical plan. Dr. Houghton set his jaw and rushed back to do the selling job of the century. It took three years. In 1945, the historic deed was signed in West Los Angeles, and the Moody Institute of Science was born, with Moon as director.

He needed men, money, and equipment. Men he could find, and equipment he could build. As for money . . . the Institute gave what it could out of a strained budget, and Moon set to work.

Actually, poverty was more help than hindrance in forming the staff of MIS. It attracted the kind of men Moon needed—men of kindred spirit with the selfless zeal and indifference to

wealth the project demanded. One man gave up a $10,000-a-year job to put in twelve to fourteen hours a day at MIS for a mere forty-eight dollars a week. Eventually Moon lined up eleven men, all experts in some field of science, many of them holders of impressive degrees.

Oddly, neither Moon nor his staff had ever had any professional movie experience. That, too, turned out to be an advantage. They went ahead blindly, accomplishing the impossible time after time without knowing it was impossible. The result was a freshness of approach and technique that drew critical raves, while it drove trained movie technicians crazy.

God of Creation, MIS's first major color production and first full-length feature, applied Moon's time-lapse technique and was a sensation. It still shows all over the world. MIS cameras explored the outer reaches of the universe through the Mount Wilson telescopes. In their own laboratory, MIS men placed specially adapted cameras into the eyepiece of a microscope to explore the miracles of life itself.

Many of the miracles of creation were photographed for the first time in history. One of those kept Moon lying on a cold floor all one Christmas eve, focusing his camera on a caterpillar, but it presented the first known color film of the metamorphosis of the swallowtail butterfly.

God of Creation set the pattern for all the "Sermons from Science." It fulfilled Moon's dream by presenting true science, unbiased and undistorted—the science of the college textbook presented to the most illiterate layman in exciting and easily grasped pictures. There was drama, humor, excitement, and superb showmanship.

That first film stirred widespread interest among the military. At one time the U.S. Air Force made "Sermons from Science" films compulsory to recruits as part of a character-guidance program.

With heightened confidence and more technical assurance, MIS produced *God of the Atom* the following year. Response to this second major production was tremendous. At Princeton University, Albert Einstein was part of an audience that saw and praised the film. Once doubtful movie critics acclaimed it with enthusiasm. In England, staid journals like the *Times* of London lost their traditional reserve. There was talk of a special Oscar.

All that was doubly remarkable because the film was made by untrained amateurs, using homemade equipment, and holding to a budget of less than $35,000. In Hollywood, where a thousand people often pour time and materials into multi-million-dollar flops, the work of MIS was regarded with greenish awe.

The next year MIS produced *Voice of the Deep.* During the war, two members of the staff—F. Alton Everest and Estes C. Wright—had done underwater research for the Navy. During that study, it was discovered that the "silent" fish were far from silent. MIS designed and built special watertight camera cases, tested them in the swimming pool of a congenial neighbor, and Moon himself donned a diving suit to make the first sound and color films of that discovery.

For years there were still hard-shell dissenters who viewed this revolutionary progress with alarm. The staff of Moody Bible Institute remained undisturbed. They recalled that back in the early 1880s Dwight L. Moody himself shocked the reactionaries of his generation by buying newspaper space to advertise his revivals. And they remembered the phenomenal physical endurance of the great shoe salesman turned evangelist. At one time Moody was rampaging across the land so tirelessly that a weary assistant groaned: "O Lord, either give me strength or make Dwight Moody tired."

Today the spirit of the great evangelist is thundering to the farthest corners of the earth on the wings of progress, clutching his Bible in one hand and a film projector in the other, his legendary tirelessness multiplied a thousandfold by the tools of science.[1]

Over the years the Moody Institute of Science has invested the effort necessary to build quality into its product. It has waited with patience to film the hard-to-get shots. When Moon had his idea for *City of the Bees,* for instance, MIS purchased a beehive from Sears, Roebuck and Company, mounted it on the top floor of its building, where the bees could come

and go through a skylight in the roof, then observed the habits of the bees for no fewer than ten years.

Photographers had to wear cumbersome bee suits, though away from the hive the bees presented little trouble—except while filming a pollination sequence on a rainy day. Rain knocks the pollen from flowers and makes work difficult for bees. Even the average human gets grumpy on a rainy day.

The task of filming bees close-up presented all kinds of photographic problems, not to mention the hazards of attack. Photographers struggled with properly illuminating their subjects, only to find, once they had solved the problem, that the heat was melting the honeycomb and bees were frying on the spot. Moon and his crew pondered the problem for

1. Robert Flood, "The Wonderful World of MIS," *Moody Monthly,* April, 1970.

Moon dons a diving suit and descends into the waters during filming of Voice of the Deep.

months. Finally they synchronized a strobe unit (electronic flash) with the camera shutter. During the one-millionth of a second in which the shutter was open, the strobe light (whose flash peaked at an illumination 5,000 times that of sunlight) could expose the film. That gave the needed light, while eliminating the deadly heat, allowing the bees to behave normally.

The bee film, almost at every turn, took incredible patience. MIS photographers stayed awake for forty-eight hours to capture the emergence of the queen from her cell. On the screen the scene takes only a few seconds.[2]

To photograph scenes for *Signposts Aloft,* Moon and Dr. George Speake flew a Beechcraft Twin Bonanza (dubbed "96 Tango") around the earth. High above the frozen Andes, "96 Tango" bit her way toward the ancient Inca capital of Cusco. At Rangoon Airport, it stopped during its global flight; at a remote desert outpost in North Africa, it refueled. A surprise downpour trapped it in Borneo mud, where friendly villagers had to rescue it with manpower. To get all the shots and footage, the trip took fourteen months and covered 125,000 air miles.[3]

The Moody Institute of Science caught the attention of the medical world when for its film called *Red River of Life* it photographed the interior valve action of the human heart for the first time. It was this kind of pioneering that earned Moon in 1980, even after he had retired, the Eastman Kodak Gold Medal Award. Moon accepted the honor from the Society of Motion Picture and Television Engineers.

"In his capacity of producer and manager of the Moody Institute of Science," read the tribute, "Dr. Moon contributed enormously in the creation of an outstanding library of visual materials utilized throughout the world."

"Perhaps Dr. Moon's most unique and significant contribution to science education," the text concluded, "was the moral and spiritual frame of reference which he built into each production."[4]

In MIS headquarters at Whittier, no fewer than fifty-seven international film awards hang in a hallway that employees have dubbed *Oscar Alley. City of the Bees* and three educational films based on it have won more awards than any

2. Jack Houston, "City of the Bees," *Moody Monthly* (April 1963).
3. Weldon Woodson, "Flying and Faith," *Moody Monthly* (September 1967).
4. "Dr. Irwin Moon Receives Highest Kodak Award," *Moody Alumni* (Spring 1981).

MIS wins the first of many international awards for advances in film photography in its City of the Bees.

other—fourteen in all. Those include the coveted Cine Golden Eagle, the Columbus Film Festival's highly regarded Chris Statuette, the Edinburgh Film Festival, and the International Film Festival of Vancouver. Yet the real awards, in the eyes of God, are the uncountable trophies of grace who have come to Christ because of a Moody Institute of Science film seen somewhere in the world.

In the Soviet Union, where atheism is government policy, more than three thousand people jam a Russian church. They are there to see a Moody Institute of Science film. More than one hundred come forward to receive Jesus Christ as their Savior.

In Brazil, seventy thousand teenagers enter a contest to win a round-trip flight to the United States after they take an exam on the content of a Moody science film. In Venezuela, officials of Kodak and a hundred commercial pilots praise a viewing of *Signposts Aloft*.

Moon interviews astronaut John Glenn, who appears in the film Signposts Aloft.

In Puerto Rico, March 30, 1977, viewers receive their first television signal from space—transmitted by a NASA ATS 6 satellite. It is the Moody Institute of Science film *Dust or Destiny* in Spanish.

A half-million people a day, somewhere around the world, view a Moody Institute of Science film.

The films have captivated Eskimos in Alaska, loggers in the Canadian wilderness, and ranchers in the Australian outback. They show up at county fairs, in museums, at state and national parks, and in the legislative halls of statehouses. Crowds have assembled to watch them on beaches, in factories, in service clubs, and at shopping malls.

Ron Mears, a U.S. Navy intelligence officer, invited his military and civilian friends to his "wetting down" party. The recipients assumed it would be a routine bash, until Mears announced it as a dry wetting down party. During the evening he and his wife showed the Moody Science film *Where the Waters Run* and shared their Christian testimonies. The response was excellent, opening doors for further witness.

From the earliest days of the Moody Institute of Science, the films have been invited into unsuspecting places. A telegram the Institute received in 1950 was signed "General Douglas MacArthur." It was just five years after the end of World War II. MacArthur had called for the help of Christian missionaries in the rehabilitation of the Far East. Now in a cable to Dr. Culbertson, he asked for copies of Moody Institute of Science films—in both Japanese and Korean.

Moody science films, now in many languages, consistently draw crowds in other lands. Some one-half million people a day somewhere in the world view a Moody science film.

The original film, *God of Creation*, took viewers out into the vastness of the universe, and also into the microscopic world. *Dust or Destiny* introduced them to such phenomena as fish that lay eggs on dry land, birds that migrate for thousands of miles without map or compass, and bats that fly through total darkness without the slightest chance of collision—all by divine plan. *Voice of the Deep* took viewers beneath the sea. *God of the Atom* documented the tremendous energies within every particle of matter.

MacArthur, in his telegram, observed how effective Moody science films had already been among the English-speaking military. "Am confident," said the wire, "these films will be source of inspiration and will give courage to Korean people who are facing the godless communist aggessors, and to the Japanese who are striving toward rehabilitation and world recognition as a democratic nation.

1973: Dr. Sweeting becomes Moody Institute of Science's new voice when he narrates the film Empty Cities. He is on location in southern Mexico.

"Also prints in any language used by United Nations forces participating in the conflict in Korea," he added, "will be welcome and useful. Your prayers and good wishes are deeply appreciated."[5]

Within weeks, Moody Vice-President Robert L. Constable was on his way to the Orient to follow up the general's request and to work out the details. Enroute he stopped in Formosa. Later, from Japan, Constable wrote:

"It was my privilege in Formosa to have dinner with Generalissimo and Madame Chiang Kai-shek. After dinner they saw the film "Dust or Destiny." They told me that if the Institute could make the films available, they would be shown throughout the Nationalist Chinese armies by teams of men especially appointed to this work."[6]

Such respect has continued to build. The films have now penetrated almost every nation upon earth and almost every stratum of society. They are shown from the executive boardrooms of American industry to the mountain villages of South America, from the American schoolroom to military bases, from churches in the free world to audiences inside the Peoples Republic of China.

For forty years, Moody films, with their unique blend of science and faith, have permeated the American scene. The face and voice of Dr. Irwin A. Moon, and more recently Dr. George Sweeting, are familiar to school children, servicemen, and college students, as well as to millions of church people. They are also known to a large segment of the people who have flocked, over the decades, to world fairs in Seattle, New York, Montreal, San Antonio, and Spokane.

At headquarters of the Moody Institute of Science in Whittier, California, film editors, in a sense of new urgency, press forward to put the Moody film line into more and more languages, for the overseas demand seems the cutting edge of the market. In 1983 and 1984 alone MIS released fifteen foreign editions—in such languages as Croatian, Norwegian, German, Japanese, Polish, Finnish, and Mandarin.

"By the year 2000," says MIS Division Manager James Adams, "the majority of Christians and missionaries will be African, Asian, and Latin. MIS must produce the tools of evangelism needed by the growing churches on these continents."

The Japan MacArthur cited in the early '50s has proved to be one of the most receptive areas of ministry for MIS films. Only 1 percent of the Japanese population professes Christianity, but almost everyone watches TV. Missionaries there began using TV in 1968, starting with two four-film series. The A. C. Nielsen Company television rating organization estimated that more than a fourth of the television sets in use at that time were tuned to the Moody Science films.[7]

The audience grew as the series progressed. Thousands responded by writing for more information. Mission agencies followed up on those who wanted more help.

In the spring of 1973, TV stations in Osaka and Tokyo carried a thirteen-week children's series that included eight Moody Science Adventure films. Some 5.5 million watched the telecasts, and almost 10,000 children responded to an offer of badges and Bible story booklets. They were personally delivered by Christians from more than 620 cooperating churches.

In Osaka, the audience was estimated at more than a million. In some churches, Sunday school attendance tripled as a result of the television outreach.[8]

The Korea that MacArthur cited also enthusiastically opened its doors. In the early 70s the Republic of Korea Army purchased twenty-three copies of the first seven MIS films. Impressed by the lives of Christian soldiers, the non-Christian Korean general supported such evangelistic efforts in hopes that a Christianized army would conteract crime and moral decay. In recent decades Korea has seen the rise of a vigorous evangelical Christianity. It has been estimated that 46 percent of those in the South Korean military are evangelical Christians.

In 1973, more than four thousand Korean servicemen accepted Christ as their Savior after

5. *Quarterly Fellowship Letter* (March 1951).
6. Ibid.
7. Lowell Saunders, "Moody Films Reach World via TV," *Moody Monthly* (January 1975).
8. Ibid.

viewing MIS films at six servicemen's centers there. On at least one occasion, more than one hundred of those were baptized in a nearby river.[9]

In Argentina, missionaries seeking to evangelize the Cordoba area set up in a town plaza and preached the gospel to a restless crowd that finally sent them retreating under a shower of insults and stones. The second night they returned, that time with a Moody Institute of Science film. Reported missionary David McGough, "The dance floor turned into holy ground as nearly sixty people pressed forward at the invitation; forty-eight proved to be sincere decisions for Christ."[10]

This kind of experience, which could be cited again and again, documents the impact of Moody science films abroad. In Latin America, too, the films have made their impact on TV. A media spokesman for the Southern Baptist Convention says, "We dare not approach large city TV management with anything less than the best. Fortunately we have found that Moody Science films are acceptable wherever we go."

Moody science films are a witness in industrial plants as well as executive boardrooms.

Moody Institute of Science films have enjoyed remarkable exposure in some industrial plants. At the McDonnell Douglas plant in Long Beach, California, a few years ago, the Douglas

Christian Fellowship closed out a series of fall-winter lunch-break showings that drew more than 20,000 viewers. At the conclusion, more than one thousand Douglas employees, their families, and management toured the MIS headquarters in Whittier during a series of open houses.

Huge corporations such as Chrysler, General Foods, General Electric, and Eastern Airlines have also used the films in employee meetings. One of the more recent ventures has taken place at the Westinghouse plant in Baltimore, it still continues today.

For five years, the Christian group at Westinghouse showed one film a month during lunch hours. Then because of the great interest, it increased the schedule to four a month. Average attendance totaled more than 500 for two years. The original Christian nucleus of four or five grew to more than fifty. Bible study groups multiplied. The coordinator of the program wrote, "One day we hope to have as many Bible studies as card games."[11]

Moody films have given Christians a medium for low-key outreach in a secular world. And their appeal even to the non-church public has been documented at five world's fairs in the past quarter century.

9. *Moody Memo* (12 July 1974).
10. "Moody Science Films Draw Crowds in U.S., Abroad," *Moody Monthly*.
11. *Moody Memo* (18 May 1979).

Dean Ortner runs a million volts through his body and lights a board in his hands.

The San Francisco World's Fair helped catapult "Sermons from Science" into prominence.

War followed on the heels of the San Franciso exposition. Not until the Seattle World's Fair of 1962 did Moody Bible Institute have another such opportunity. As in San Francisco years before, area Christian businessmen helped make the potential on Puget Sound a reality.

By that time Irwin Moon had long since retired from his regular demonstrations in order to orchestrate the organization that had grown up around him. The front man was George Speake, former Navy pilot and mechanical engineer trained at the University of Pennsylvania, who had met Moon back in 1939 after he had seen him perform at the San Francisco fair. Warm and personable, a man who could think on his feet, Speake joined Moon in 1947 and for years challenged military audiences around the world.

At Seattle, Speake demonstrated a "talking flashlight" and supported objects on invisible pillars of sound. Like Moon had done, he also set a pine board on fire by permitting a million volts of electricity to run through his body. Moody science films alternated with Speake's live demonstrations. Purposely, the program piled up evidence of an orderly and marvel-filled universe, the handiwork of an all-wise Creator. Speake's lectures pressed the Bible as true and authoritative.

At the close of each program, many in the 300-seat auditorium filed to counseling rooms where workers, mobilized by Seattle-area evangelical churches, stood ready to speak individually with everyone. Many received Christ.

A congressman and his family exited the auditorium greatly impressed, went on to Canada, and returned the next week. This time they talked with counselors and found assurance of salvation—the congressman, his wife, two sons, and a brother. By the fair's close, 417,000 had attended, and many of these went home, like the congressman, to a new life.[12]

The New York World's Fair followed in 1964-65. Christian businessmen again extended the invitation. The Moody Institute of Science

12. "From Science to Faith at the Seattle Fair," *Moody Monthly* (July-August 1962).

In the 1960's Sermons from Science draws huge crowds at world fairs in Seattle, New York, and Montreal (above). When Montreal Mayor Dean Drapeau turns his fair into the permanent exhibition "Man and His World," he asks Sermons from Science to stay.

questioned whether it should commit a substantial amount of its productivity for two years to such a gigantic task.

Fair officials at first refused to grant the land. The project almost slipped away. The head of a world-famed electronics corporation, himself an outstanding Christian businessman, intervened. The fair granted twenty-thousand square feet of choice exhibit space, then later doubled it. Two years later another 1,358,000 people had visited "Sermons from Science," and again thousands became new Christians.

Montreal two years later proved even more exciting. Crowds jammed twenty shows a day. Non-English-speaking visitors heard the film sound tracks in their choice of four languages. Live lecture-demonstrations provided simultaneous translation into French. When the summer of Expo '67 closed, 850,000 had seen the films and demonstrations. The spiritual response had been dramatic. More than a quarter million had attended follow-up sessions in the counseling room.

But it did not end there. Montreal's Mayor Jean Drapeau turned the fair into a permanent exhibition, "Man and His World," and asked "Sermons from Science" to stay. Should they? Could it staff the pavilion for another summer? Could it finance the project?

"Sermons from Science" stayed not just one year, but another eight years. On September 6, 1971, the Montreal pavilion opened its doors for the 10,000th time, and Montreal Mayor Drapeau was there to cut an eight-foot-long cake to celebrate. As the only pavilion to reach this milestone, Mayor Drapeau called it "evidence of man's abiding interest in eternal realities." Citing the pavilion's record attendance, "Man and His World" publicist Nicole Mongeau wrote in a Montreal newspaper: "Could it be because this pavilion has learned how to reach the deepest part of one's being while at the same time discarding that which simply solicits but never satisfies?"[13]

About the time Montreal opened, a group of Texas businessmen formed a non-profit organization called "Alive, Inc." and called on the product and counsel of Moody Institute of Science for an outreach at HemisFair '68 in San Antonio. While not an official MIS project, the venture exposed 455,000 to Moody films during the fair's

six-month run. Add to this another 380,000 at the Spokane World's Fair in 1972. At six world fairs, Moody attendance totaled nearly 4.5 million, with almost three-quarters of a million people responding for spiritual counseling.

Though Moody decided to bypass the World's Fair in Knoxville, Tennessee, in lieu of other priorities, and George Speake has now retired, the Sermons from Science outreach goes on. Speake's successor is Dean Ortner, who is on the road in the United States several months out of the year. Ortner was converted in Fargo, North Dakota, during a Billy Graham crusade. From the science faculty of North Dakota University, Ornter enrolled for a year in Moody's Advanced Studies Program then joined MIS in 1973 at the encouragement of Dr. George Sweeting. His combined audiences total about 40,000 people a year.

In the tradition of his predecessors, Ortner still performs the high-voltage act. Although the coil he stands on for fifteen seconds produces a million volts, it does not permanently harm his body. Yet each performance leaves him drained, his muscles aching, and his blood and body temperature affected.

Why doesn't the shock kill him?

"Your body's electrical system and muscles are in tune with sixty cycles," Ortner explains. "We change the standard sixty cycles to 65,000 cycles. At sixty cycles your muscles contract so fast that if it were used on the coil it would throw your dead body across the room."

Why does he risk it?

"No other illustration shows so vividly how one can be in tune or out of tune with his source of power. If you are not in tune with God, you cannot tap into His source of power."[14]

Ortner has had some anxious moments. In 1977, he broke his wrist when a new coil threw him off on the first test run in the lab. "It had a short which didn't show up in the preliminary tests," he says. "While I was in the air I yelled 'Off!' If my assistant had not turned it off before I hit the ground, the electricity would have grounded through my body and killed me."

13. *Moody Memo* (15 October 1971).
14. Gary L. Wall, "The Man on the Coil," *Moody Monthly* (March 1979).

As Irwin Moon approached his retirement in the early 70s, he suggested that the new president of Moody Bible Institute, George Sweeting, replace him as the narrator and host of future Moody Institute of Science films. In 1973, Dr. Sweeting narrated his first science film, *Empty Cities,* which takes viewers to the scene of once great civilizations in central and south America. Today one finds on these sites either decadence or no civilization at all. The film has produced devastating evidence against the theory of social evolution, which assumes that man's progress is ever upward.

Three years later, in its thirtieth anniversary year, MIS released *Where the Waters Run* and *In the Beginning . . . God,* the latter a glimpse into the universe by means of radioastronomy. Later in the decade it released *Energy in a Twilight World.*

A few Moody films, like *Survivor Number Three* and *The Ultimate Adventure,* have been biographical. One follows the life and impact of a missionary in Mexico; the other follows a motorcyclist across the Sahara desert.

Signposts Aloft also took the MIS film crew into the desert to trace the mysterious disappearance of a World War II plane called the "Lady Be Good." Its wreckage was eventually found in the Libyan desert, hundreds of miles beyond its Bengali destination, on the north coast of Africa. The flight crew, returning from a night mission, had apparently ignored their radio compass when it told them they had reached Bengali hours ahead of schedule. Caught unknowingly in an extremely high tail wind, identified today as the "jet stream," the pilots had trusted their logic, rather than their instruments. The lesson: "There is a way that seemeth right unto a man, but the end thereof are the ways of death" (Proverbs 14:12).

At least two-thirds of the elementary and secondary schools in America have access to Moody Institute of Science educational films. So also do numerous major universities. Linked to educational curriculum, they are often the most used films in the school library.

Educational film versions must be non-sectarian and cannot present God's plan of salvation. "But that does not mean," explain MIS officials, "that we cannot refer to God as Creator, or to the existence of absolute moral laws." Nor does it mean that the films cannot point to "God's provision for our spiritual as well as our physical lives." In view of the naturalistic orientation of today's public education, Moody Science films stand in sharp contrast.

Some churches have used Moody films in creative ways. The First Baptist Church of West Los Angeles showed one film a week in their church parking lot, and called it "An Evening Under the Stars." But during the week the film was also available to anyone in the church who wanted to use it in a neighborhood outreach or on the job. Some films enjoyed as many as ten showings.

A survey of five-thousand pastors revealed that more than 70 percent of them had used Moody Institute of Science films to strengthen the faith of their congregations.

In the early 80s, MIS began to release films featuring Dr. John MacArthur, including a series on *The Family: God's Pattern for Living* and *The Christian's Walk in the Eighties.* Does this signal a major departure from the science format? "Not necessarily," says MIS manager James Adams, who points to MIS's Bible adventure films for children, Bible background filmstrips, and teacher-training filmstrips as examples of non-scientific products that have been in the MIS line for years.

In early 1985 MIS premiered "The Journey of Life," the story of seeds and how they travel—by wind, water, animals, land, fire. Final minutes of the film remind the viewer that God created still another seed—man, and he too has a God-ordained journey.

Whatever the theme of a Moody Institute of Science film, it will lead the viewer to one common conclusion: there *is* a God of creation. And to know the Creator, the film may also pursue, is to know, first of all, Jesus Christ.

Today the films are widely used even beyond the Iron Curtain and in the People's Republic of China. Two factors insure the growing significance of Moody Science films in any global strategy: the enormous respect for science and technology in Third World countries, and the culturally neutral content of the films.

May these nations "see and recognize and consider . . ." (Isaiah 41:20).

A few of Moody Press's 1984 book releases. It has more than one thousand titles in its line.

Chapter 19

BOOKS FOR
TODAY'S WORLD

Books have long shaped the minds of men. The Bible has altered hundreds of millions of lives since the days when its earliest translators put it into the hands of the masses. *Das Capital* and *Mein Kempf*, on the other hand, helped destroy the freedoms of half the world and lead millions to their destruction. Today's outpour of pornography may add to the calamity.

Early statesman Daniel Webster saw the need of Christian books on the American scene:

"If religious books are not widely distributed among the masses in this country," he said, "I do not know what is to become of us as a nation. If truth be not diffused, error will be. If the evangelical volume does not reach every hamlet, the pages of a corrupt and licentious literature will."[1]

Dwight L. Moody saw the issue too, and as a result he introduced the inexpensive religious paperback decades before the paperback became standard in the book world. The heritage of his pioneer groundwork and foresight is today's Moody Press, one of the nation's largest Christian publishers.

In 1894, Dwight Moody brought William Norton from Northfield, Massachusetts, to manage the Bible Institute Colportage

1. Robert Flood, "They Put Their Stamp on History," *Moody Monthly* (July-August 1981).

Early days in the offices of the Bible Institute Colportage Assocation (BICA). William Norton, Moody's handpicked first administrator of the Colportage ministry, sits at center.

Association, a publishing operation and network of traveling salesmen which Moody himself had established. Norton found the operation housed in the basement of a frame building at 260 North LaSalle, with four women employees and a stock clerk. Today its employees number in excess of forty, and Moody Press's annual sales exceed fifteen million dollars.

Walk into one of the thousands of Christian bookstores across the country, and whether you are looking for children's books, a commentary or a Bible reference work, books on Christian living or Bible doctrine, or even fiction, you will find many choices in each category with the Moody Press label. Moody Press has more than one thousand titles in its line.

The major national book chains like B. Dalton and Walden Books, or the book department of firms like J. C. Penney, will probably also have a few books from Moody Press, including the *Ryrie Study Bible* and *The Bible in Pictures for Little Eyes.*

In Chicago, the Moody Press operation is located ten miles north of the main campus on the border of Evanston. In a Moody-owned building that was once the national headquarters of the A. C. Nielsen television rating firm, editorial, marketing, and production people busily orchestrate the Moody Press publishing program. The Moody Press distribution center lies further northwest in suburban Northbrook.

Dwight L. Moody once said, "If we believe the gospel is the best news that ever came to the world, then let us publish it to everybody we can reach." He planted the foundations of what became Moody Press when, after a series of meetings in Madison, Wisconsin, in 1894, he searched for a booklet on Christian growth to leave with his new converts. He found none. Moody continued to search for Christian books in the cities in which he preached, but with little success.

Moody urged several Christian publishers to publish inexpensive Christian literature on a mass basis, but all were reluctant to take the risk in the absence of general demand. So he decided to do it himself. In November of the same year, he formed the Bible Institute Colportage Association of Chicago—forerunner of Moody Press.

His first books were reprints from the line of publisher Fleming H. Revell, his brother-in-law. They were pocket-sized paperbacks, sold at ten cents each, by outstanding Christian authors of the day. Revell provided the plates to each book and was happy to do so, since it was Moody who had urged him to enter the publishing field in 1869.

While Moody Press has long helped anchor the mainstream of the Christian publishing industry, today's expansive Christian bookstore movement is a relatively modern day phenomenon. Few Christian bookstores existed before the middle of this century. Instead, Moody Bible Institute distributed its books through a vast network of "colporters," who sold directly to the consumer on a generous commission basis. Even as late as 1944, the Bible Institute Colportage Association of Chicago employed more than two thousand salespeople.

Today the job is handled by a small sales force of seven men, who call personally on the larger Christian bookstores in their assigned regions, and by the use of telephone WATS lines out of Moody Press's offices. Their customers are the several thousand Christian bookstores that have emerged on the American scene within the last three decades.

The major event of the year for Christian booksellers is an annual trade convention held every July, usually in cities like Dallas, Washington, D.C., or Anaheim. The gathering of the Christian Booksellers Association (CBA) has become so gigantic that only a few of the nation's convention centers can accommodate the week-long event, despite the fact that it is not open to the public.

At the CBA convention Moody Press and scores of other religious publishers, along with Christian music publishers and other firms that supply the Christian bookstore trade, assemble a vast exhibit floor of products that would boggle the eyes of the uninitiated. Between time spent in workshops and seminars on how to better manage their stores (there are dozens of such sessions from which to choose), store operators roam the exhibit

Moody Press's exhibit at the 1984 convention of the Christian Booksellers Association (CBA) in Anaheim, California, where Christian bookstore buyers meet their suppliers. The annual event is now one of the largest trade coventions in the nation.

floor, scanning product lines and placing orders with publishers and suppliers. Their biggest challenge: how to cover it all, and make the right choices, in a week's time.

The scene is all the more amazing, however, to those who realize that the vast Christian Booksellers Association, which did not even exist thirty-five years ago, had its birth at the Moody Bible Institute.

For years requests for counsel and information on how to open and operate Christian bookstores had poured into Moody Press. William Moore, an employee of the Press at the time, and Ken Taylor, then its director, called together several Chicago area Christian book dealers to explore the idea of forming a Christian association. In April 1950, Moody Press hosted several luncheon meetings devoted to the subject.

Out of this came their first convention at Chicago's LaSalle Hotel in September 1950. Two months later the Christian Booksellers Association incorporated as a nonprofit corporation in the state of Illinois.

CBA used the facilities of Moody Press

until 1959, when it moved to its own offices in suburban Chicago, then relocated in Colorado Springs in 1970. John Bass resigned as personnel director of the Moody Bible Institute to become CBA's full-time executive director. Still in that position today, Bass and CBA have played a key role in the phenomenal rise of the Christian book industry. The association has grown to become a worldwide operation, providing book dealers all over the globe with information on how to better operate their stores. The CBA convention has become one of the ten largest trade shows in the US. Nearly every key executive with CBA at one time or another has worked at Moody Bible Institute.

Moody Press today releases about seventy-five new titles a year. At its expansive distribution center, workers standing at long conveyors pick and pack about $4,000 worth of books and Bibles a day. Computer reports flag each title when it reaches a predetermined minimal inventory so that Moody Press's production department can rush another printing of the book before the stock is depleted.

The original Moody Colportage Library published two books per month during its first year and one per month in subsequent years. The criteria: it had to be in readable style, by a well-known author, strictly evangelical and nondenominational, well printed but inexpensive. The first book was *All of Grace* by Charles Spurgeon; the second, *The Way to God* by Dwight Moody. Both books are still in print, after more than ninety years, the latter in a new, cleanly designed cover, anticipating Moody Bible Institute's centennial year.

The press runs of those early years were large. The first edition of *The Way to God* by Moody totaled 100,000 copies. High press runs helped keep the unit cost low, but of course at that time there were few other books in the line to market simultaneously. Typical press runs of a title today are 10,000—necessary to keep inventory trim, especially with such a large line.

Dwight Moody began the first book club in the United States when he urged people to sign up to receive a new book each month. It was an idea that surfaced long before its time. By 1903, the five books in print by Dwight Moody had already sold nearly one-half million copies. Moody himself, of course, sold thousands of books around the country wherever he preached.

Moody was determined to stop, if he could, the "awful tide of impure reading matter" in his day. He was also determined to reach the non-churchgoer, to help Christian workers

evangelize, and to get the printed page into the hands of prisoners behind bars.

The mass network of colporters in earlier days gave many Christians a satisfying source of full-time or bonus income. Young people who wished to train for Christian work often were able to finance their schooling through colportage work.

Not all books were sold. To reach special segments of society, funds were established to provide free literature. Some such funds were geographical: Africa, Alaska, India, Latin America, French Louisiana (a fund to reach the half-million French Catholics). There were funds for seamen, railroadmen, prisoners, lumbermen, miners.

For nearly a half century, however, the colportage work was incorporated separately from the Institute itself. In 1941, it became an official part of Moody Bible Institute and was split into two divisions. The printing and sales division was called Moody Press, and the missionary literature work became known as the Colportage Department, later Moody Literature Mission, and still later Moody Literature Ministries.

Moody Press entered the textbook line in 1955, calling heavily upon the faculty of Moody Bible Institute to help launch the program. Their primary market: other Bible institutes, Christian colleges and seminaries, along with pastors and laymen. Moody Press textbooks cover such areas as theology, Bible study, comparative religions,

Computers advance and make more efficient many spheres of Moody Press publishing. An editor with a word processor (left) is able to cut his editing time in half, and telephone WATS and ordering systems (right) increase sales and inventory potentials.

Tom Olsen examines a copy of The New Unger's Bible Handbook. *A complete line of Bible reference books help anchor the broad Moody Press line. The Institute's entrance into Bible publishing in the 1960s now adds substantial dollar volume to Moody Press sales.*

Christian education, church music, church history, missions, archaeology, psychology, homiletics, and biblical languages.

Major Bible reference books, introduced in the 1960s, also help anchor the Moody Press line. These include *The Wycliffe Bible Commentary*, produced by some forty-nine scholars from a cross-section of denominations, *Unger's Bible Handbook, Nave's Topical Bible,* and *Unger's Bible Dictionary.* The *Wycliffe Bible Encyclopedia,* many years in the making, followed in 1975. The consistent sales of these books year after year, along with other substantial references, help give Moody Press great stability.

But perhaps Moody Press took its biggest step when it decided to enter the field of Bible publishing.

Such a move might have seemed natural for Moody Press, and for an established organization like Moody Bible Institute, but still it was a major decision. The investment would involve millions of dollars, especially if it were to produce quality, leather-bound Bibles.

Until the 60s, Moody Press's only track record in Bibles had been with *The New Testament in the Language of the People* by Charles B. Williams, a pioneering venture because most people were reluctant to read anything but the King James Version. It became an immediate success.

Then in the 1960s Moody Press, by arrangement with the Lockman Foundation, became one of only five distributors of the *New American Standard Bible,* in a variety of formats and prices. More recently it released a new *Thinline* edition, made possible as the printing industry developed paper that is ever lighter, yet also strong and durable.

In 1978, Moody Press released the *Ryrie Study Bible,* which contains a broad spectrum of cultural, theological, historical, and linguistic material in the notes of Dr. Charles Ryrie, former professor of systematic theology at Dallas Theological Seminary. It was offered in both the King James and the *New American Standard* versions, and in a broad range of colors and cover grades. It has become the leading Moody Press product.

Ken Taylor's *Bible in Pictures for Little Eyes,* which had long been a part of the Moody line, became a Moody Press all-time best seller. Its total sales now surpass 1,000,000 copies, and it has been published in forty languages—more than any other single Moody Press title.

In the children's line, Moody Press stands as one of the major publishers in the industry. Among its children's books are several well-established series, including the quality-produced Muffin Family series, by Gilbert Beers, the Children's Bible Basics, by Carolyn Nystrom, the Peggy series, by Dorothy Martin, the People of the Bible series, by Ella Lindvall, and several other mystery and adventure series.

Once a manuscript is accepted by a publisher, it usually takes nine months to a year before the book is on the market—sometimes longer. Manuscript editors may spend weeks, even months, in meticulous work on a single book, especially if it is a major reference work or textbook. When Moody Press released in 1980 its two-volume *Theological Wordbook of the Old Testament,* the work of several scholars, it had been more than ten years in the making.

Good management requires that slower-selling titles be trimmed from the line on a regular basis to control inventory, make way for new books, and keep the line from becoming unwieldy. Such decisions are not easy—either for editors or for authors. In the final analysis, though, it is primarily the public that dictates the decision.

Recognizing the extra strain on potential book buyers during the economic recession, Moody Press released some of its basic reference books in a no-frills format it called the "Affordables." In a sense, it was Moody Press's response to the generic trend.

From its earliest days, Moody Press has majored in books on practical Christian living. Dwight Moody wrote on *Prevailing Prayer,* Reuben Torrey assembled his popular *Vest Pocket Companion,* and today authors like Warren Wiersbe and John MacArthur write *Live Like a King* and *The Ultimate Priority.* But add to this today a wide scope of newer products, including several popular-level works that reach the masses without compromising biblical basics. Moody Press has tried to touch people where they are.

In addition to Moody's own campus bookstore, it also owns a flourishing bookstore on Chicago's south side and now three stores in Charleston, West Virginia, donated on 1 October 1984, by Bill and Sylvia Stevens. In 1980, rising overhead forced a reluctanct close to its store on Adams Street in the heart of the Chicago Loop, a store which drew heavy business during the downtown Chicago lunch hour, much of it a non-church crowd.

One of those touched by the ministry of the Loop store was Jill Wilson, a manager in the sprawling book department at nearby Marshall Field. Through visits to the Moody Bookstore, she became a Christian. She eventually left Marshall Field to come to the Institute and later managed the Loop store and then Moody's campus

Today Moody Press continues to publish an extensive line of children's books, as it has done for years. Prominent on this store rack are the books of Carolyn Nystrom and the Muffin Family series by Gilbert Beers.

bookstore. More recently she was named Adult Trade Editor of Moody Press. The director of Moody Retail, Barbara Goodwin, also came to Christ through the ministry of the old Loop bookstore.

Moody' original concept of free literature on a project basis has not been lost. This function is carried on year after year by what is now Moody Literature Ministries. MLM has given millions of dollars over the years to supply Christian books for schoolchildren in Appalachia, book stalls in Latin America, and sailors at sea. It has sent tons of books and tracts to men in prison, masses behind the Iron Curtain, and struggling pastors in the Third World, where theological libraries are almost non-existent. It has sent free book sets to U.S. public libraries, large

print books to every nursing home in America, and funds to translate Moody Press's own books into other languages. And it has helped to open Christian bookstores around the world.

The Moody Bible Story Book is widely used in the schools of Japan, and so also in the schools of Africa, where very few educational books of any kind exist. Military chaplains in the U.S. Army, Navy, Air Force, and Marines put Moody literature into the hands of servicemen around the globe. Funds have sent millions of tracts, tailored for almost every culture, to the peoples of the world.

Even Evangelical Literature Overseas (ELO), a U.S. based service agency established to lend technical assistance in literature to mission groups worldwide, has partial roots at Moody Bible Institute. Though not affiliated with the Institute, it was conceived in part by former Moody Press directors Ken Taylor and Peter Gunther, both of whom had extensive experience in Christian literature overseas. Gunther retired in 1983 as director of Moody Press's international sales. In an annual report to management shortly before his retirement, Gunther wrote:

> I have been privileged to be a part of the ministry of Moody Press and Moody Literature Ministries for thirty-three years. The blessings we receive from our Lord Jesus Christ are new every day and never fail to excite me. Take for instance the delightful experience of receiving a small parcel from the Philippines. In it are six sample copies of our *Pictorial Pilgrim's Progress* in the southern Kalinga dialect. Or a parcel from Kenya with six sample copies of *How to Begin the Christian Life* in Swahili. Or a parcel from Thailand with six copies of *Gladys Aylward* in the Thai language. I still get goose bumps when these books are received, realizing that the Moody Press ministry is extended to people who speak and read a "strange" language.[2]

Daniel Webster and Dwight L. Moody would be pleased. The books of Moody Press go out daily across the nation, shaping the lives of Americans in city, suburb, and hamlet. But that is only part of the picture. They are also going around the world.

2. Peter Gunther, "Annual Report," Moody Press, 1983.

MONTHLY

Moody

THE CHRISTIAN FAMILY MAGAZINE

THE WORLD'S LEADING PEDIATRIC SURGEON ON SOCIETY'S MOST CONTROVERSIAL ISSUE

C.E.Koop M.D.

Chapter 20

THE MAKING OF A MAGAZINE

In 1980, Moody Monthly poses Surgeon General C. Everett Koop for the cover of its most widely-circulated issue of all time.

What has been called "America's foremost Christian family magazine" now reaches into a quarter million homes in America, plus a few thousand readers abroad, most of them missionaries. One subscriber in Alaska wrote that he saw an Eskimo reading *Moody Monthly* while driving his dogsled!

Today's *Moody Monthly* bears little resemblance to the small bi-weekly paper called *The Institute Tie*, first published on November 7, 1891, for the alumni of Moody Bible Institute. The first publication lasted little more than a year, until it had to shut down because of general economic conditions. In September 1900, it resurfaced, this time as a copyrighted monthly magazine, with A. P. Fitt as editor.[1]

Despite its name, *Moody Monthly's* audience extends far beyond the alumni and close friends of Moody Bible Institute. It has established itself as a general consumer magazine in its field—the largest periodical in the country, perhaps, that is affiliated with a school, either Christian or secular. Few magazines attached to an institution have been able to achieve this kind of exposure.

In reality, *Moody Monthly's* outreach may be closer to a million. Each *Moody Monthly* household represents an average of about three people. Add to this the pass-along factor.

The fact that *Moody Monthly* carries the advertising of other Christian schools and publishers which, from a purely self-serving point of view, might be seen as competition, further establishes the magazine's position as a genuine journal for the evangelical public at large.

When in 1907 James M. Gray and R. A. Torrey took over as co-editors of the old *Institute Tie*, they immediately altered its format to more of an educational one, in order to reach out beyond MBI's alumni and close circle of friends. The new format included contributed articles, book reviews, sermon outlines, and religious news. Readers could also find Bible study, Bible commentary, and a question and answer column. It was a wise first step toward becoming more than just another house organ.

Gray wrote a biblical exposition for each issue, beginning with Genesis, and moved month by month through the whole Bible. It took him ten years. In 1910, the publication changed its name to *The Christian Workers' Magazine*, further evidence that even then it had expanded its target market. The same year it added such regular departments as "Studies in Personal Soul Winning" by William Evans (the Institute's first graduate), "The Gospel in the World," and "The International Sunday School Lesson." The latter feature ran for sixty years. Not until 1920 did the magazine become *The Moody Bible Institute Monthly*. The words "Bible Institute" were dropped from the logo in 1938.[2]

The *Moody Monthly* of today would seem a far cry from the drab-looking, type-crowded magazine of those years, yet its heartbeat and doctrine remain unchanged. The style of journalism has changed, and its graphics have been updated to capture and hold the attention of today's reading public. But its mission is the same.

The genius of a magazine, by its very

1. Getz, p. 151.
2. Ibid., p. 258.

name, is variety. Unlike a book, it changes pace. Every good magazine has a clear editorial "formula," yet also a clear focus that gives that same variety cohesiveness. *Moody Monthly* is obviously evangelical, and also family-oriented. That is part of its focus. Pick up a typical issue, and you can also detect its editorial formula: Christian living, news, Bible study, testimony, doctrine, current issues, Christian education, church matters, book reviews, parental help, and more.

Some issues will be themed. The subject may be the "Fruit of the Spirit," "Discipleship," "Religious Freedom," or a seasonal thrust. Yet *Moody Monthly*'s typical issue is large enough to accommodate many other features as well.

As an example, a May 1983 emphasis on the theme "Can Persecution Bind the Church?" took readers behind the Bamboo Curtain, cited believers from Assam to Zimbabwe who are suffering for the cause of Christ, interviewed Brother Andrew on the responsibility of free world Christians to the suffering church abroad, and also blended into its theme an article on "The Theology of Suffering." Yet in that same issue were no fewer than twenty-six *other* features and articles.

One of *Moody Monthly*'s most far-reaching special editions of recent years was its May 1980 issue on the abortion controversy. Although not a subject that everyone likes to face, it drew widespread attention and response. The Midwest edition of *U.S. News & World Report* carried a full page ad on this particular edition, with a special subscription offer. *Moody Monthly* met Surgeon General C. Everett Koop, an evangelical and staunch anti-abortionist, at O'Hare Airport for a special interview and cover photo.

Moody Monthly's "Letters to the Editor" column ranks high in readership. The magazine does not ban negative letters, especially if they are well expressed. A lively letters column reflects a healthy magazine and confirms that readers are involved with its content. Reader comments often uncover new and rich facets of an issue or sometimes cite legitimate flaws. Not all published reader criticisms are legitimate, and some views expressed are not even scriptural, but *Moody*

Monthly assumes that most of its readers have enough intelligence and spiritual maturity to tell the difference.

News also always ranks near the top in reader surveys. This may be in part because there are few sources that provide the Christian public a biblical slant on the news.

Although some Christians prefer a magazine without advertising, *Moody Monthly* has long seen this as a legitimate function of its ministry. Its pages are a veritable shopping guide to some of the best products on the market: books, Bibles, church products, music, Sunday school materials, and more. Some readers even admit that they "read the advertising first." Several years ago news commentator Paul Harvey wrote in his syndicated column that evangelist Billy Graham enrolled in a Florida Bible school because "his mother saw the ad in *Moody Monthly*."

Moody Monthly tries to maintain a high standard, however, on the kind of advertising it will accept, both in light of basic doctrine and good taste. Yet the magazine has had the courage to refuse, graciously, as much as $75,000 worth of advertising a year in order to maintain its standards and its reader trust.

The paid circulation of *Moody Monthly* in 1921, according to earliest available figures, was 19,431. By 1935, it hovered around 40,000. When Will Houghton became president of Moody Bible Institute and assumed the magazine's editorship, he promoted it vigorously and circulation climbed to a new high of around 75,000. By the early sixties it had topped 100,000, where it essentially remained at the end of the decade.

In 1972, *Moody Monthly,* sensing a much greater potential market, stepped out in an aggressive national direct mail campaign, mailing to 2.5 million prospects. It also introduced a special edition parallel *New Testament/Wycliffe Commentary* as a premium. Circulation in the next two years climbed to one-quarter million.

For a magazine to maintain this kind of circulation, an average of about one thousand subscriptions—either new or renewal—must flow into *Moody Monthly* every working day. The

In the era of Will Houghton, Moody Monthly *climbs from 40,000 to 75,000 circulation, with help from editors Ernest Christie (right) and Clarence Benson. In the early 1970s it spirals from 100,000 to one-quarter million. With the advent of offset, its printing moves in the 1960s from Illinois to high-speed presses in Milwaukee.*

heaviest mail comes usually before Christmas (many give the magazine to others at this time of year) and in February, after the magazine's biggest mailing. It is interesting that young people who sell the magazine to friends and relatives, or door-to-door for subscription agencies, generate nearly 15,000 subscriptions a year. Through the assistance of Moody Literature Ministries, *Moody Monthly* can also be found in many U.S. public libraries.

In the earlier days of *Moody Monthly,* and even as late as the era of Will Houghton, Moody Bible Institute presidents took an active part in the magazine's day-by-day editorial operations. But as the multi-faceted operations of the Moody Bible Institute imposed growing demands on the president's time, this kind of arrangement became impractical. Shortly after William Culbertson assumed office, the Institute hired Wayne Christianson, a former newspaperman and graduate of Iowa State's school of journalism, as its first full-time executive editor. The president then carried the title editor-in-chief.

Wayne Christianson, executive editor, provides two decades of leadership for Moody Monthly. *Under him the magazine modernizes its format and sharpens its focus.*

For the next two decades the editing skills and remarkable Christian spirit of Wayne Christianson, who still serves as Senior Editor Emeritus, inspired all who worked under him. By the 1960s, *Moody Monthly* had improved in its design and editing and had introduced full-color covers. The magazine implemented graphic

improvements a step at a time, lest some readers complain that it was not "the old *Moody Monthly.*" To remedy the magazine's type-heavy appearance, the designer began to "loosen up" the magazine and give the copy more breathing room. On at least one occasion, an old-time Moody alumnus on campus for Founder's Week dropped into the editorial offices to charge the editors with "wasting the Lord's money with all that white space." But the vast majority of readers responded favorably. The magazine had become more readable.

Even greater strides would follow. But so would the competition. New magazines appeared on the Christian scene, often targeted to a specialized segment of the Christian market, but nonetheless giving Christian readers more options. Other Christian magazines, once drab, also began to sparkle. As the American family spent more hours before the television set, some media surveys even forecasted that magazines would become obsolete. Such predictions proved wrong. Yet Christian magazines could no longer assume that people would pick them up, unless they appeared inviting and delivered substance.

Good covers have always been a major challenge to magazine editors. They are especially critical to magazines which sell on the newsstand. Although *Moody Monthly* sells primarily through subscriptions, except for sales in churches and Christian bookstores, a good cover can still encourage a subscriber to lift the magazine from his coffee table. Cover subtleties can please or sometimes trigger adverse reaction.

A February 1977 *Moody Monthly* cover carried the painting of an exhausted vacation Bible school teacher, with crayons and papers on the floor around her after her students had left the room. To the editors the scene conveyed an amusing Norman Rockwell kind of humor. But one VBS superintendent complained that it would discourage prospects in her recruitment of VBS teachers.

An October 1980 issue with the cover story "Russia Eyes Israel's Oil" carried the painting of a glowering bear—symbolic of the USSR in prophecy. The manager of a Christian bookstore reported that this issue did not sell well in his store because, in his observation, "mothers and their children reacted to the scary-looking bear."

Sometimes editors go to great lengths for what they hope will be a creative cover. To illustrate a February 1977 cover story on "Reaching Athletes for Christ," a *Moody Monthly* editor arranged for the University of Illinois card section to spell out "Moody" during the halftime of one of its football games. The scene doubled both as a cover photo and "Moody" cover logo. The cover photographer had just fifteen seconds to get off his shot when the cards went up. Crowds on the other side of the field may still be wondering how "Moody" got into the card sequence.

Moody Monthly won its first "Periodical of the Year" award from the Evangelical Press Association in 1957. It repeated that again in 1976, and in the past decade it has earned dozens of individual EPA categorical awards. The Evangelical Press Association represents more than three hundred periodicals with a combined circulation in the millions.

Surveys have documented that *Moody Monthly* subscribers, as a whole, are heavily active in their local churches. About half of them, or around 125,000, are Sunday school teachers. While *Moody Monthly* is making its own impact upon its readership, its readers in turn have demonstrated themselves people of action. They are not simply armchair Christians. *Moody Monthly's* one-time label, "The Christian Worker's Magazine," may still accurately define its market, although since then its audience has multiplied by many times.

The making of a magazine—a quality Christian magazine—demands many professional skills. It also demands that its editors be sensitive to the needs of readers and, above all, to the mind of the Lord. A Christian magazine is not an end in itself. What counts most, in the eyes of its editors, is how God can use it to change lives and to refine the faith of the people of God.

In 1975: Moody Monthly *celebrates its 75th anniversary with this nostalgic cover.*

A postman delivers mail to the Moody Correspondence
School in an earlier era.

Chapter 21

THE NATION'S
CLASSROOM

At his home near the southern shores of Lake Erie, Andre Thornton, first baseman of the Cleveland Indians, settles down in his study and opens a Bible and the Moody Correspondence course on the book of Hebrews. It is his third course from Moody, and he is one of the school's more than 30,000 enrollees. Already a recipient of awards for "humanitarianism" and "exemplary Christian spirit" in professional baseball, Thornton presses on in his Christian growth.

James Grant is an oil geologist in Wichita, but he is also a Bible student. He was brought to Christ years ago when his wife taught the Moody Correspondence course *Memorize the Word* as part of the school's group study plan. Since then Grant has taken more than thirty groups through the same course himself.

Without leaving his home in Mercer, Pennsylvania, Reverend Edward Johnson has rounded out an impressive Bible school education. Since the early forties, he has finished twenty-six courses. In 1982, Carol Ann Morrical of Mt. Carmel, Illinois, a former missionary housewife, donned her cap and gown as the first Moody graduate to complete her work entirely by correspondence in the new Certificate of Graduation program.

People of almost every background, occupation, and social level have taken the courses of the Moody Correspondence School. In more than three-quarters of a century its roster has included a senator, a movie actor, the wife of a billionaire, and a Michigan convict who came to Christ after murdering five men.[1] On its rolls also have been an army of pastors and missionaries, not to mention a host of Christian laymen.

By means of printed lessons, carefully prepared exams, and personal grading, this ministry brings Bible study within the reach of those who cannot go to a Bible institute or even attend night classes. It reaches the young person who cannot begin training immediately but hopes to in the future, the pastor or other Christian worker who feels the need for further study, the layman or laywoman who wants to be a more effective worker. It also serves the many who simply find personal Bible study a key to spiritual growth.

If all of those currently enrolled in a Moody Correspondence course were brought together onto one campus, it would equal the student bodies of Harvard, Yale, and Notre Dame combined.

Fifteen offered courses are college level. (Others are categorized as adult credit courses.) Moody's long-established Correspondence School dovetails beautifully with the current trends in continuing education.

As in other ventures, Moody Bible Institute found itself in on the ground floor of the emergence of the correspondence school phenomenon in America.

The Chautauqua movement brought music, education, and culture to the byroads of early America. Though founded to train Sunday school teachers, it became a secular school. Chautauqua was the first American institution to establish correspondence courses.[2] The first course was offered in 1879 by William Rainey Harper,

1. Wayne Christianson, "The Bible School That Comes to Students," *Moody Monthly* (January 1976).
2. Getz, p. 121.

then a professor of Hebrew at Yale.

Harper brought the correspondence school concept from the Chautauqua movement to the University of Chicago, where he became its president in 1892. His work helped establish correspondence study "as a part of the educational scene" in America.[3] D. L. Moody was familiar with the Chautauqua movement, points out Gene Getz, and he "also knew many of the authorites in the seminary and university world (he spoke at Princeton in 1876 and at Yale in 1878). R. A. Torrey also knew the trends in general education, having received his A.B. and B.D. at Yale, where Harper taught Semitic languages."[4]

Whatever the precise connection, the early leaders of the Institute saw the potential and began to talk of a correspondence school program as early as 1895. By 1901, Moody had released the first two courses—"Bible Doctrine" and "Practical Christian Work," both written by Torrey. This made its "school by mail" the first of its kind in the Bible institute movement.[5]

It should be noted, however, adds Getz, that C. I. Scofield prepared a "Comprehensive Bible Correspondence Course" and began distributing it as early as 1896. Scofield's course, covering the whole Bible, seems to have been the first evangelical correspondence Bible study program ever circulated. Scofield handled the course privately for a number of years, then sold it in 1915 to the Institute. The *Scofield Course* then became a part of the Moody Correspondence School curriculum and has remained so ever since.[6]

The Scofield course, in fact, which takes three years to complete, is still the most demanding single course. But those who invest in it find it worth the effort. A psychotherapist from New York wrote of the Scofield course: "In my Scripture study what was once tedious is now pleasurable. What I once avoided I now look forward to and, miracles of miracles, I can now pray! Distractions are gone. Christ has become a person to me."[7]

A student could complete Torrey's Bible Doctrine course in two years with just several hours of study a week. But in those days men worked ten to twelve hours a day. Torrey had that

problem resolved too. He had the lessons prepared in sections that could be easily folded. In this way a student could study while traveling to and from work on the street car or on the recently completed elevated trains.

The street cars no longer exist in many American cities, but some students still use train time. Today's commuter, though, can flip a Moody Correspondence School audio cassette into his tape deck and settle back to listen as his car crawls into or out of the city during the rush hour. Of course, he can't try to write out an exam too!

There are still other variations of Moody's Bible study by mail program.

3. Ibid.
4. Ibid.
5. Ibid., p. 122.
6. Ibid.
7. Kay Oliver, "Thousands Study Bible by Mail," *Moody Monthly* (February 1971).

One of them uses radio. On September 21, 1926, simultaneously with the first broadcasts of Chicago's WMBI, the Radio School of the Bible went on the air. It was an innovation not only in the religious world, but also in the secular world, since regular schools-of-the-air did not come into prominence for several years. Not only did the Institute pioneer in offering Bible subjects over the air, but also in making course outlines available to listeners for individual study and by sending listeners examinations, which were then returned for grading. Upon successful completion of each course, a special certificate of recognition was issued to each student, which could be transferred to credit in the Day or Evening school. Today's Radio School of the Bible enrolls up to 1,000 students each year.

All college level correspondence courses are also taught in the Evening School, and those who live in the Chicago area or near one of

A women's group in Chicago listens to a WMBI broadcast of Radio School of the Bible. The courses presented on the radio are published by the correspondence school.

Moody's satellite evening schools sometimes combine the two into their program toward a Correspondence School Certificate of Graduation. Nancy Weeks Wong, who earned a B.A. in education with high honors from the University of Tennessee, graduated from the Moody Correspondence School in 1981 by doing some of her work in the Evening School. So did Eugene Pond of Naperville, Illinois, who already held a B.S. and M.S. in computer science from the University of California but wanted to get "a richer knowledge of God's Word so that I might teach others." After completing his Moody work, Pond pursued a doctorate at Northwestern University. M. David Johnson, lanky civil engineer involved in Chicago's deep tunnel project, who graduated from the Correspondence School in 1982, is another talented person who was attracted to a Moody Correspondence School education.

Moody Bible Institute college level Correspondence School courses are transferable both into the Day School and the Evening School, as well as to other Bible institutes and colleges offering equivalent courses. Many secular universities also recognize these as credit courses in religion, in the same way they recognize credits from the Moody Day School.

In 1970, the school added New Testament Greek Grammar to its college level courses, making it possible for those who want to read the New Testament in the original language to pursue study of Greek by mail. Later it also added a more advanced Greek grammar course. Both are four semester hours, and are the equivalent to the same course offered in Moody Day School. Written by Donald Wise of the MBI faculty, the course guides the student in his study by using cassette tapes with recorded instruction for each of the eighteen lessons. The tapes help the student's pronunciation, enhance his understanding of the text, and guide his progress in completing the work sheets. Wise also helps the student make spiritual applications from the Greek text. In addition to taped instruction, the course includes a leatherette Greek New Testament, the textbook, *Essentials of New Testament Greek,* and a loose-leaf binder containing study guides, supplementary material, work sheets, exams, and vocabulary cards. A student has one year to complete each course.

In 1979, the Moody Correspondence School introduced Hebrew, giving students by mail access to the foundational language of the Old Testament. Publishing Hebrew I and II was one of the most ambitious projects ever undertaken by the Correspondence School. It introduces the student to the Hebrew alphabet, grammar, tenses, and sentence structure. Extensive reading assignments are given in the Hebrew text from the book of Ruth. Written by Dr. Douglas C. Stephens, MBI professor of Bible, the course was several years in the making. Typesetting alone took nearly two years, for only a handful of printers in the nation have the equipment to typeset Hebrew! By the time Hebrew I went onto the market, sixty-seven students were ready to enroll immediately, and 1,500 had asked for information about it.

When Dwight L. Moody pushed the religious paperback, one of his target markets was the US prison population of his day. With advent of the correspondence course, it too found its way into the prisons, usually with the encouragement of chaplains. Today over four thousand prisoners, who do not only have time but need as much activity as they can find, are enrolled in the Moody Correspondence School yearly. Dr. Will Norton, chairman of the Department of Journalism at the University of Mississippi, wrote about one of them, Tommy Tarrants, in the September 1980 *Moody Monthly:*

> A tall, lean, dark-haired man in his mid-twenties leaned forward at his desk and finished the last line of a Greek assignment. But he wasn't your average student. He studied in the austere compound of Camp 3 in the Mississippi State Penitentiary at Parchman.
>
> Despite his surroundings, Tommy Tarrants was grateful. His beginning course in New Testament Greek offered through Moody Bible Institute's Correspondence School was part of his pursuit to absorb all he could about his new commitment to Christ.
>
> Neither was Tarrants an average prisoner. During the late 1960s, he was a leader of Mississippi's dreaded White Knights of the Ku

Tommy Tarrants, former KKK leader and convict, finds spiritual growth through the Moody Correspondence School.

Klux Klan. As one of the most violent organizations in the United States, it was responsible for nine murders and more than 300 bombings, burnings, and beatings. . . .

He made headlines when he was identified as a Klan terrorist and was captured by police and sharpshooters and FBI agents June 29, 1968, in Meridian, MS.[8]

Norton describes in his article a dramatic chase and shootout in which Tarrant finally ran face to face into the shotguns of the FBI and was gunned down, yet he miraculously escaped death.

In prison, Tarrant continued to defy authorities until a passage in the book *Legacy of Freedom* by John C. Roach turned him toward the Bible in a search for truth. There, writes Norton, "Tommy saw himself as God saw him, and it crushed him. He wept bitterly and asked Jesus to save him."

After eight years in prison, Tommy was released to attend the University of Mississippi. "Today," writes Norton, "he is in full-time ministry teaching God's Word and discipling new believers. He wants to provide a Christian perspective to an unstable world facing political extremism. Tommy Tarrants has found a new cause."[9]

Jimmie Johnson was sentenced to ten years in Sing Sing Penitentiary for armed robbery and at one time served on a chain gang. Known as the "Beau Brummel" robber, he would return several days later to the scene of the crime, in suit and tie, and see if the victims recognized him. But even while awaiting trial, he had asked for a Bible and read the New Testament from cover to cover. Eventually transferred to minimum security, he began taking Moody Correspondence courses. In five years he earned twenty-two MCS diplomas and started the Scofield Reference Bible Course. In the years after his release from prison, Jimmie's wife died of alcoholism, and he

8. Will Norton, Jr., "Manhunt," *Moody Monthly* (September 1980).
9. Ibid.

Axel Bolin (right), Protestant chaplain of New Mexico State Penitentiary, confirms the impact of Moody Correspondence courses in prisons. Here he accepts the MBI Alumnus of the Year award from Tim. S. Ostrander.

eventually married a veteran missionary to France. Today they are missionaries in Chad, a French-speaking country in Africa.[10]

Axel Bolin, Protestant chaplain of New Mexico State Penitentiary, uses Moody Correspondence School courses extensively. Men readily accept them as they enter prison, says Bolin, and he has seen numerous prisoners enter the Christian ministry after their release.

The option of group study built into the Moody Correspondence School program lends itself not only to the student, but also to the one who wants to teach—and pass on Christian truth to others.

One day in 1959 a woman came to Nydia Worrall of Indianapolis and asked, "Will you teach me the Bible?"

"That's a tall order," Nydia replied, "but I'll try."

She and her husband spent their three-week vacation attending classes that summer at Moody Bible Institute. The time passed quickly, yet they hungered for more. They asked each other, "How can we keep learning and growing in the Lord?" Nydia asked Moody advisers to help her. They told her of the Moody Correspondence courses.

"Can I become a teacher?" she asked.

They answered a strong yes.

Nydia opened her home to Bible study and began to reach out into her neighborhood. Others, too, opened their homes. Seventeen years later, in 1977, when she was named Moody Correspondence School's "Outstanding Class Leader of the Year," she tallied up the number of students she had enrolled: 3,623. By then, her Bible study groups were meeting all over Indianapolis—even in a bank.

But that did not measure the full impact. As students moved away, they started their own groups—in Ohio, Texas, Florida, even Germany. "One of my students," says Nydia, "has become a public school teacher in Ecuador. I know what a beautiful Christian witness she has taken there."[11]

For evangelistic outreach, the Moody Correspondence School offers The Good News course, by William MacDonald, for less than the price of a hamburger. Under the MCS "Harvester Plan," these can be purchased at bulk discount by churches, missions, and evangelistic organizations. Other outreach courses and booklets have been used over the years at fairs, as follow-up to gospel films, in door-to-door visitation, and on college campuses.

Servicemen, too, take Moody Correspondence courses, sometimes at the encouragement of their chaplains. Lessons come regularly from those stationed abroad and at sea.

Some churches find the Moody Correspondence School courses ideal for adult electives or for a young people's Sunday school class. Other churches have essentially built evening Bible institutes around the courses. Class leaders may still do some of the teaching, but the Correspondence School course establishes the curriculum and the homework. And upon completion of the class, students earn their certificates.

Dr. Don Engram pastors the flourishing Church of the Open Door in Elyria, Ohio. There he started an Evening Bible Institute, which has now ordered more than 2,000 Moody Correspondence School courses as it reaches out to the community.

At its Howard Street offices on the northern edge of Chicago, the deeply-committed Moody Correspondence School staff processes more than 500 lessons a day. Exams flow in and out, grades are recorded. Notes in red ink encourage students or offer help where needed. Longer letters, often with booklets or other materials, go out to students grappling with complex problems. Counsel is given about enrollment, while others work on courses to be released in the future.

Amid all this, the staff finds time to rejoice when an unsaved student has trusted Christ as Savior or made some other important decision. Just as important, however, is the Christian growth the staff can detect as students pursue their studies.

Wrote a student from San Francisco of the Scofield Course: "You wouldn't understand how

10. Rosemary Rausch, "Confined to Study Scripture," *Moody Monthly* (November 1983).
11. Mary Sue Best, "Nydia's Tall Order," *Moody Monthly* (November 1981).

Don Engram, who pastors Elyria, Ohio's Church of the Open Door, orders more than 2,000 Moody Correspondence School courses to reach his community.

much that class I finished has helped me. Everyone at church wants your address because I've changed so much."

In the minds of some people, especially in years past, the correspondence school education has been looked upon as inferior. And it has sometimes been unfairly linked with the disreputable fly-by-night schools that only bilk the public. But in today's academic circles, that image is fast giving way to one that sees the correspondence school as a legitimate and growing part of the American educational scene.

Some in fact have argued that the correspondence school student is a far more serious and self-motivated one than many of those on today's typical campus. He is older, more mature, more settled and established. The time he invests in study is undiluted by campus social pursuits. Correspondence school students often turn in superior performances over those in the classroom, perhaps in part because they can proceed at their own pace until they feel they have truly learned the material, and can schedule their exams when they feel prepared.

The far-reaching ministry of the Moody Correspondence School, over the years, has attracted administrative directors of versatile talents. These included men like Dr. Phillip R. Newell, author of the gospel song "At Calvary"; Dr. Edward Curdry, who later headed the Conservatory of Music at Wheaton College; Robert Constable, who became executive vice-president of Moody Bible Institute and in his retirement continued to counsel students in the Scofield Course; the late Herbert Klingbeil; Harold Shaw, later founder of his own publishing house, and Wayne Buchanan, who left the director's position to become president of the National Sunday School Association, then later founded his own business in Nashville.

The Moody Correspondence School may well stand on the threshold of its most exciting days, especially as the dimensions of church growth overseas opens new potential to enroll thousands in Bible study by mail.

Chapter 22

MOODY AFTER HOURS

The inner campus as Chicago's Evening School crowd arrives for classes.

Twilight settles over Chicago. Most of the several hundred employees of Moody Bible Institute have long before exited the campus. Day School students and faculty have dispersed to their homes or dorm rooms. But suddenly the campus comes alive with a new influx of people carrying Bibles, notebooks, and textbooks. It is an obviously older group on the whole, yet the range could be seventeen to seventy.

These are students of the Moody Evening School who gather on the campus three nights a week. They are office workers, housewives, local pastors. They are salesmen, college students, factory workers, teachers, computer technicians. The majority are not in full-time Christian work, nor is that necessarily their goal. They simply want to pick up courses—in counseling, Bible, Christian education, and other areas—that will make them more effective in their local churches.

More than two thousand are enrolled, but they are not all on Moody's Chicago campus. Nearly five hundred can be found at a satellite evening school network in northeast Ohio— Cleveland, Youngstown, Medina. Some are in nearby suburban settings like Wheaton, Mt. Prospect, and Highland, Indiana. Other schools are in East Moline, St. Petersburg, and Boynton Beach, Florida.

The Evening School program offers a smorgasbord of nearly one hundred and fifty courses. Bible subjects are basic—Old or New Testament survey, book studies, doctrine, Bible background—but there are also classes in Christian education, missions, evangelism, sacred music, and communications. One can find courses to help him build a successful home, Sunday school, or church library. There are courses in journalism, audio-visuals, creative teaching methods. The church organist, the pastor's wife, the camp worker—all will find courses tailored for them.

More than one third of the Evening School faculty comes directly from the Moody Day School. The others are local pastors and other Christian workers who are carefully screened before given status as "special instructors."

The Evening School student enjoys the privilege of picking up courses at his own pace. He may only take a course or two in his lifetime, or he may set graduation as his goal.

One Chicago area man, employed by General Electric, attended Evening School until 9:00 two or three nights a week, even though he also arose each morning at 3:30 for work. Today he has earned his Evening School Certificate of Graduation and is working in home missions.

One woman first enrolled in Evening School in 1925. Family and other responsibilities took her away from the course until the 1970s. In 1975—fifty years later—she received her certificate.[1]

Until 1951, the curriculum of both the Day and Evening Schools was much the same. That is no longer so says Dr. Jay Fernlund, MBI's former dean of continuing education and newly appointed director of the Correspondence School. The programs today are entirely different. Day School requires ninety-two hours of instruction, while Evening School, tailored primarily for adult education, requires thirty-six.

Fernlund points to the historical change in the philosophy of the church and the church worker as the reason the Institute changed its Evening School format. "There's been a real shift in emphasis on how churches perform their ministry," he says. "When Dwight L. Moody began our school, the concept was very strong that you had a professional staff who did the church work. The pastor, the music director and his assistants performed the work of the ministry. But Moody felt that the scriptural way is for the whole church, the laypeople, to be involved. The pastor and his staff become trainers or facilitators."[2]

The change is significant, and who can measure the contribution Dwight L. Moody has made to the Protestant lay movement and voluntarism of the twentieth century? An earlier generation of churchmen might have looked askance at such a trend, but today it has become the very element of evangelical Protestantism which even much of the Roman Catholic Church admires.

While the Moody Evening School is basically lay-oriented, many people prominent in Christian circles today have MBI Evening School courses somewhere in their backgrounds. One is the late Cameron Townsend, founder of the Wycliffe Bible Translators, now the largest missionary organization in the world. Peter Deyneka, founder and director of the Slavic Gospel Assocation, with headquarters in Wheaton, attended Evening School as a young man, shortly after becoming a believer. It was there that he heard the challenge to witness to others. "Right away the Slavic speaking people were on my heart," he remembers. And thus was born a movement which now reaches into the Iron Curtain countries, by radio, with tremendous impact.

Edward Zegan, executive director of Child Evangelism for Southern California, spent one night a week for four years at Moody Evening School. "I couldn't wait to get to the Institute each night," he recalls, "the studies were so interesting and helpful." It was at Evening School, too, that he met the Chicago director of Child Evangelism Fellowship, whose encouragement led him to his present work.[3]

Many Chicago blacks have found the Moody Evening School an excellent place to ground themselves more deeply in the Scriptures and to pick up ideas in church methodology. Black church history is a part of the Moody Evening School curriculum.

The Evening School attracts people of diverse backgrounds, but the enthusiastic spirit and unity of the crowd becomes apparent as one sits in on a class or mingles with students in the

1. "Education After Hours," *Moody Alumni* (Summer 1980).
2. Ibid.
3. Calvin Biddle, "Evening Classes That Make a Difference," *Moody Monthly* (December 1974).

Students that have day jobs in secular environments find Evening School courses especially refreshing.

Coffee Cove. Common faith helps transcend the wide range of age and social backgrounds.

The story of Jesse Howard, former Chicago street gang member, is a case in point. Fifteen years before his graduation from the Moody Evening School, Jesse helped attack Moody student Richard Gleason because Gleason was moving into the gang's territory to set up a mission. Gleason wound up in the hospital, Jesse Howard in the hands of the law. Police rounded up the gang, and Gleason identified them from his hospital bed. But he refused to press charges. Instead, he secured their names for personal follow-up.

Gospel singer Mahalia Jackson learned of Gleason's plight and paid his hospital bill. When two of the gang went on trial for murder in another incident, only Gleason showed up in court to befriend them. In time Gleason brought Jesse Howard to the Lord and channeled him into the Moody Evening School.

The impact of the Evening School directly upon Chicago is overwhelming. Many students apply knowledge gained in class to their own sermons and Sunday school lessons. As can be seen in this picture, the black community is especially served by Moody's wide selection of courses.

"Before I was saved, I was always the dumbest kid in school," says Howard. That changed when he became a Christian and found new motivation. He graduated from Moody Evening School a year ahead of schedule, then went on to earn a certificate from the Illinois Institute of Banking and also one in community law from DePaul University. Today he is busy in Chicago sharing the good news of Christ, both as a sociologist and youth worker.[4]

Dwight L. Moody would have rejoiced in such reports. At his old Northside Tabernacle he had established evening school classes even before the existence of Moody Bible Institute. One purpose of such classes had been to teach new immigrants to read English by using the English Bible. "Here again," says Moody historian Dorothy Martin, "was the combination always present in Moody's work: the social and the evangelistic."

The original evening work disbanded for a few years in the 1890s, because of economic depression. But in 1903 the Evening Department became firmly established. Classes met four nights a week that first year, with about 125 students each evening. The next year the schedule changed to three nights a week. A student could complete the evening program in three years and receive the same diploma as a day school graduate, but because of the long working day in those times, it was not an easy route.

Moody Bible Institute's growing program of continuing education has other promising horizons—among them telecommunications. The Institute is already testing a program that would develop video cassettes for distribution to churches or organized extension schools.

4. "Jesse Howard—from Chicago's Gangs to MBI Graduation," *Moody Memo* (15 December 1972).

The concept of offering courses at night is not new to Moody. Dr. William Evans, the Institute's first graduate, teaches an Evening School course near the turn of the century.

Evening School students in 1935 head out to minister in their weekly assignments. This practice is still carried on in the Day and Evening Schools.

The use of visuals such as charts, diagrams, and on-location photography can make classroom teaching more precise. But beyond this, video programs could have wider application through cable television and in Theological Education by Extension on the mission field.

It is almost a century too late to capture Dwight L. Moody on videotape. But if he were on the scene today, you could be sure that he would tell someone, "Push it."

Chapter 23

FROM SANKEY TO SATELLITE

1953: The Moody Chorale, with Don Hustad conducting, sings at Easter sunrise services in the Hollywood Bowl.

The pages of a standard church hymnal abound with hymns penned by men once associated with the Moody Bible Institute—D. B. Towner, Charles Alexander, James M. Gray, and many others. Sing gospel songs like "Great Is Thy Faithfulness," "My Anchor Holds," "Trust and Obey," "I Know Whom I Have Believed," and you are singing the heritage of Moody Bible Institute.

Listen to one of today's popular cantatas—be it the Easter or Christmas season, or some other occasion—and chances are it has been written by John Peterson, Don Wyrtzen, or Larry Mayfield. All studied at the Moody Bible Institute.

Attend a Billy Graham crusade, anywhere in the world, and the organist will probably be John Innes. He too graduated from the Sacred Music program of Moody Bible Institute.

Listen to a concert of the Moody Chorale, and you will be hearing a group that has toured both America and Europe and earned an international reputation.

When asked by a newspaperman in 1890 what studies he proposed to include in his new training school, D. L. Moody listed three—study of the English Bible, evangelism, and music, "both vocal and instrumental. I believe music is one of the most powerful agents for good or for evil."[1]

Moody and Sankey created and popularized the kind of music known as the "gospel song." It was easy music to sing and

1. Getz, p. 140.

remember. The average man could relate to the gospel song's testimonial message. Yet the Moody-Sankey crusades taught the public to handle such music with dignity.

There is evidence that the New Testament church enjoyed congregational singing for the first few centuries of its existence. But with the advent of cathedrals and liturgy, the "voice of the congregation was stilled in public worship" for nearly one thousand years. It was the Protestant Reformation that freed the tongues of the congregation once more. "The same conviction which motivated Luther's translation of the Bible into the vernacular of the people," wrote the great church musician W. J. Reynolds, "also produced the desire for congregational song in the language of the common man."[2] That is why Luther is classified by some as the first "evangelical hymn writer."

As the twentieth century unfolded, Moody Bible Institute sought to upgrade the music of the church at large and to promote the church's rich heritage of majestic hymnody. It sought balance. Wrote former Sacred Music Department director Donald Hustad in 1961:

Gospel hymns are widely used in our constituent evangelical churches. And our interest in and support of them is for spiritual as well as cultural reasons. We believe the gospel hymn is a vital subjective expression of our "know-so, say-so" faith. It is our personal testimony in song, and it is effective partly because it is couched in simple words and music.

However, we are thankful that our churches are also regaining some of their lost heritage of historic hymns of worship and doctrine. I'm thankful for the example set by our church leaders here at MBI; it is not hymns *or* gospel songs, but *both*. This means spiritual, as well as musical, balance.[3]

2. Williams Jensen Reynolds, *A Survey of Christian Hymnody*, p. 17.

3. Donald Hustad, "Gospel Songs Fading?" *Moody Memo* (May 1961).

D. B. Towner takes over the Institute's music department in 1893. He eventually publishes more than 2,000 songs, among them the melody to James M. Gray's "Only a Sinner." Today's hymnbooks abound with songs written by those once associated with Moody Bible Institute.

Moody Bible Institute came into existence during a period when the gospel song had just emerged. The Moody-Sankey campaigns popularized it. Most of those songs had an "evangelistic text," a "tuneful melody," a "catchy rhythm," and "simple harmony." With Moody the key evangelist of his time, it should have been no surprise that the school he founded would shape church music for decades.

In 1889, the MBI Musical Department had as its stated aim to train students "to become singers, leaders, or organists" who could "assist evangelists and pastors, and do a work on the mission fields, both at home and abroad." Hugh H. McGranahan, nephew of famous gospel composer James McGranahan, was appointed MBI's first music director. Subjects included notation, sight reading, harmony, solo and part singing, vocal training, conducting, normal training for teachers, and composition.

When Ira Sankey began to go blind in 1884 and could no longer lead music in the campaigns, Mr. Moody had to search for a successor to the author of "The Ninety and Nine." Daniel Brink Towner, a music teacher in Cincinnati, attracted Moody's attention with his stirring solos. Towner became Moody's song leader, and for fifteen years the two lived in hotels and Pullman cars together, as they held revivals across America.

In 1893, Towner took over the Institute's music department and laid out its curriculum. "Taken as an all-around . . . teacher, conductor, soloist, composer and author," said the late E. O. Sellers, Towner's associate on the Moody music faculty, "D. B. Towner doubtless had no equal." He had every potential to develop into a concert and oratorio singer, which had been his ambition until he met Moody. "As a composer," said Sellers, "Dr. Towner is credited with over 2,000 published songs . . . He edited and published many songbooks, also a line of textbooks for his class work, and in those days they were widely used. He is gratefully remembered by literally thousands of his students now scattered in every part of the world."[4]

A list of the prominent and successful song leaders, composers, and music professors

Towner helped train includes Charles M. Alexander, J. B. Trowbridge, Harry Loes, Homer Hammontree, Dr. I. E. Reynolds, George S. Schuler, among many others. After studying at Moody, he traveled with R. A. Torrey in evangelistic work to Australia and Great Britain. "It has been published," cited Sellers, "that during the four and one half years Torrey and Alexander labored together, one hundred and fifteen thousand persons made professions of faith in Christ as the result of their work."

Some of the more familiar songs that Towner wrote included "Trust and Obey," "My Anchor Holds," "Anywhere with Jesus," "Redeemed," "Nor Silver nor Gold," "Grace That Is Greater Than Our Sins," and "For God So Loved the World." The latter was written after years of trying to find a fitting tune for that text.

D. B. Towner also wrote the music to some of the lyrics penned by James M. Gray, including the melodies for "Only a Sinner" and Moody Bible Institute's official school song. Towner served as director of the music department until just a few months before his death in 1919.

Harry Dixon Loes, who graduated from the Bible-Music course in 1915 and later returned in 1939 to teach into the 1960s, composed more than three thousand gospel songs, many of which were published and became popular in thousands of churches and Sunday schools. Two of his most well known are "Blessed Redeemer" and "All Things in Jesus."

George S. Schuler, after studying at Moody periodically from 1903 to 1906, became a member of the faculty in 1909 and taught there for forty-two years. During this time he contributed regularly to *Etude,* a music magazine, and composed a number of songs, among them "Overshadowed" and "Make Me a Blessing."

William J. Reynolds, noted Southern Baptist hymnologist whose father, George W. Reynolds, attended Moody, says, "Moody Bible Institute made a significant contribution for church music development over the last half century among Southern Baptists."[5]

4. DeRemer, p. 39.

5. Getz, pp. 156-57.

One with the Lord

FELLOWSHIP SONG

JAMES M. GRAY   D. B. TOWNER

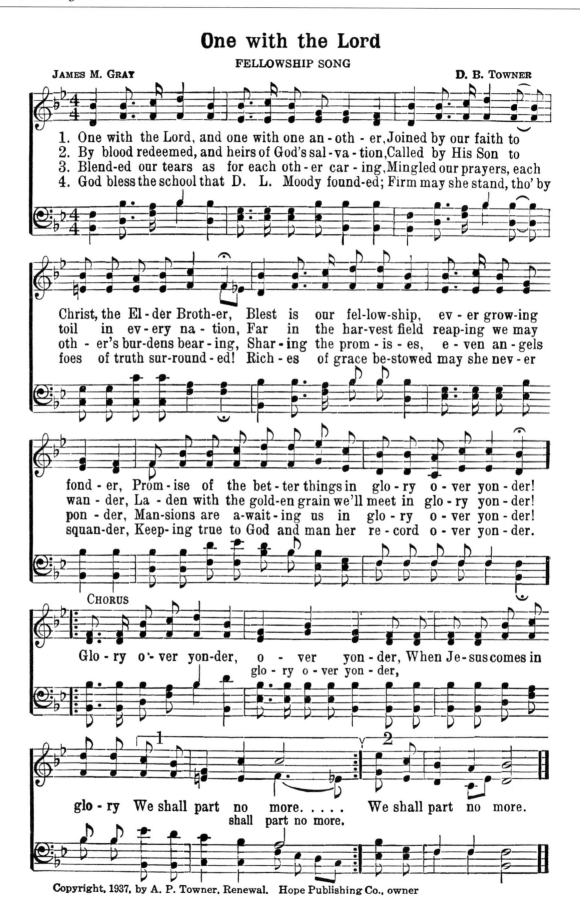

1. One with the Lord, and one with one an-oth-er, Joined by our faith to
2. By blood redeemed, and heirs of God's sal-va-tion, Called by His Son to
3. Blend-ed our tears as for each oth-er car-ing, Mingled our prayers, each
4. God bless the school that D. L. Moody found-ed; Firm may she stand, tho' by

Christ, the El-der Broth-er, Blest is our fel-low-ship, ev-er grow-ing
toil in ev-ery na-tion, Far in the har-vest field reap-ing we may
oth-er's bur-dens bear-ing, Shar-ing the prom-is-es, e-ven an-gels
foes of truth sur-round-ed! Rich-es of grace be-stowed may she nev-er

fond-er, Prom-ise of the bet-ter things in glo-ry o-ver yon-der!
wan-der, La-den with the gold-en grain we'll meet in glo-ry yon-der!
pon-der, Man-sions are a-wait-ing us in glo-ry o-ver yon-der!
squan-der, Keep-ing true to God and man her re-cord o-ver yon-der.

CHORUS

Glo-ry o-ver yon-der, o-ver yon-der, When Je-sus comes in
glo-ry o-ver yon-der,

glo-ry We shall part no more..... We shall part no more.
shall part no more.

Copyright, 1937, by A. P. Towner, Renewal. Hope Publishing Co., owner

Avis B. Christiansen wrote the lyrics to such songs as "Fill All My Vision" (music by Homer Hammontree), "Only One Life" (music by Merrill Dunlop), and "Love Found a Way."

T. J. Bittikofer authored "Complete in Thee." E. O. Sellers wrote "Wonderful, Wonderful Jesus" and "Thy Word Have I Hid in My Heart." William M. Runyan wrote the music to "Great Is Thy Faithfulness." George C. Stebbins originated the music for "Jesus Is Calling" and "Take Time to Be Holy." Al Smith is compiler of the hymnal *Living Hymns,* released in 1972. It contains more than seventy of his own numbers, among them "My Father Planned It All" and choruses like "For God So Loved the World" and "Isn't He Wonderful?"

James M. Gray wrote the words of MBI's school song, D. B. Towner the music. The melody is familiar to young and old alumni alike.

George Schuler teaches music at Moody for forty-two years and pens such songs as "Overshadowed" and "Make Me a Blessing."

Merrill Dunlop, long owner of his own music publishing firm, wrote the music to "Only One Life" and "He Was Wounded for Our Transgressions" and both words and music to "My Sins Are Blotted Out, I Know!" Eugene Clark, with Back to the Bible Broadcast, wrote over fifty gospel songs (among them "Nothing Is Impossible") and four cantatas. Though blind and bedfast the last seventeen years of his life, he continued to write music by using a dictating machine. He produced twenty record albums, and his choral arrangement books sold more than 200,000 copies.

All these men were associated with the Moody Bible Institute.

In 1928, MBI expanded its music course to three years and added such subjects as advanced theory, counterpoint, history of music, and hymnology. The intent was twofold: to turn out a "finished product" and to reverse what the Institute saw as a deteriorating trend in church music. Men like Sankey, Stebbins, Bliss, and others of like caliber had handled the gospel song with dignity, but the same was not true of some who followed. James M. Gray analyzed it as "a case of smaller men copying a master and, as is not unusual, making that sometimes ridiculous which he [Sankey] made an art."[6]

In 1930 the Institute created a combined Christian Education/Music course major. Gray defined the rationale:

> There are many churches today in smaller towns and with limited budgets, which desire a director of church music and also a director of religious education, but which cannot afford both. Could they obtain the two in one their need would be met, and to meet this need is one of our objectives.[7]

When Moody Bible Institute moved from the term to the semester plan in 1951, the Sacred Music course was expanded again to include four programs of study: piano, organ, voice, and composition. With creation now of the Department of Sacred Music, other music courses appeared—among them music theory, choral conducting, survey of music literature, music in the church service, advanced sight singing, sight playing, choral compositions, survey of music

history, plus training in any of the orchestral instruments. By 1966, students could earn a Bachelor of Arts or a Bachelor of Sacred Music degree by combining Moody study with additional college and university work. In the 1950s, recitals became a curricular requirement for all music students.

The stage was set, now, for the meteoric rise of the Moody Chorale.

Choral groups had been a part of Institute life since before the turn of the century—including a male chorus and a ladies' chorus. But they were designed to help students develop their voices, not to give regular public performance—at least not until 1921. At that time Dr. James M. Gray had started holding services every Sunday afternoon in the Moody Bible Institute auditorium—an event designed as a model to teach pastors how to conduct a service properly. He asked Guy Latchaw of the music faculty to form a choir from the student body, a group that promptly became known as the "Auditorium Choir." A quarter-century later, in 1946, under James Davies, its name was changed to the Moody Chorale.

Moody was the first school in the United States—Christian or secular—to attach the name "chorale" to its choral group. The next year it took its first extended tour. Within little more than a decade it would become one of the most outstanding and well-known choral groups in the religious world.

The Moody Chorale climbed into international prominence under the directorship of Donald Hustad, who joined the Institute's faculty in 1947. Cross-country Easter tours became standard. In 1953, the Moody Chorale sang in Easter sunrise services at the Hollywood Bowl. The next year it made its first European tour. It returned there four years later. In 1958, the Moody Chorale sang in scores of churches and auditoriums in several European countries to a total audience of 65,000. It also released its first recording, "O for a Thousand Tongues," produced by Word Records.

6. Donald P. Hustad, "Problems in Psychology and Aesthetics in Music," *Bibliothecra Sacra* (July 1960), p. 216.
7. Getz, p. 142.

A flutist concentrates on her music. After attaining international stature with the Moody Chorale, the Institute adds two glee clubs, a handbell choir, a concert band, and an orchestra. The groups travel cross-country and also abroad.

By this time the Moody Bible Institute was spinning off other choral groups as well—a Women's Glee Club in 1957, a Men's Glee Club in 1958. They too began making cross-country tours. The Institute could send each one in a different direction, expanding its musical coverage and ministry into as many as twenty or more states on simultaneous tours.

Winter and Easter tours provided great opportunity for singing groups to share their faith not only in churches and auditoriums, but also in homes and on buses. Even bus drivers came to personal confessions of the Savior. One year, as the Moody Chorale was leaving the Grand Canyon on a sightseeing sidetrip, the bus driver took the microphone, interrupted informal singing, and announced that his life was not right with God. He asked the group to pray with him. Two weeks later the Chorale flew him to Chicago for their annual home concert. The concert crowd was moved by the genuine quality of the bus driver's testimony.

By 1963, the Women's Glee Club, now also with a Handbell Choir, traveled abroad, giving fifty concerts in England, Scotland, Ireland, and Wales, and closing with concerts in Paris. In London, the girls presented a concert at the Whitechapel Foundry, where their handbells had been made. It was the first time some of the workers had ever heard a choir use the bells the foundry so carefully crafted.

While director of Moody Bible Institute's Department of Sacred Music, Don Hustad, well known for his arrangements, also helped edit the *Worship and Service Hymnal*, a major contribution to the churches of America. Used by almost every

Protestant denomination, this book soon sold over a million copies. Hustad left Moody Bible Institute to travel worldwide as organist for the Billy Graham crusades. Today he is professor of church music at the Southern Baptist Theological Seminary in Louisville.

Construction in the mid-fifties of the four-story William H. Doane Memorial Music Building, along with adjacent Torrey-Gray Auditorium, proved a gigantic step in Moody Bible Institute's music program. It incorporated the latest in acoustical and architectural planning. It contained thirty-eight practice rooms, four classrooms, thirteen studios, a music library, two choir robing rooms, and administrative offices.

William Howard Doane rose from bookkeeper to become president of the J.A. Fay Company, serving in Connecticut and Chicago. In a serious bout with heart disease as a young man, he vowed to commit his musical talents to the Lord if the Lord spared his life. God did heal him, and over the next fifty-two years Doane wrote more than 2,300 compositions, many of them in collaboration with the blind hymnwriter, Fanny Crosby. His most famous is "To God Be the Glory."[8]

Doane was never officially associated with the Moody Bible Institute, but a generous memorial gift from the estate of his daughter made possible the much-needed music building. It also bought the four-manual, sixty-four-rank Möller organ in Torrey-Gray Auditorium. With 4,000 pipes, it is one of the largest pipe organs in Chicago. Doane Memorial houses four other pipe organs and seventy pianos, including eighteen grands.

Other major musical groups emerged at Moody as the program grew, first an orchestra, then a concert band. In 1975, music from Moody was heard from Maracaiba to Honolulu as the Concert Band toured Venezuela and the Men's Glee Club sang its way around Hawaii. In Latin America, public officials joined standing-room-only crowds. Four band students spoke Spanish well enough to share their Christian testimonies in the language of the people.

In 1976, the Women's Glee Club and Handbell Choir, under Robert Carbaugh, toured the British Isles for a second time—Ireland, Scotland, England, Wales, then France.

The next year, in 1977, Dr. Sweeting and the Moody Chorale toured Europe in a concert itinerary that took them into the Netherlands, Belgium, England, West Germany, Austria, and France. In Holland, they performed live via the Dutch Television Network, and in Heidelberg, West Germany, they sang at the largest American army base chapel.

Each of the choirs perform some fifty concerts a year. But there are special events on the campus as well.

During the Christmas season, for instance, Moody's Oratorio Chorus sings Handel's Messiah, plus another major choral work in the spring. The 250-voice Oratorio Chorus comprises nearly 20 percent of the student body. In addition, the annual "Candlelight Carols," which also involves all choral groups, concert band, and orchestra, has had to move from two concerts to three in order to accommodate more than six thousand who drive from as far as Indiana, Wisconsin, and Michigan to hear it. Home concerts, graduation concerts, Founder's Week, and other special events add to the schedule.

The 1970s saw at least two great "Festivals of Praise" at off-campus locations, two at Chicago's historic, seven-tiered Auditorium Theatre and one at McCormick Place. The groups have also staged May noon-hour outdoor concerts in Chicago's Daley Center plaza, by arrangement with City Hall.

Students use their musical talents almost weekly, of course, in their churches, or in other practical Christian ministries. The nearby presence of WMBI gives some of the more talented students radio experience—as accompanists or as participants in ensembles.

The Institute's location gives students convenient access to world-famous musicians and musical groups—both sacred and secular—at places like Orchestra Hall, Grant Park, the University of Chicago, Northwestern University, and Ravinia Park. One Moody graduate, Kathleen

8. *Moody Memo* (12 March 1982).

John W. Peterson, *publisher of many choral cantatas and more than a thousand gospel songs.*

Lund, has played for ten years in the Grant Park Symphony.

Moody Bible Institute encourages exposure to the classics, and students often learn to master the works of great composers. Guest artist concerts have brought to the campus such figures as organist Virgil Fox, harpsichordist Dorothy Lane, and basso Jerome Hines of the New York Metropolitan Opera.

In the late 1940s, a Moody student sold ten songs for forty dollars to radio evangelist Percy Crawford. One of those songs was "It Took a Miracle." The composer was John W. Peterson.

Peterson later flew one hundred flights over the Himalaya Mountains during World War II. It gave him many lonely hours to view the world's tallest mountains and contemplate God's protection, no matter what the circumstances. Although "It Took a Miracle" was eventually recorded by well-known performers, including Kate Smith and Eddie Arnold, Peterson recalls his time in Chicago as the period when he and his wife, Marie, lived in a series of one-room apartments. While at the Institute he worked at WMBI and continued to write songs.

Singspiration's Don Wyrtzen—*composer, arranger, pianist and publisher.*

Composer/arranger Larry Mayfield, *who also studied at Moody.*

Moody's Oratorio Chorus, in a performance of Handel's Messiah, *offers a glimpse of the Institute's musical depth.*

Moody's Concert Band performing at Moody Church under its founder, Gerald Edmonds. The band is now under the direction of Henry Hecht, who at one time played for and conducted the United States Navy Band.

John Innes, who for many years has been organist for the Billy Graham crusades.

John Peterson worked with several music publishers and went on to become president of Singspiration in 1963 (he now has his own company, Good Life Productions). In his forty-five year career he has published many choral cantatas and more than a thousand gospel songs—among them "Jesus Is Coming Again," "Springs of Living Water," "So Send I You," "Over the Sunset Mountains," "I Believe in Miracles," "Surely Goodness and Mercy," and "Heaven Came Down and Glory Filled My Soul."[9]

Don Wyrtzen, concert artist, composer, arranger, and one of today's leading spokesmen in Christian music, has arranged and composed over 200 anthems and sacred songs, including such favorites as "Yesterday, Today and Tomorrow," "Love Was When," and "Worthy Is the Lamb." As director of music publications at Singspiration Music in Grand Rapids, Michigan, Wyrtzen

lectures widely on church music in many of the major Christian universities and seminaries in America.

Christian music has undergone some major changes in recent years.

"High technology," says Gerald Raquet, chairman of the Department of Sacred Music, "has made music, including church music, more available. We now have digital recordings, and soon we will have laser recordings. Recordings are inexpensive, and people listen to music almost constantly."

Raquet sees another frontier in the study of ethnomusicology—the study of the music of other cultures. It is obviously of importance to those who would communicate the gospel on the mission field.

"We are looking forward to accreditation by the National Association of Schools of Music for our diploma program," says Raquet. "A record album for the 1985-86 centennial is in production. We hope to remodel North Hall to provide a large recital hall and rehearsal room. And we look forward to extending the music ministry of Moody Bible Institute by satellite."

The music of Moody has come a long way—from Sankey to satellite. But its basic message, and its musical basics, have not changed.

Ira Sankey knew the power of song. But he saw its greatest power in his own singing only when he backed it in prayer "with the same earnestness," writes composer Al Smith, "that he would have used had he been called to be a preacher." When he did so, Sankey acquired a style with convincing power about it.

As Moody musicians seek that same convincing power, and tap modern technology, the gospel in music will continue to move the hearts and minds of men in America—and to the far corners of the earth.

9. "Music Is Ministry" (Winter 1980-81).

Moody Bible Institute, rising in the foreground, looks out
to the world around it.

Chapter 24

A CENTURY IN CHRIST'S SERVICE

G od had His hand on the life of Dwight L. Moody. It is also clear that God has had his hand on the Chicago institution that Moody founded.

In his book *The Story of Moody Bible Institute,* Gene Getz has analyzed, from a human perspective, why Moody Bible Institute became so influential. He presents several factors:

Its strategic location. When Dwight L. Moody, on impulse, hopped a train to Chicago on that day in 1857, that move ultimately decided the geographical location of the school he later founded. The choice of site turned out to be not only strategic, but timely. It might have seemed otherwise when the great Chicago fire, in only a matter of hours, turned Moody's church, his home, and his city mission field to ashes. But no fire could stop Moody. It was simply another open door for the gospel, and he was one of the first to lead the forces of rehabilitation. Within only months, a new city rose from the ashes. In ten years it would have a population of one-half million, and by 1890 more than one million. The World's Fair came to Chicago in 1893, and Moody, mobilizing the Christians of Chicago and the forces of his newly-established Chicago Evangelization Society, stepped into the midst of that international event. From its earliest years, the school was in the right place at the right time.

An urgent objective. The Moody Bible Institute was born in an era of widespread concern about the nation's urban crisis. In Chicago, conflict between management and labor had boiled over into the Haymarket Riot of 1886.

"Chicago's large immigrant population," noted one analyst, "also included a nucleus of men nurtured on anarchism and Marxian dialectics then spreading over Europe." "Either these people are to be evangelized," said Moody in March 1886, "or the leaven of communism and infidelity will assume such enormous proportions that it will break out in a reign of terror such as this country has never known."[1] Moody had enough faith to believe that the gospel could help to defuse the crisis, right wrongs, and reverse ominous trends. But it would have to start, he believed, with the conversion of individual citizens.

A well-known founder. Dwight L. Moody had become an international figure long before the official birth of the Moody Bible Institute. He could innovate, and he could implement. "Moody's ideas and ventures," Getz points out, "did not have a history of failure."[2] So if D. L. Moody proposed a school in Chicago, the Christian public reasoned that it must be worth backing.

Many important friends. From the school's outset, Moody drew top people of Chicago's business realm into the school's circle of earnest supporters. Cyrus McCormick, T. W. Harvey, John Farwell, and other men of their caliber constituted the Institute's first board of trustees. After Moody's death, the Institute could no longer rely on keeping the Moody Bible Institute afloat primarily on the large financial gifts of a few. But such names helped give the Institute early respect as a religious institution. The evangelist's many

1. Getz, p. 49.
2. Ibid., pp. 49-50.

contacts also brought some of the world's greatest Bible scholars to his school's Chicago campus. "These men," says Getz, "became outstanding 'publicity agents' as they left the premises of the institute and traveled back to their native states and countries."[3]

An interdenominational venture. Moody had no use for needless schism and narrow sectarianism. By design he refused to identify, in membership, with any single denomination, or even to become ordained, so that he might minister with freedom to all. He cooperated with a broad spectrum of the evangelical churches of his time, especially as he helped lead the great Sunday school convention era to its peak in 1886 and as he brought mission agencies closer together. As a result, Moody Bible Institute, from its outset, attracted students from a great

evangelical spectrum and fed its graduates back into countless denominations and Christian agencies.

MBI dared to teach the Bible as the authoritative Word of God. As the fundamentalist-liberal theological controversy grew, especially after the turn of the century, Moody Bible Institute positioned itself firmly as the defender of historic evangelical theology and an inerrant Bible. Yet it did so on the basis of solid biblical scholarship from the pens and lips of men like R. A. Torrey and James M. Gray. Thus its own graduates were solidly grounded as they went forth. Such influence prompted church observer Jasper Mossee to write in 1923, "In my judgment, the constituency that has gone out

3. Ibid., p. 51.

from the Moody Bible Institute during the last ten years has saved the evangelical churches of the country."[4]

MBI dared to innovate. Dwight Moody himself set the pace as one who dared to innovate and pioneer. Those who later picked up the torch pioneered as well—in Christian education, in Christian radio, in gospel science films, in missionary aviation. All of this helped to establish Moody as an institution of influence.

But even all of those factors are inadequate, apart from recognition that behind it all lies God's sovereign design and plan. By design God sent His Son into the world to bring salvation to all who will respond. By design God raises up men and institutions to spread that good news. He uses people who admittedly have "feet of clay," yet the plan and the mission is no less divine.

Today Moody Bible Institute looks back not simply to bask in past glories, but to understand more fully what God has done. It looks back also in order to plot the future with intelligence and spiritual insight—to know the mind of God in these times. The start of its second century looms even more exciting, and more demanding, than its first. On the threshold of a new era, Dr. Sweeting has asked alumni and Christians across the nation and around the world to pray that "a sense of *urgency* would characterize all we do at the Moody Bible Institute."

Dwight L. Moody knew that sense of urgency.

Woodrow Wilson, while president of Princeton, sat in a barber shop one day when another customer entered and sat in the chair next to him.

"Every word that he uttered," said the man who would later become president of the United States, "showed a personal and vital interest in the man who was serving him; and before I got through with what was being done to me, I was aware that I had attended an evangelistic service, because Mr. Moody was in the next chair."

By the time Moody walked out the door, observed Wilson, he had changed the climate of the shop. The barbers, he said, "talked in undertones. They did not know his name, but they knew that something had elevated their thought."

Moody focused on individuals and at the same time moved the masses—and even the world.

Dwight L. Moody would want nothing more than to see the Bible institute he founded continue on with that same urgency of spirit—proclaiming the gospel of Jesus Christ everywhere: Teaching the Word, and reaching the world.

4. Rollin Lynde Hart, "The War in the Churches," *The World Book* (September 1923), p. 472.

Dr. Sweeting kneels at the grave of Dwight L. Moody in Northfield, Massachusetts. After a century Moody's legacy continues to grow, but the Institute's greatest years may yet lie head.

**MOODY
BIBLE
INSTITUTE**

**BOARD OF
TRUSTEES**

Robert G. Dunlop
Tequesta, Florida

Dr. John Elsen
Evanston, Illinois

Richard E. Gildner
Mason City, Iowa

Edgar A. Harrell
Rock Island, Illinois

Edward L. Johnson
San Marino, California

Paul H. Johnson
Birmingham, Michigan

Dr. John MacArthur, Jr.
Canyon Country, California

James N. Mathias
Wheaton, Illinois

William F. Mitchell, Sr.
Boca Raton, Florida

Roy Nyholm
Spokane, Washington

Wallace L. Pepin
Willoughby, Ohio

Dr. George Sweeting
Chicago, Illinois

E. Richard Tallmadge
Barrington, Illinois

Gerrit Wit
Glen Ellyn, Illinois

MBI Management

CABINET

Dr. George Sweeting—President
Mr. Donald Hescott—Executive Vice President and General Manager
Mr. Marvin Beckman—Vice President, General Counsel, and Manager of Investments
Mr. Brandt Gustavson—Vice President and Administrator of Development
Dr. Kenneth Hanna—Vice President and Dean of Education
Mr. Donald Leach—Vice President and Treasurer
Mr. Frederick Rudy—Vice President of Administrative Services

Managers

Mr. James Adams—Moody Institute of Science
Mr. Gary Canaday—Facilities Management & Planning
Mr. Charles Connon—Controller
Mr. Kenneth Epp—Dean of Enrollment Management
Dr. Brent Garrison—Dean of Student Services
Mr. James Gwinn—Division of Public Ministries
Mr. Jerry Jenkins—Publishing Division
Mr. Robert Neff—Broadcasting Division
Dr. Richard Patterson—Dean of Continuing Education
Mr. David Stewart—Information Systems
Dr. Howard Whaley—Academic Dean

Directors

Mr. Donald Barber—Headmaster, Keswick Christian School
Miss Betty Burdick—Constituency Services
Mr. Bruce Cain—Audio Visual
Mr. Donald Cole—Radio Pastor
Mr. Charles Davis—Distribution
Mr. Jim Dillon—Engineering Services
Mr. Lloyd Dodson—Personnel
Dr. Jay Fernlund—Correspondence School
Miss Barbara Goodwin—Moody Retail
Mr. Raymond Lahikainen—Visual Arts
Mr. Bill Leber—Construction Services
Mr. John Maddex—Broadcast Stations
Mr. Delmar Mohler—Treasury Operations
Mr. Victor Nischik—Accounting
Mr. Timothy Ostrander—Alumni
Mr. Gerald Raquet—Sacred Music
Dr. Leonard Rascher—Practical Christian Ministries
Mr. Daniel Redka—Service
Mr. Dick Reed—Moody Keswick Bible Conference
Mr. Marvin Rhodes—Buildings and Grounds
Mr. Richard Schock—Library
Mr. Robert Shackelford—Student Development
Mr. Wayne Shepherd—Programming
Mr. Ken Simmelink—Missionary Aviation
Mr. Alan Terwilleger—Food Service
Mr. Philip Van Wynen—Registrar & Director of Student Records
Mr. Jim Wick—Public Relations

APPENDIX A:
DOCTRINAL STATEMENT

Article I

God is a Person who has revealed Himself as a Trinity in unity, Father, Son and Holy Spirit—three Persons and yet but one God (Deut. 6:4; Matt. 28:19; 1 Cor. 8:6).

Article II

The Bible, including both the Old and New Testaments, is a divine revelation, the original autographs of which were verbally inspired by the Holy Spirit (II Tim. 3:16, II Pet. 1:21).

Article III

Jesus Christ is the image of the invisible God, which is to say, He is Himself very God; He took upon Him our nature, being conceived by the Holy Ghost and born of the Virgin Mary; He died upon the cross as a substitutionary sacrifice for the sin of the world; He arose from the dead in the body in which He was crucified; He ascended into heaven in that body glorified, where He is now, our interceding High Priest: He will come again personally and visibly to set up His Kingdom and to judge the quick and the dead (Col. 1:15; Phil. 2:5-8; Matt. 1:18-25; I Pet. 2:24, 25; Luke 24; Heb. 4:14-16; Acts 1:9-11; I Thess. 4:16-18; Matt. 25-31-46; Rev. 11:15-17; 20:4-6, 11-15).

Article IV

Man was created in the image of God but fell into sin, and, in that sense, is lost; this is true of all men, and except a man be born again he cannot see the kingdom of God; salvation is by grace through faith in Christ who His own self bare our sins in His own body on the tree; the retribution of the wicked and unbelieving and the reward of the righteous are everlasting, and as the reward is conscious, so is the retribution (Gen. 1:26, 27; Rom. 3:10, 23; John 3:3; Acts 13:38, 39; 4:12; John 3:16; Matt. 25:46; II Cor. 5:1; II Thess. 1:7-10).

Article V

The Church is an elect company of believers baptized by the Holy Spirit into one body; its mission is to witness concerning its Head, Jesus Christ, preaching the gospel among all nations; it will be caught up to meet the Lord in the air ere He appears to set up His kingdom (Acts 2:41; 15:13-17; Eph. 1:3-6; I Cor. 12:12, 13, Matt. 28:19, 20; Acts 1:6-8; Thess. 4:16-18).

The LaSalle Drive frontage of Moody Bible Institute.

Appendix B:
Buildings and Grounds

1889 Purchased vacant lot at 80 West Pearson Street (later 153 Institute Place)
Purchased three houses at 228-32 LaSalle Avenue (now 812-18 North LaSalle Street)

1889-90 Construction of three-story 153 Building; dedicated January 16, 1890

1892 Two more stories added to the 153 Building

1893 Purchased east lot at 152 Institute Place

1897 Purchased three more houses on LaSalle Avenue

1901 Purchased property at 242 LaSalle Avenue (now 826 North LaSalle Street)

1907 Purchased west lot at 152 Institute Place

1909 Constructed men's dormitory at 152 Institue Place (later Norton Hall)

1910 Constructed women's dormitory at 830 North LaSalle Street (Smith Hall)

1911 Purchased property at 820-24 North LaSalle Street

1916 Purchased property at 158 Institute Place, 828 North LaSalle, 116 West Chestnut

1917 Purchased property at 118-20 West Chestnut

1918 Purchased Moody Church at corner of Chicago and LaSalle
Purchased Guild House at 150-52 Chicago Avenue

1920 Purchased property at 900-902 North LaSalle, 148 West Locust (sold in 1951), 904-6 North Wells

1922 Purchased property at 829-33 North Wells

1923 Purchased property at 29 East Division, 159 West Chestnut (Flat Building), 153 West Chestnut, 843-45, 837-41 North Wells (Ransom Hall and annex), 161, 163-73 West Chestnut (Houston Row), 835 North Wells

1925 Purchased property at 154 West Locust

1927 Purchased property in Addison, Illinois

1927-28 Constructed radio building in Addison, Illinois

1930 Purchased property at 848 North LaSalle

1935 Purchased property at 1032 North LaSalle (sold in 1950)

1937-39 Constructed the twelve-story Administrative Building at 820 North LaSalle; dedicated February 4, 1939 (renamed Crowell Hall in 1945)

1938-39 Constructed the basement of Torrey-Gray Auditorium

1946 Leased space at the Elmhurst Airport and constructed a Quonset hangar

1947 Puchased the rest of the block area along Chicago Avenue, Wells Street, and Institute Place (included sixteen stores and sixty-four apartments) Cleared for parking space in 1953

1950 Moved airport facilities to the Wood Dale Airport

1950-51 Constructed ten-story women's dormitory, Houghton Hall, at corner of Chicago and LaSalle Dedicated October 30, 1951

1954 Took full possession of the Wood Dale Airport
Purchased the Butler Building for MIS in Los Angeles, California

1954-55 Completed Torrey-Gray Auditorium and Doane Memorial Music Building
Dedicated February 1, 1955

1955 Purchased property at 152-54, 158-60 West Chestnut
Rented property and opened South Side Bookstore

1957 Rented Cleveland property for radio station WCRF-FM

1958 Purchased Bank of America Building in Los Angeles, California

1959 Purchased property at 162-64 West Chestnut
Purchased building at 24-26 East Adams in Chicago "Loop"
Razed three top floors in 1959 and opened for bookstore business on May 2, 1960
Leased Moline property and constructed own building for radio station WDLM
Rented property and opened Des Plaines Bookstore

1960 Purchased five-story building at 828-36 North Wells for Moody Press storage

1960-62 Constructed four-story academic building, Fitzwater Hall.

1965 Purchased property in Whittier, California, for Moody Institute of Science

1967 Acquired airport property at Elizabethton, Tennessee

1968-69 Constructed twenty-story men's dormitory, William Culbertson Hall, at corner of Chicago and Wells

1968 Purchased former Masonic Temple on North LaSalle (renamed North Hall)

1971 Construction of new student Dining Hall beneath upper plaza

1973 Remodeled Smith Hall for offices, student housing

1974 Acquired new Norton Building at 2101 W. Howard St. from A. C. Nielson Co.

1975 Purchased Moody Press Distribution Center at Northbrook, Illinois.

1977 Purchased Brittany Terrace Nursing Home on LaSalle (renamed Dryer Hall)

1978 Bill and Marge Caldwell donate to the Institute Southern Keswick Ministries in St. Petersburg, Florida. Valued at more than three million dollars, the property includes a beautiful Christian conference grounds, two radio stations (WKES and WGNB) and a K-12 Christian school.

1980 Sold Osborne Hall, Osborn Row, Chestnut Street

1983 Purchased lots between Wells and Franklin streets for athletic field and future projects

1984 Acquired three bookstores in Charleston, West Virginia, donated by Bill and Sylvia Stevens

APPENDIX C:
WMBI MILESTONES

1926

July 28
WMBI begins broadcasting on a wavelength of 288.3 meters, pioneering as an educational and religious station

September 19
Miss Edna Johnson organizes the KYB Club

September 21
Radio School of the Bible originates

October 1
Wendell P. Loveless transfers from the Extension Department to Radio, as program director and chief announcer

1927

February 1-5
First broadcast of a Founder's Week conference brings a wide response from listeners

March 12
Special test program 1:00 to 3:00 A.M. brings letters and wires from almost every state in the union, including six from California. WMBI was then only 500 watts

June 15
WMBI begins operating at 1140 kc dividing time with Chicago radio station WJAZ

1928

January 20
Dedication broadcast of a new 5,000 watt transmitter at Addison, Illinois

October 7
WMBI assigned a new frequency of 1080 kc, sharing limited time with WCBD in Zion, Illinois

1929

First Letter Week is held to encourage listeners to comment on WMBI programming

1939

First course in radio broadcasting added to the Moody Bible Institute curriculum

January 8
First broadcast from new tower studios in Crowell Hall

1941

March 4
FCC grants permission for construction of an FM station

March 29
WMBI changes frequencies from 1080 to the present 1110 kc, still dividing time locally with WCBD for several months

July 6
Full daytime operation begins

1943

October 1
Moody Bible Institute begins operating the first non-commercial religious FM station in the country, W75C

1950

Tapes are put into use, allowing editing of programs and greatly improving sound

1958

November 23
WCRF begins FM operation in Cleveland

1960

April 3
  WDLM, East Moline, Illinois, goes on the air

July 25
  WMBI-FM is reactivated, receiving a non-commercial educational license for 90.1 hr. mHz

1964

May 26
  WMBI wins the 16th Alfred P. Sloan Radio-TV award at the Waldorf-Astoria, New York City

1965

July 28
  WMBI-FM puts into operation a new transmitter, boosting its FM power to 100,000 watts

1972

October 9
  WMBI-FM begins broadcasting many programs in stereo

1973

July 1
  MBI's voice in the south, WMBW, begins FM operation in Chattanooga

July 28
  WMBI's newly remodeled stereo studios are dedicated

1974

January 1

WMBI-FM begins operating twenty-four hours a day

January 5
  WMBI begins weekly Spanish programming

July 1
  KMBI-AM-FM, Spokane, goes on the air

1976

July 28
  WMBI celebrates fifty years of transmitting

1978

January 1
  Southern Keswick Ministries in St. Petersburg, Florida, is donated to the Moody Bible Institute, including WKES and WGNB

1979

January 20
  WDLM begins FM in East Moline, Illinois

April 15
  WRMB begins FM operation in Boynton Beach, Florida

1981

April 28
  MBI board of trustees approves launch of new satellite radio ministry.

1982

May 1
  Moody Broadcasting Network commences twenty-four hour a day service to the continental U.S.

APPENDIX D:
MIS HISTORICAL HIGHLIGHTS

1945 MIS becomes a part of the total ministry of Moody Bible Institute, beginning in West Los Angeles with four employees

1946 "God of Creation" released as the first Sermons from Science film

1947 Foreign Film Committees established in England and Mexico (eleven committees presently assist in the foreign ministry)

1948 Sermons from Science films placed in U.S. military chaplains' programs

1949 First foreign versions, *God of Creation* translated into nine languages

1952 Filmstrip production begins with Christian education emphasis, "Successful Teacher Training" series

1953 Education Film division launched with two films, *How Many Stars?* and *Human Machine*

1955 Film rental libraries established throughout the U.S. and Canada

1956 MIS begins television ministry with 1,800 programs scheduled on network television

1957 *Red River of Life,* a Sermons from Science film, now translated into thirteen languages and used in forty-eight countries, gives medical science its first opportunity to study heart valves as they perform in normal, low, and high blood pressure conditions

1962 Seattle World's Fair—417,000 attend the Sermons from Science Pavilion

1963 MIS receives its first international award for *City of the Bees*

1964 New York World's Fair attracts 1.3 million people

1965 MIS moves from Los Angeles to Whittier

1967 Montreal World's Fair attracts 820,000

A high speed color processing laboratory is installed, and the equipment is used to print and process an average of 2.5 million feet of film per year

1968 Foreign television ministry launched in Latin America and twenty-two countries view Sermons from Science films in Spanish and Portuguese

1969 MIS announces twenty-fifth anniversary project: Operation Mobile Missionary

1970 MIS celebrates twenty-five years of ministry

1972 Sermons from Science films shown at the XX Olympiad in Munich; shown in all five official languages, the effort produces decisions for Christ from thirty-five countries

1973 Dr. George Sweeting narrates his first Sermons from Science film *Empty Cities*

1974 Spokane World's Fair exhibit draws 390,000

1975 MIS 30th anniversary *Where the Waters Run* and *In the Beginning . . . God* released

1976 Thousands are reached through films and live demonstrations at the XXI Olympiad in Montreal; *To the Unknown God* released

1977 First Moody films transmitted via satellite, *Survivor Number Three* released

1978 MIS films penetrate the Iron Curtain

1979 MIS educational films (five titles) approved for use in science classroom of the People's Republic of China

1980 MIS thirty-fifth anniversary Dr. Irwin A. Moon honored by the Society of Motion Picture and Television Engineers with the presentation of the prestigious Eastman Kodak Gold

Medal Award; in Detroit, Sermons from Science help celebrate 200th anniversary of the Sunday school in America

1981 MIS produces its first series with Dr. John MacArthur, Jr.—*The Family: God's Pattern for Living*

1982 Sermons from Science films begin a witness in China and Israel

1983 Trustees approve installation of video production studio

1984 First shipment of Moody films to major universities in China

1985 MIS celebrates fortieth anniversary and releases "The Journey of Life," a film on seed dispersal.

Moody Institute of Science headquarters at Whittier, California.

BIBLIOGRAPHY

BOOKS

Alumni Directory, Moody Alumni Association (1981-82).

Appleby, David P. *History of Church Music.* Chicago: Moody, 1965.

Bailey, Albert E. *The Gospel in Hymns.* New York: Scribner's, 1950.

Bailey, Faith Coxe. *D. L. Moody—The Valley and the World.* Chicago: Moody, 1959.

Benson, Clarence H. *A Popular History of Christian Education.* Chicago: Moody, 1943.

Blanchard, Frances C. *Life of Charles Albert Blanchard.* New York: Revell, 1932.

Bradford, Gamaliel. *D.L. Moody—A Worker in Souls.* New York: Doran.

Cairns, Earle E. *Christianity in the United States.* Chicago: Moody, 1964.

Chapman, John Wilbur. *The Life and Work of Dwight L. Moody.* Philadelphia: Winston, 1900.

Daniels, W. H. *D. L. Moody and His Work.* Hartford: 1876.

Day, Richard Ellsworth. *Breakfast Table Autocrat.* Chicago: Moody, 1946.

————. *Bush Aglow.* Philadelphia: Judson, 1936.

DePlata, William R. *Tell It from Calvary.* New York: Calvary Baptist Church, 1972.

DeRemer, Bernard R. *Moody Bible Institute: A Pictorial History.* Chicago: Moody, 1960.

Drummond, Henry. *Dwight L. Moody.* New York: McClure, Phillips, 1900.

Eavey, Charles B. *History of Christian Education.* Chicago: Moody, 1964.

Erdman, Charles R. *D. L. Moody—His Message for Today.* New York: Revell, 1928.

Farwell, John V. *Early Recollections of Dwight L. Moody.* Chicago: Winona Publishing, 1907.

Findlay, James F. *Dwight L. Moody—American Evangelist.* Chicago: University of Chicago, 1969.

Fitt, A. P. *Moody Still Lives.* New York: Revell, 1936.

————. *The Life of D. L. Moody.* Chicago: Moody, 1982.

Flood, Robert. *America, God Shed His Grace on Thee.* Chicago: Moody, 1975.

Gasper, Louis. *The Fundamentalist Movement.* Paris: Mouton, 1963.

Gaustad, Edwin Scott. *Historical Atlas of Religions in America.* New York: Harper & Row, 1962.

Getz, Gene. *MBI: The Story of Moody Bible Institute.* Chicago: Moody, 1969.

Gundry, Stanley. *Love Them In—The Proclamation Theology of D. L. Moody.* Chicago: Moody, 1976.

Glover, Robert Hall. *The Progress of World-Wide Missions.* Reprint. New York: Harper and Row, 1960.

Hall, J. H. *Biography of Gospel Song and Hymn Writers.* New York: Revell, 1914.

Harkness, Robert. *Reuben Archer Torrey, the Man, His Message.* Chicago: Bible Institute Colportage Assn., 1919.

Head, Sydney W. *Broadcasting in America.* Boston: Houghton-Mifflin, 1956.

Hopkins, C. Howard. *History of the Y.M.C.A. in North America.* New York: Assn. Press, 1951.

Houghton, Will H. *A Watchman on the Wall.* Grand Rapids: Eerdmans, 1951.

Houghton, Will H., and Cook, Charles T. *Tell Me About Moody.* Chicago: Moody, 1937.

Jenkins, Jerry B. *The Night the Giant Rolled Over.* Waco: Word, 1981.

Jones, Clarence. *Radio, the New Missionary.* Chicago: Moody, 1946.

Living Hymns, edited by Alfred B. Smith. Montrose: Encore, 1972.

Loveless, Wendell P. *Manual of Gospel Broadcasting.* Chicago: Moody, 1946.

Mann, Chester A. *Dwight L. Moody, A Mighty Man of God.* Grand Rapids: Zondervan, 1937.

————. *The R. A. Torrey Year-Book.* New York: Revell, 1929.

Martin, Dorothy. *God's Power in Action.* Chicago: Moody, 1977.

————. *The Story of Billy McCarrell.* Chicago: Moody, 1983.

Metcalf, Edith B. *Letters to Dorothy from the Bible Institute.* New York: Revell, 1893.

Moody, Emma Powell. *Heavenly Destiny*. Chicago: Moody, 1943.

Moody, Paul D. *My Father*. Boston: Little, Brown, 1938.

Moody, William R. *The Life of Dwight L. Moody*. New York: Revell, 1900.

———. *D. L. Moody*. New York: MacMillan, 1930.

Pollock, John. *Moody: The Biography*. Chicago: Moody, 1984.

———. *Moody*. New York: Macmillan, 1963.

Reynolds, William Jensen. *A Survey of Christian Hymnody*. New York: Holt, Rinehart & Winston, 1963.

Robinson, Margaret Blake. *A Reporter at Moody's*. Chicago: Bible Institute Colportage Assn., 1900.

Runyan, William M. *Dr. Gray at Moody Bible Institute*. New York: Oxford, 1935.

Ryckman, Susan. Compiler, *D. L. Moody's Travels—Moody's chronology alphabetized by city*. Chicago: Moody Bible Institute Library, 1979.

Sellers, E. O. *Evangelism in Sermon and Song*. Chicago: Moody, 1941.

Shanks, T. J. *D. L. Moody at Home*. New York: Revell, 1886.

Smith, Wilbur M. *An Annotated Bibliography of D. L. Moody*. Chicago: Moody, 1948.

Torrey, R. A. *Why God Used D. L. Moody*. Chicago: Moody, 1923.

Sweet, William Warren. *The American Churches*. Nashville: Abingdon-Cokesbury, 1948.

———. *The Story of Religion in America*. New York: Harper, 1942.

Thiessen, John Caldwell. *A Survey of World Missions*. Rev. ed. Chicago: Moody, 1961.

White, Paul. *The Moody Church Story*. Chicago: Moody Church. N. d.

Williams, A. W. *Life and Work of Dwight L. Moody*. Chicago: Ziegler, 1900.

Witmer, S. A. *The Bible College Story: Education with Dimension*. New York: Channel, 1962.

Worship and Service Hymnal. Chicago: Hope, 1961.

ARTICLES AND PERIODICALS

"A Bucket of Cold Water," *Moody Monthly* (January 1973).

Aldridge, L. M. "Moody Press Distributes 1,500,000 Bible Portions in Many Lands During Year," *Chicago Daily News* (27 June 1936).

"Alumni Couple Build Drive-In Ministry," *Alumni News* (Spring 1979).

Alumni News. Vols. 17-30, no. 3. Chicago: Moody Alumni Association.

"Alumni Who Served in China Retire to Work Among Chinese in Washington," *Alumni News* (Fall 1980).

"Alumnus Conducts Business for Christ," *Alumni News* (Summer 1979).

Arch 1983.

Balk, Alfred. "Dwight Moody: The Man Who Spoke to 100,000,000," *Sunday Digest* (24 July 1960).

———. "West Point of the Gospel," *Coronet* (June 1959).

Berg, Roland H. "First Pictures Ever Taken Inside the Beating Heart," *Look* (October 1957).

Best, Mary Sue. "Nydia's Tall Order," *Moody Monthly* (November 1981).

Biddle, Calvin. "Bible Study in the Newsroom," *Moody Monthly* (February 1973).

———. "British Campaign Over but Outreach Goes On," *Moody Monthly* (April 1974).

———. "Evening Classes That Make a Difference," *Moody Monthly* (December 1974).

———. "Moody Pilots—They're More Than Good Flyers," *Moody Monthly* (March 1974).

Cadman, S. Parkes. "Famous Revivalists of the United States."

Carlen, Doug. "The Person and Work of Harv Russell," unpublished paper.

The Chautauquan, 20 (January 1895).

Chicago Tribune (23 January 1886).

The Christian Worker's Magazine. Vols. 11-20. Chicago: Moody Bible Institute, 1910-1920.

Christianson, Wayne. "The Bible School That Comes to Students," *Moody Monthly* (January 1976).

———. "The Little Station That Went On and On" *Moody Monthly* (July-August 1976).

Cipriani, Frank. "The Sinner Saver," *Chicago Sunday Tribune* (24 January 1937).

Clapp, Rodney. "Keeping the Faith Downtown," *Christianity Today* (6 August 1982).

Coder, Samuel Maxwell. "The Philosophy of Education of MBI," Moody Alumni

Association. N. d.

Crider, Bill. "Moody Bible Institute Pilots Train Cross-Country," *Alumni News* (Summer 1979).

Culbertson, William. 1966 Founder's Week message.

———. *Review of Moody: A Biographical Portrait* in *Moody Monthly* (August 1958).

DeRemer, Bernard R. "D. L. Moody and the Chicago Fire of 1871," *Moody Alumni* (Winter 1981-1982).

Doering, Jeanne. "They Were Willing to Die," *Moody Monthly* (June 1981).

"Dr. Irwin Moon Receives Highest Kodak Award," *Moody Alumni* (Spring 1981).

"Dr. Irwin Moon Speaks to Military Chaplains," *Moody Monthly*. N. d.

"Dr. Sweeting Challenges Fellow Broadcasters," *Moody Alumni* (Summer 1981).

"Dr. Sweeting Talks to Alumni," *Alumni News* (Winter 1978-1979).

"Dwight L. Moody." Obituary. *Chicago Times Herald* (23 December 1899).

"Education After Hours," *Moody Alumni* (Summer 1980).

Elliott, John H. "An American Great-Heart," *Christian Endeavor World* (14 December 1911).

Evans, M. Stanton. "The Private School Boom," *National Review* (16 May 1960).

Everest, F. Alton. "Acoustic Treatment for Small Projection Rooms," *American Cinematographer* (July 1953).

———. "Acoustic Treatment of Three Small Studios," *Journal of the Audio Engineering Society* (July 1968).

———. "Challenges Before the American Scientific Affiliation," *Journal of the American Scientific Affiliation*, 16 (March 1964).

———. "The Efficient Use of Light in Macrocinematography," *Journal of the Society of Motion Picture Engineers*, 71 (September 1962).

———. "Parabolic Reflector for Sound Recording," *Tele-Tech and Electronic Industries* (March 1955).

Everest, F. Alton, and Hargett, G. Keith. "Photography of Heart Valves with the Cardiac Pulse Duplicator," *Journal of the Biological Photographic Association*, 25

(November 1957).

Everest, F. Alton, and Moon, Irwin. "A Film-Processing Machine of Flexible Characteristics," *Journal of the Society of Motion Picture Engineers*, 67 (November 1958).

———. "Multiple-Camera Control," *Journal of the Society of Motion Picture Engineers*, 64 (September 1955).

Findlay, James. "Moody, 'Gapmen' and the Gospel: The Early Days of Moody Bible Institute," *Church History*, 31 (September 1962).

Finley, Deanna. "Here's Hope for Saturdays," *Moody Monthly* (July-August 1981).

Flood, Robert. "Jerry Moritz: Navy Chaplain," *Moody Monthly* (November 1980).

———. "The Wonderful World of MIS." *Moody Monthly* (April 1970).

———. "They Put Their Stamp on History," *Moody Monthly* (July-August 1981).

———. "They're Still Pioneering the Rural Frontier," *Moody Monthly* (July-August 1966).

———. "Who's Helping the Youth Pastor?" *Moody Monthly* (October 1980).

"From Science to Faith at the Seattle Fair," *Moody Monthly* (July-August 1962).

Gilbert, David. "Jailed Women to Lose a Pal," *Chicago Tribune* (25 August 1969).

Gray, James M. "A Forward Step by the Moody Bible Institute," *Moody Bible Institute Monthly* (June 1922).

———. "Our New Adventure in Music," *Moody Bible Institute Bulletin* (May 1930).

———. "Radio," *Moody Bible Institute Monthly* (March 1926).

Gunther, Peter. "Annual Report," Moody Press, 1983.

Hamlin, Teunis. "The Evolution of Northfield," *Northfield Echoes*, Vol. 3. East Northfield: E. S. Rostall, 1896.

Hart, Rollin Lynde. "The War in the Churches," *The World Book* (September 1923).

Hartzell, Wesley. "Bicentennial Rally Stirs Chicago," *Moody Monthly* (April 1976).

"Hitchcock Retires as Nursing Home Director," *Moody Alumni* (Spring 1982).

Hitt, Russell. "Main Street in Evangelicalville," *Eternity* (November-December 1981).

Houston, Jack. "City of the Bees," *Moody Monthly* (April 1963).

Hunt, Ridgely. "Moody Through a Reporter's Eyes," *Chicago Tribune* (16 April 1975).

Hustad, Donald P. "Church Music—the Pastor's Responsibility," *Bibliotheca Sacra*, 118 (October 1960).

————. "Developing a Biblical Philosophy of Church Music," *Bibliotheca Sacra*, 117 (April 1960).

————. "Gospel Songs Fading?" *Moody Memo* (May 1961).

————. "Music for Worship, Evangelism, and Christian Education," *Bibliotheca Sacra*, 118 (October 1960).

————. "Problems in Psychology and Aesthetics in Music," *Bibliotheca Sacra*, 118 (July 1960).

Hutchens, Paul. "D. L. Moody's Platform Methods," unpublished paper.

"Inside Moody Bible Institute," *Moody Monthly* (December 1960).

Institute Tie. Vols. 1-10. Chicago: Moody Bible Institute, 1900-1910.

Interview with Richard Jensen in *News in Engineering.* Published by Ohio State University. Excerpted in *Moody Alumni* (Spring 1983).

"Jesse Howard—from Chicago's Gangs to MBI Graduation," *Moody Memo* (15 December 1972).

Johnson, Titus. "Storm in the Congo," *Moody Monthly* (March 1961).

"Joseph's Tailor Ministry to Black Americans," *Moody Alumni* (Fall 1981).

Livingston, Lisa. "Celebrating a Centennial in Korea," *Moody Monthly* (September 1983).

"Long Distance Broadcasting," *Moody Memo* (7 August 1981).

"MBI Aviation Complex Rises in Tennessee," *Moody Monthly* (September 1969).

"MBI Graduates Make Impact in Chaplaincy," *Moody Monthly* (April, 1968).

McCulley, Dale. "Colportage Was His Challenge," *Christian Life* (August 1947).

McKinley, Mary Jean. "History of Chorale Goes Back to '21," *Moody Student* (21 April 1949).

Moody Alumni. Vol. 30, No. 4-34. Chicago: Moody Alumni Association.

Moody Alumni News. Vols. 1-6, 1926-1932; 1-16, 1949-1966. Chicago: Moody Alumni Association.

Moody Bible Institute of Chicago Bulletin. Vols. 1-23. Chicago: Moody Bible Institute. 1915-1944.

Moody Bible Institute Monthly. Vols. 11-38. Chicago: Moody Bible Institute, 1920-38.

Moody Literature News. Vols. 1-26. Chicago: Moody Bible Institute, 1951-77.

Moody Memo (15 October 1971).

————. (17 November 1972).

————. (20 April 1973).

————. (12 July 1974).

————. (18 September 1974).

————. (18 May 1979).

————. (12 March 1982).

Moody Monthly. Vols. 39-85. Chicago: Moody Bible Institute, 1938-1985.

"Moody Press Widens Activities in Trade Publishing," *Publishers Weekly* (April 1945).

"Moody Science Films Draw Crowds in U.S., Abroad," *Moody Monthly.* N. d.

Moody Student. Vols. 1-50. Chicago: Moody Bible Institute, 1918-66.

Moon, Irwin. "A Photoelectric Film Cuing System," *Journal of the Society of Motion Picture Engineers*, 49 (October 1947).

"Music Is Ministry," *Moody Alumni* (Winter 1980-1981).

Norton, Jr., Will. "Manhunt," *Moody Monthly* (September 1980).

Oliver, Kay. "In the Steps of D. L. Moody," *Moody Monthly* (September 1971).

————. "Paul Robinson: Winging It," *Moody Monthly* (September 1975).

————. "Thousands Study Bible by Mail," *Moody Monthly* (February 1971).

"Our Alumni in the Caribbean," *Moody Monthly* (March 1970).

Parrish, Emma K. "Early Days on the Great West Side," *Chicago Daily News* (7 February 1929).

Philpott, P. W. "Moody Bible Institute—Old Fashioned Gospel for Modern Times," from *Midwest* (27 January 1974).

————. "Moody Mighty Reconciler, Like Lindbergh," *Chicago Tribune* (5 February 1928).

Pippert, Wesley. "The Making of a Jungle Pilot,"

Moody Monthly (March 1972).

Pugyao, Leonard. As told to Robert Griffin. "Filipino Full Circle," *Beyond* (July-August 1983).

Quarterly Fellowship Newsletter (March 1951).

———. (March 1960).

———. (June 1960).

———. (June 1961).

———. (March 1967).

———. (June 1968).

———. (June 1982).

Rausch, Rosemary. "Confined to Study Scripture," *Moody Monthly* (November 1983).

Saunder, Lowell. "Moody Films Reach World via TV," *Moody Monthly* (January 1975).

Schlafly, Phyllis. "Silent Censorship," Copley News Service, 1983.

Scot, Darrin. "World's Biggest Little Studio," *American Cinematographer* (August 1961).

Siemens, Jr., David F. "The Mathematics of the Honeycomb," *The Mathematics Teacher* (April 1965).

Smith, Wilbur M. "In the Study," *Moody Monthly* (January 1952).

"Soldiers on the Homefront," *Moody Monthly* (April 1961).

Streyckmans, Felix B. "Sermons from Science," *Kiwanis Magazine* (March 1951).

Sweeting, George. "Land of the Morning Calm," *Moody Monthly* (September 1983).

———. "Love Is the Greatest," *Moody Monthly* (February 1982).

———. "Northfield's Reminder," *Moody Monthly* (November 1979).

———. "Pioneer for Our Grandson's Grandsons," *Moody Monthly* (May 1984).

———. "Thirty-five Years to the Glory of God," *Moody Monthly* (April 1976).

Taylor, Kenneth. "Gold Behind the Ranges," *Christian Life* (June, 1948).

Thorogood, Horace. "Moody—Salesman of Salvation," *Evening Standard* (4 February 1937).

"Three Generations of Alumni Serve Christ," *Moody Monthly* (Summer 1979).

Torrey, R. A. Letter to the editor, *Moody Monthly* (October 1923).

"Vick Heads Wichita Fellowship of Christian Police Officers," *Moody Alumni* (Winter 1981-1982).

"Volunteers on the Foreign Field," *Moody Monthly* (September 1961).

Wall, Gary L. "The Man on the Coil," *Moody Monthly* (March 1979).

Wells, John, and Arnold, Glenn. "Winging the Word," *Christian Herald* (September, 1981).

Woodson, Weldon D. "Flying and Faith," *Moody Monthly* (September 1967).

———. "Those Inspiring Sermons from Science," *Business Screen* (April 1961).

Woodward, Ann. "Our Incredible Missionary Translators," *Moody Monthly* (May 1968).

LETTERS, REPORTS, AND OTHER MATERIALS, PUBLISHED AND UNPUBLISHED

Arnold, Glenn F. "A comparative study of the present doctrinal positions and Christian conduct codes of selected alumni of MBI," 1945-1971. Unpublished.

Blanchard, Charles A. Unpublished manuscript describing the events leading to the founding of Moody Bible Institute, February 1916.

Beers, V. Gilbert. "The Work and Influence of D. L. Moody in the Field of Christian Education." Master's thesis, Northern Baptist Theological Seminary, 1953.

Boon, Harold W. "The Development of the Bible College or Institute in the United States and Canada Since 1880 and Its Relationship to the Field of Theological Education in America." Ph. D. diss., School of Education, New York University, 1950.

Campbell, Wilbur Fred. "Dwight L. Moody and Religious Education." Master's thesis, Divinity School, Yale University, 1949.

Chicago Bible Work. Annual reports. Prepared by Emma Dryer. 1874, 1875, 1885-86.

Chicago Evangelization Society. First annual report, 1888.

Christian Booksellers Association. Bylaws.

Committee on Research, Division of Correspondence Study. An annotated Bibliography of Correspondence Study, 1896-1960. National University Extension Association, 1960.

Cook, Harold R. "Factors Affecting the Accuracy of our Missionary Statistics." June 1964.

Dryer, Emma. Unpublished manuscript describing Emma Dryer's associations with D. L. Moody before and after the founding of the Chicago Evangelization Society, January 1916.

Everest, F. Alton. "Chronology of Sermons from Science." 27 February 1963.

Everest, F. Alton, and Moon, Irwin. "Proposal for a Christian Laboratory." December 1944.

Findlay, James. "D. L. Moody." Ph. D. diss., Northwestern University, 1960.

Getz, Gene A. *Report of the Presidential Questionnaire.* 4 vols. Chicago: Moody Bible Institute Printing Plant, 1964.

McBirnie, William S., Jr. "A Study of the Bible Institute Movement." Ph. D. diss., Southwestern Baptist Theological Seminary, 1952.

McCormick, N.F. Letter to D. L. Moody, 15 July 1887. Photostat in Moodyana file. Original in Cyrus H. McCormick Family Papers, Wisconsin State Historical Society.

Moody Martyrs. Chicago: Moody Bible Institute, 1972. Unpublished material.

Palmer, Joy E. "The Contributions of Clarence H. Benson to the Field of Christian Education." Master's thesis, Wheaton College, Wheaton, Illinois, 1958.

Photographic file in Moodyana, Moody Bible Institute.

Reed, Lenice. "The Bible Institute Movement in America." Master's thesis, Wheaton College, Wheaton, Illinois, 1947.

Whaley, Howard. "The Effects of American Revivalism 1726-1828 on Missions." Master's thesis, Wheaton College, Wheaton, Illinois, 1963.

PAMPHLETS AND CATALOGS

A Brief Story of the Bible Institute Colportage Association of Chicago. Chicago: Bible Institute Colportage Association, 1940.

Here We Stand, George Sweeting. Chicago: Moody Bible Institute. N. d.

Moody Evening School Catalog. Moody Bible Institute, 1984-85.

Moody Institute of Science—A Story of God at Work. Moody Bible Institute, 1977.

Moody Institute of Science Film Catalog. Moody Bible Institute, 1983-84.

Moody Press Catalog. Chicago: Moody, 1984.

Moody Trains for a Ministry in Music. Chicago: Moody Bible Institute. N. d.

Story of WMBI and WMBI-FM. Chicago: Moody Bible Institute, 1951.

Moody Press, a ministry of the Moody Bible Institute, is designed for education, evangelization, and edification. If we may assist you in knowing more about Christ and the Christian life, please write us without obligation: Moody Press, c/o MLM, Chicago, Illinois 60610.

CREDITS

Cover and Type Design: Kent Puckett Associates
Interior Layout and Design: Joe Ragont Studios

Ambassador Steel, p. 138
Australian Tourist Commission, 162
Bookstore Journal, 216
Russ Busby, 249
Chicago Historical Society, 23, 31, 36
Chicago Tribune, 45, 140
Drive-In-Churches, Inc., 122
Dynamic Media, Inc., 106, 108-09, 112
Lynn Ekblad, 214
Charlotte Ellison, 213
Evangelism International, 17
Eric Fellman, 91
Robert G. Flood, 135, 168
French Government Tourist Office, 159
Anne Gavitt, 18, 46, 56, 66, 78, 88
Good Life Productions, 247
HCJB, 168
Kent Puckett Associates, 210
Larry Mayfield, 247
Charles McIlhenny, 120
NASA, 173
Ohio State University, 139
Phil Lasz Galleries, 154, 158
River Valley Ranch, 135
Singspiration, 247
TEAM, 153
United States Navy, 144
Wycliffe Bible Translators, 124, 150, 172, 191
Youth For Christ, 132-33